| SOUTHWARD | | | Siding Capacity | | | | TIME TABLE No. 7 | | | | | | |
|---|---|---|---|---|---|---|---|---|---|---|---|---|---|
| THIRD CLASS | SECOND CLASS | FIRST CLASS | | | Distance from Joplin | Maximum Grade | STATIONS | Maximum Grade | Station Numbers | Telegraph Call | CLASS | SECOND CLASS | THIRD CLASS |
| **323** Local Freight | **11** Manifest Freight | **1** Passenger | Pass. | Other | | | Effective 12.01 A.M. SUNDAY February 25, 1945 | | | | **2** Passenger | **12** Freight | **324** Local Freight |
| Tues. Thurs. Sat. | Daily | Daily | | | | | | | | | Daily | Daily | Mon. Weds. Fri. |
| Lv 8.00AM | Lv 9.30AM | | | | 1.17 | | DN {JOPLIN..CTWX} 19.70 | | 0 | JO | Ar 4.50PM | Ar 4.05PM | |
| 8.40 8.50 | 10.20 10.35 | Lv 6.30AM | 18B | 23 | 19.70 | 0.80 | D {NEOSHO...WY} 6.54 | 0.50 | 20 | N | Ar 7.05PM | 4.10 3.35 | 3.25 3.15 |
| 9.11 | 11.00 | f 6.45 | 20B | 2 | 26.24 | 0.80 | AROMA 4.16 | 0.00 | 26 | | f 6.49 | 3.15 | 2.55 |
| 9.26 | 11.15 | s 6.55 | | 23N | 30.40 | 0.80 | STARK CITY 6.71 | 0.80 | 30 | | s 6.39 | 3.00 | 2.40 |
| 9.46 | 11.35 | s 7.10 | 44B | | 37.10 | 0.80 | FAIRVIEW 4.18 | 0.80 | 37 | | s 6.24 | 2.40 | 2.20 |
| 10.01 | 11.50AM | s 7.20 | 44B | | 41.29 | 0.80 | D WHEATON........W 4.96 | 0.30 | 41 | HN | s 6.14 | s 2.30 | 2.00 |
| 10.15 | 12.04PM | f 7.32 | 18B | | 46.25 | 0.80 | RIDGLEY 5.61 | 0.72 | 46 | | f 6.02 | 2.05 | 1.35 |
| 10.36 | 12.25 | s 7.45 | 35B | | 51.86 | 1.10 | D {WAYNE} 9.43 | 0.60 | 52 | WN | s 5.49 | 1.50 | 1.20 |
| 11.01 11.31 M-12 M324 | 12.50 1.20 | 8.03 8.13 | Yd. | | 61.29 | 0.00 | DN {SELIGMAN..TW} 2.22 | 1.14 | 61 | SI | 5.31 5.21 | 1.20 12.50 M11 | 12.50 12.20 M11 |
| 11.40AM | 1.29 | 8.21 | 12B | | 63.51 | 0.50 | PENDER 7.85 | 2.60 | 64 | | 5.13 | 12.30 | 12.08PM |
| 12.05PM M12 | 1.50 | f 8.38 | 42B | | 71.36 | 0.40 | WALDEN 2.29 | 1.58 | 71 | | f 4.56 | 12.05PM M323 | 11.35AM |
| 12.10 | 1.55 | f 8.45 | 18B | | 73.65 | 0.84 | BEAVER 3.79 | *1.04 | 74 | | f 4.49 | 11.52AM | 11.22 |
| 12.20 | 2.05 | f 8.57 | 27B | 27 | 77.44 | 1.25 | JUNCTION...CWY 1.81 | 0.00 | 77 | | f 4.40 | 11.45 | 11.15 |
| 12.30 | | s 9.08 | | 51 | 79.25 | 0.00 | D EUREKA SPRINGS 1.81 | 0.00 | 79 | AW | s 4.26 | | 10.58 |
| 12.45 | 2.30 | f 9.18 | | | 77.44 | 1.75 | JUNCTION...CWY 2.52 | 1.25 | 77 | | f 4.16 | 11.22 | 10.43 |
| 1.00 | 2.45 | f 9.25 | | 7S | 79.96 | 1.75 | TUNNEL 4.57 | 0.00 | 80 | | f 4.10 | 11.07 | 10.28 |
| 1.18 | 3.03 | s 9.36 | 37B | | 84.53 | 1.50 | GRANDVIEW 4.07 | 1.75 | 85 | | s 3.59 | 10.45 | 10.05 |
| 1.33 | | f 9.48 M324 | 17B | | 88.60 | 1.90 | FREEMAN...WY 2.58 | 1.75 | 89 | | f 3.48 | 10.30 | 9.48 M1 |
| 1.45 | | s 9.58 | 32B | 29 | 91.18 | 0.00 | D BERRYVILLE 2.52 | 0.00 | 91 | B | s 3.38 | | 9.30 |
| 2.08 | 3.28 M2 | f 10.08 | | | 88.66 | 1.75 | FREEMAN...WY 3.09 | 1.90 | 89 | | f 3.28 M11 | | 9.15 |
| 2.23 | 3.40 | f 10.18 M12 | 26B | | 91.75 | 1.75 | URBANETTE 3.99 | *0.00 | 92 | | f 3.18 | 10.18 M1 | 9.00 |
| 2.37 | 3.54 | f 10.29 | 43B | | 95.74 | 1.75 | CISCO 4.52 | *1.75 | 96 | | f 3.09 | 10.00 | 8.45 |
| 2.58 M2 | 4.15 | s 10.41 | 20B | 25 | 100.56 | 1.49 | D GREEN FOREST 5.81 | 1.75 | 101 | KN | 2.58 M323 | f 9.45 | 8.30 |
| 3.23 | 4.40 | f 10.54 | 21B | | 106.37 | 1.75 | COIN 4.65 | 1.75 | 106 | | 2.45 | 9.20 | 8.15 |
| 3.43 | 5.00 | s 11.04 | 32B | 8 | 111.02 | 1.75 | D ALPENA........W 6.40 | 1.75 | 111 | PA | 2.34 | s 9.00 | 7.55 |
| 4.18 | 5.35 | f 11.21 | | 4N | 117.42 | 1.41 | BATAVIA 2.58 | *1.40 | 117 | | f 2.18 | 8.35 | 7.40 |
| 4.36 | 5.43 | f 11.28 | 27B | | 120.00 | 0.00 | CAPPS 6.33 | *1.75 | 120 | | f 2.11 | 8.25 | 7.25 |
| Ar 5.00PM | Ar 6.05PM | Ar 11.44AM | Yd. | | 126.33 | | DN HARRISON....CTWX | 1.75 | 126 | DS | Lv 1.56PM | Lv 8.00AM | Lv 7.00AM |
| Tues. Thurs. Sat. | Daily | Daily | End Connected B—Both N—North S—South | | | | 126.33 135.05 | | | | Daily | Daily | Mon. Wed. Fri. |
| **323** | **11** | **1** | | | | | | | | | **2** | **12** | **324** |

Via KCSRy.  Via StL-SF

## Northward trains are superior to trains of the same class in the opposite direction.

See Page 4 for "special instructions," first district. See Page 4 for speed restrictions. See Page 4 for overhead structures that will not clear man on top or side of car.

Trains will assume no rights on this timetable between Joplin and Neosho, or between Wayne and Seligman, but will run under direction of and as per timetable of Kansas City Southern Railway Co. and the St. Louis-San Francisco Ry., respectively.

All trains must get proper clearance card at Neosho, Seligman and Harrison.

SPUR TRACKS BETWEEN STATIONS
See Page 8

ADDITIONAL FLAG STOPS FOR PASSENGER TRAINS
Monarch Springs, Mile 24.72 no track
Elk Ranch, Mile 75.06 no track
Little Arkansas Mile 115.00 no track

# The North Arkansas Line

En route from Seligman to Harrison, a freight train of the Arkansas & Ozarks crosses a bridge near Beaver on the sunny Memorial Day holiday in 1958.

*(Richard S. Prosser)*

# The North Arkansas Line

## THE STORY OF THE MISSOURI & NORTH ARKANSAS RAILROAD

By James R. Fair, Jr.

HOWELL - NORTH BOOKS

BERKELEY, CALIFORNIA

THE NORTH ARKANSAS LINE

*Printed and bound in the United States of America*
Library of Congress Catalog Card No. 78-96727
SBN No. 8310

Published by Howell-North Books
1050 Parker Street, Berkeley, California 94710

# Preface

This is the story of an Ozark Mountain railroad that in its turbulent history had as many ups and downs as its sawtooth topographical profile might indicate. It ran for 365 miles from Joplin, Missouri, to Helena, Arkansas, on the Mississippi. Its colorful career came to an end in 1949 when its abandonment marked the largest, in route miles owned, of any in United States railroad history.

It was on a warm, sunny morning in June 1930 that I became acquainted with the Missouri & North Arkansas railroad. My family and I had traveled in Pullman luxury before arriving at the small town of Kensett, Arkansas, the day before. Now, we were on the last lap of a journey to the Ozark Mountain town of Shirley, where my grandmother's hired hand would meet us and drive us across some very rough roads to the Stone County seat of Mountain View, Arkansas. After an early breakfast we proceeded to the mustard-and-brown Missouri Pacific depot adjacent to the M. & N. A. crossover. As we waited on the cinder platform I suddenly caught sight of the train, backing in from the yards to the north, that shortly would be ours to board.

The train was something of a shock to me. Instead of the dark green of the Frisco and Missouri Pacific, the cars were painted a dark red, and they were grimy from the previous day's run. At the head of the four cars was an engine that, compared with the monsters I had come to know, was diminutive indeed. To my surprise, as I entered the coach, I saw a pot-bellied stove! But the car was clean and, being at the rear of the train, would afford me the pleasure of peering out at the track and right of way.

Our ride that day was generally uneventful. At the several stops I overheard interesting conversations between the trainmen and the local residents. My rear view showed me several substantial cuts, fills, and bridges. The station buildings were neatly painted in yellow with brown trim. The crossties were spaced by a profusion of weeds. The whole operation was intriguing, and I resolved to look further into this interesting railroad. I could hardly wait to return home to look it up in my new and prized possession, the *Official Railway Guide*.

From that point on I maintained a more-than-casual interest in the M. & N. A. In many travels throughout Arkansas with my father I was able to see many facets of the railroad, such as the substantial stone depots at Eureka Springs and Leslie; the neat shops and yards at Harrison; the red ball freight rolling through the typical mountain town of Shirley, pulled by an ex-Big Four locomotive; the wiggly main line rails threading their way through the verdant weeds near Cotton Plant and Wheatley; the "blue goose" streamlined rail cars rolling into Heber Springs; and the early morning steam display at the Kensett shops. And in the 1940s, when making regular trips through Kensett on the Missouri Pacific's *Southerner* or *Texan,* I wondered whether some of my fellow passengers might not have wondered about those light and unballasted rails that approached from the hill country to the north; appeared to hesitate before the big, shiny, double-tracked iron of the Missouri Pacific; and then, after crossing, disappeared into the cotton and rice flatlands to the south.

When the road shut down in 1946 I was away from Arkansas and could only see the forsaken facilities occasionally. When most of the rails were taken up in 1949-1952 I was remorseful for not having made some effort to save them. And finally, in 1961 when the last real vestige of the road, a short line called the Arkansas & Ozarks, gave up the ghost I resolved to look into the history of this railroad that had come and gone almost unnoticed by the outside world.

Hence this book. It has been a labor of love and, I hope, of some value to others as well as to me. I have been surprised to learn of incidents which gave the railroad an important, though fleeting, place in the sun. And I have been impressed by the number of people having a latent, yet deep, concern over the old M. & N. A. Many of them have been extremely helpful, and their contributions are acknowledged elsewhere in the book. May this written record help them continue to keep a soft spot in their hearts for "The North Arkansas Line."

# Acknowledgments

A work of this type depends heavily upon the input of many people. The author hesitates to list any of them for fear of making prominent, though innocent, omissions. Nonetheless, important contributors must be identified; such is small compensation for their undue generosity.

Special recognition must go to E. G. Baker of Louisville, Kentucky. As a boy and young man living in Harrison, Arkansas, he alone had the foresight to record photographically the trains and facilities of the North Arkansas Line. The many pictures in this book credited to him attest to his abilities as a historian as well as a cameraman. His assistance and encouragement throughout this project were both generous and unfailing.

Another individual meriting special acknowledgment is Lewie A. Watkins, Harrison resident and for many years top executive officer for the railroad. He not only encouraged preparation of the manuscript but also kindly consented to review critically those portions covering his tenure as receiver and president.

Special thanks go to Rev. Paul Wobus, for his early encouragement of the project; to S. R. Wood, H. L. Goldsmith, and Charles Winters, for providing basic data on North Arkansas locomotives; to John and Mary Roberts, of the National Museum of Transport, for making available that institution's files and for providing numerous leads to sources of information; to J. W. Barriger, for permitting use of his vast private library which, happily, contained much unpublished information on the railroad; to Mrs. W. A. Spalding, for providing memoirs and photos relating to her husband's interest in the railroad; to W. D. Kirkpatrick, who provided materials and information gathered by his father, Carlos Kirkpatrick; and to Mrs. Catherine Osterhage, librarian at Eureka Springs, Arkansas, who as a "flat land furriner" showed great interest and assistance in a project involving her newly found home.

Others, providing photographs, materials, reminiscences and general encouragement, include the following.

| | | |
|---|---|---|
| Ashley, James H. Sr. | Harlow, Lester | Moore, Max |
| Bishop, Mrs. Inez | Hoffman, G. E. | Newman, |
| Braswell, E. R. | Holder, Lon | Mr. and Mrs. J. R. |
| Braswell, O. Klute | Hull, C. E. | Prosser, Richard |
| Brock, Leonidas | Husa, W. J. | Riddle, Eugene |
| Brown, Mrs. Homer | Johnson, A. B. | Roberts, C. C. |
| Brown, Lynn | Johnston, Fred | Rothfus, R. R. |
| Campbell, D. G. | King, Roy T. | Sarno, Donald |
| Cartwright, Olin | Lack, Mrs. Loren | Saunders, Earl |
| De Golyer, E. L. Jr. | Lambert, J. B. | Stindt, Fred A. |
| Gooden, O. T. | Lamberton, H. C. | Stowe, Robert |
| Goodwin, Louis W. | Ligett, D. A. | Vaughan, Oran |
| Gray, J. M. | McCann, Bennie | Vollrath, H. K. |
| Ham, William | McGaughey, Merritt | |

Searches for materials took the author to many archives. Those providing him with assistance beyond the normal call include the De Golyer Collection of the Fondren Library, Southern Methodist University, Dallas, Texas; the Federal Records Center (I.C.C. files), Springfield, Virginia; the Missouri Historical Society, St. Louis; the Historical Society of Missouri, Columbia; the Arkansas History Commission, Little Rock; the Little Rock Public Library; and the New York Public Library.

Finally, the author wishes to thank his immediate family: his wife, Merle, and the children—Rud, Beth, and Rich. They showed great patience, provided encouragement, and seemed to understand when "Daddy headed off on his railroad project."

JAMES R. FAIR, JR.

*St. Louis, Missouri*
March, 1969

# Table of Contents

Richard Kerens, left, was first president and largest stockholder of the Eureka Springs Railway. Powell Clayton, right, was a guiding light in the promotion and construction of the railway.

*(Two pictures: Eureka Springs Carnegie Library)*

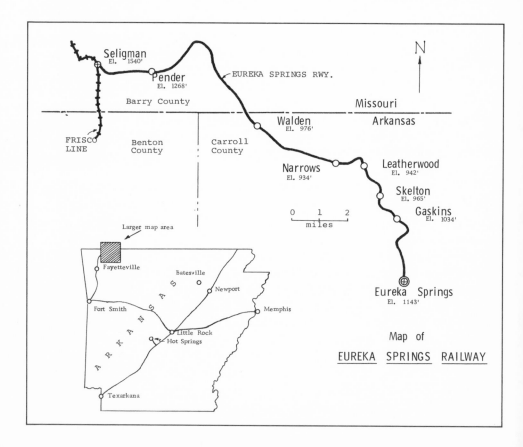

# CHAPTER ONE

# *1879-1899*

# *Eureka Springs and its Railroad*

---

The Ozark Mountain region of Northwest Arkansas was, in 1879, a remote, primeval and peaceful place. Post-Civil War foraging parties had long since gone, the Osage Indians had moved west, and governmental control from Little Rock seemed adequate now that the carpetbaggers had been dispossessed. The small communities in the mountains owed their existence to trading or county government, and were connected with each other by the merest of wagon trails. Supplies came in from the St. Louis & San Francisco Railroad (The Frisco Line) at Pierce City, Springfield, and other Missouri towns far to the north. Such isolation was taken philosophically by the settlers, many of whom were of pure Anglo-Saxon stock, as they hacked a livelihood out of soil and tree.

A man who knew this peaceful region well was Dr. Alvah Jackson, who covered the trails by horseback selling a quack preparation called "eye-water." He surreptitiously collected the liquid at an old spring in Carroll County that he had discovered back in 1854. The spring was one of many in the immediate vicinity and had been used by Indians as well as by convalescing Confederate soldiers from Pea Ridge, Prairie Grove, and other nearby scenes of encounter during the Civil War. The water really seemed to have curative power and the doctor acquired a substantial, if somewhat local, prominence.

In May 1879, Dr. Jackson elected to take a friend, Judge L. B. Saunders, to the spring to attempt treatment of an "incurable" leg sore. Saunders camped at the site, bathed the leg regularly, and as

1

the reader would suspect, received the cure. Saunders was not one to keep this discovery quiet, he spread the word, and by July 1 some 20 families were at the spring seeking cures for their various ailments. Shortly afterward, at the suggestion of Saunders' son, the site was named "Eureka Springs."

The tenor of the times was such that news of "miracle healing waters" would attract multitudes who had or thought they had incurable ailments. Spas such as Saratoga, French Lick, and White Sulphur had already come into prominence. Eureka Springs appeared to offer such waters and the news burst forth rapidly from this remote sector of northwest Arkansas. Families by the wagon load started coming in from Arkansas and from outstate and before many weeks had passed permanent dwellings were under construction.

The rapid genesis of Eureka Springs has been described in other writings, and it is sufficient here to report that on February 14, 1880 Eureka Springs was incorporated, and by census time that year could record 3,984 permanent inhabitants. In less than a year the city had become one of the six largest in Arkansas. Growth was largely unplanned and haphazard, many of the dwellings were shacks or lean-tos. But Eureka Springs had more than just curative water in its favor; it was located in a beautifully-wooded and mountainous area with a sufficient elevation to capture cool breezes in the summertime and yet not undergo unusual rigors of cold winter weather.

But a city of 4,000 permanent population, plus countless transients needed transportation facilities far beyond those provided by the wagons and stages connecting it with points on the railroad. The rough, 55-mile stage ride from Pierce City was enough to jeopardize further the health of anyone seeking treatment at Eureka Springs. Fortunately, the Frisco railroad had begun steps that would help alleviate this problem.

The Frisco had planned a route from St. Louis to Texas in 1879 and on June 18, 1880 was granted charters in Missouri and Arkansas to build from Plymouth, Missouri (about 5 miles east of Pierce City on the line from Springfield to the Indian Territory) generally south through Fayetteville to Fort Smith, Arkansas, with ultimate objectives of Paris and Dallas in Texas. The line was chartered as the St. Louis, Arkansas & Texas Railway; construction started July 9, 1880 and by November the line was completed 32 miles to the Arkansas border. Just north of the state line was platted the town of Seligman, so named for a New York banking house that had handled portions of the Frisco financing.

Seligman was situated high on the Ozark Plateau, and though only about 20 miles from Eureka Springs was separated from it by the White River Valley. A connecting wagon road was soon fashioned that followed Butler Creek from its source at Seligman down a winding and narrow valley to the river for a ferry — or fording-crossing. It then followed another White River tributary, Leatherwood Creek, up to its source at the springs. Health-seekers could now travel by train to Seligman and then suffer only a four to five-hour stage ride before reaching Eureka!

The Frisco construction plan had not gone unnoticed by the Eureka Springs citizens. They had to have a railroad and in 1880 promoted the Eureka Springs Railway Co. of Arkansas. On June 26, 1880 this company was granted a charter to build from the Missouri line to Eureka Springs (and beyond to "a point on the Osage River in Carroll County," according to the charter). The Missouri portion of the Frisco connection was chartered separately September 21, 1880, as the Missouri & Arkansas Railroad Company of Missouri. But the usual difficulties of financing appeared, and by the time the Frisco reached Seligman there was little hope for the beginning of construction.

The Frisco annual report for 1880, written by General Manager Charles W. Rogers on January 2, 1881, indicated some optimism: "The station of Seligman . . . is 18 miles from the famous Eureka Springs . . . a place with eight thousand people, although but 18 months old. Travel to the Springs is growing larger every month, and will, I believe, prove to be of value to this road. Parties are now preparing to construct a branch line from Seligman to Eureka Springs, intending, it is stated, to extend such line through to Little Rock via Harrison."

Central figure in the promotion of the railroad to Eureka Springs was a colorful, one-armed gentleman named Powell Clayton. He was a Pennsylvanian who had been a practicing civil engineer before the Civil War. During the war he fought for the

Union in Missouri and Arkansas, and rose to the rank of briga-
dier-general before being mustered out in 1865. He then bought
40,000 acres of land near Pine Bluff and became a wealthy cotton
farmer. He was elected a Republican Governor of Arkansas and
served 1868-1871 before being elected United States Senator
from Arkansas. He was an extremely controversial public figure,
and his suspect manipulation of state funds appeared often to
work in favor of the railroads of Arkansas. Much has been written
about Clayton, most of it bad. But he was acknowledged to be a
master organizer and effective promoter and these talents made
significant and lasting contributions to Eureka Springs and its
railroad.

Clayton was attracted to Eureka Springs soon after its establishment. He had taken up residency in Little Rock in 1877 after
his term in Congress, and by 1880 was spending a great deal of
time on his Eureka Springs Railway project. He was elected
president of both the Missouri and the Arkansas portions of the
proposed line, and throughout 1881 was at work lining up financial support for the venture. He worked through close Republican
friends in St. Louis and Little Rock (there had not yet been time
for the development of Eureka Springs capital), and by early 1882
he had enough subscriptions to take forthright action. And at this
time he relocated his residence to Eureka.

Clayton and his colleagues filed articles of consolidation of the
two proposed railroads with the Arkansas Secretary of State on
February 27, 1882. The new company would be simply the Eureka
Springs Railway, with authorized capital stock of $500,000. Sub-
scribers met on April 28 at one of the leading Eureka Springs
hotels, The Southern, and deliberated over plans for construction.
They also agreed on the rather sizable funded debt of $500,000 in
6% first mortgage bonds and $500,000 in 6% second mortgage in-
come bonds.

Estimates showed that about $500,000 initial outlay would be
needed to place the road in operation. Arrangements with the
Frisco had been made for the use of rolling stock and also for an
interesting traffic agreement. For example, the Frisco would pay
the Eureka Springs 10% of its gross receipts from interchange
passenger fares for travel to or through junctional or terminal

points on the Frisco. Similar arrangements applied to the interchange of freight. The payments to the Eureka Springs would be up to but not in excess of the interest payments on the 6% first mortgage bonds, or $30,000 per year. In exchange for this generosity, the Frisco would receive 1,000 shares of common stock ($100,000 par), a like amount of second mortgage bonds and, to be sure, the opportunity for increased business.

As was the custom of the times, construction of the line would be handled by a separate company formed for the purpose, the Western Construction Co. of Little Rock. All securities of the railroad would be issued to this company which, in turn, would issue its securities to the investors. Total securities of $1,500,000 for an 18-mile road costing around $25,000 per mile was clearly a case of overcapitalization, but this also was a custom of the times. Just what the breakdown of bondholders was is not clear, but the principal common stockholders were identified:

| Richard Kerens, St. Louis | 1,593 shares |
| Frisco Railroad | 1,000 " |
| Logan H. Roots, Little Rock | 683 " |
| Powell Clayton, Eureka Springs | 569 " |
| Bernard Baer, Fort Smith | 294 " |

Kerens was a prominent St. Louisan who had been a military colleague of Clayton and who had prospered in the overland mail business before moving to St. Louis in 1876. He was identified with the building of several railroads, and in later life would serve on the Continental Railroad Commission and would be U. S. Ambassador to Vienna. Like Clayton, he fell in love with the beauties of Eureka Springs. Because of this interest as well as his significant investment, he was elected president of the Eureka Springs Railway.

Logan Roots was another military compatriot of Clayton and had prospered in various businesses after moving south to Little Rock. He was elected treasurer, and was largely responsible for "front" activities of the Western Construction Co.

Powell Clayton was elected vice president and general manager of the line, and he turned at once to the business of getting it built and into operation. He placed an order for the required rail and fastenings, choosing a 56-pound per yard weight that was currently being used on the Frisco main lines. He also ordered a steam locomotive, being guided by the advice of the Frisco motive power experts. After that, it was necessary to dust off the preliminary survey data for redevelopment. Because of his civil engineering background he was able to make his own technical contributions, but also called on experienced engineers S. C. Martin and Major M. M. Randall to supervise the work directly.

The survey party was in the field by May and located the river crossing such that a contract for the bridging could be let to the Delaware Bridge Company. On June 19 Clayton and Kerens took the Frisco overnight train to Seligman to review the construction work with possible contractors, to let a contract for crossties, and to deal with the problem of procuring land. The survey was complete, except for a final decision on the specific location of the Seligman connection. Attempts had been made to tie in with the Frisco south of the depot but the terrain just wouldn't permit. It was after July 1 that the decision was finally made to tie in north of town and require that Eureka Springs trains back into or out of the depot.

Finally, construction contract bids were opened July 10 in Room 24 of the Planters House in St. Louis. Clayton, Roots, and Kerens officiated, and Judge John McClure from Arkansas gave them legal advice. Six bids were submitted, and the winner was Jones and Cowen, of Fort Worth, Texas, at an announced sum of $200,000. (Interstate Commerce Commission records indicate that a smaller amount was actually paid.) The senior contracting partner was Morgan Jones, quite prominent in railroad construction in Texas, and destined in 1883 to become president of the Fort Worth & Denver City Railroad. There appeared to be no question as to Jones' qualifications for the job at hand.

By August 1882 trees were being cleared, earth was being moved (by mule-powered dragbuckets), and protruding bluffs were being blasted away. The survey called for a precipitous 2.6% drop out of Seligman for about two miles followed by a more gently-descending grade of 1.6% or less until the White River was reached. In this 11-mile stretch the elevation changed from 1540 to 934 ft., and the right of way twisted and turned according to the vagaries of Butler Creek. A level stretch of about two miles along and across the river was followed by about five miles of continuous ascending grade along Leatherwood Creek, with the maximum gradient of 1.25% just outside Eureka. The profile of the line resembled a giant roller-coaster dip.

Butler and Leatherwood Creeks cut narrow canyons only near their headwaters, and grading was not difficult. There were two outstanding examples of rockwork that proved to be quite photogenic. Just north of the White River crossing it was necessary to blast a narrow shelf under Poker Bluff and directly adjacent to the river. And just south of the crossing it was necessary to blast a 60-foot deep cut out of a narrow limestone ridge that separated the White and Leatherwood watercourses. This incision was only about 100 feet long and took the name of "Narrows Cut." The story goes that Powell Clayton had genuine difficulty in dispossessing a settler whose house at the top of the Narrows Ridge was right where it shouldn't have been!

By November grading was essentially complete, many of the trestles were in, and track had been laid to the river. Bridge crews were able to complete the river crossing by the end of the year, and it appeared that certain right of way concessions by the town of Eureka, contingent on reaching there by February 1, 1883, would be gained.

An important event of late 1882 was the arrival of EUREKA SPRINGS No. 1, a heavy consolidation-type locomotive built by Pittsburgh Locomotive Works. (Motive power for the tracklaying operation had been supplied by the Frisco.) Its specifications were influenced by those of Baldwin locomotives delivered to the Frisco in 1881 and 1882. The No. 1 weighed about 50 tons, with 45 of them on the relatively small 44-inch drivers. The tractive effort of about 20,000 pounds put the No. 1 on a par with any freight locomotive on the Frisco system and equipped it for the task of moving tonnage up the 2.6% grade into Seligman.

There was excitement indeed among Eureka residents in January 1883, and they thronged to watch the placing of rails on crossties down in Leatherwood Valley, and also to observe the splendor of No. 1. By working all night the tracklayers put rails to the depot site on January 24, and thousands turned out to see the arrival of the first passenger train at one o'clock that afternoon. Some 55 passengers made the trip, presumably most of them from Seligman. The *Missouri Republican* stated that "the passenger depot will be a fine structure. The car houses and freight depot are completed. The road will be formally opened for travel on February 1 . . ."

The *Arkansas Gazette* of February 3, 1883, presented word direct from Eureka Springs regarding the formal opening:

> The people of this place made subscriptions payable upon the railroad reaching here by February 1. Although the train has been running to the depot for nearly a week, the depot is just outside the corporate limits. Wednesday night, Harry Pratt, the conductor, before unloading at the depot had the train pulled into the corporate limits, and the locomotive seemed endowed with superior power as it whistled and bellowed a sound of grand triumph. Although it was decided to postpone the special pomp and ceremony commemorative of the event until some future day, yet all the persons who have invested in the enterprise are present, and today there have been other notables present, and joy has reigned supreme and Eureka's boom is swollen to the fullest extent. Its permanency is not a question, but a fixed fact.

The Harrison, Arkansas, *Times* added this information: "The road is reported as first-class in every particular and the most expensive for its length in the United States. The fare is $1.75 one way, $3.50 round trip, between Seligman and Eureka Springs."

Yes, Eureka had her railroad, and it was a fine one. The *Railway Age* dated February 1 announced completion of the line and that ". . . through Pullman palace sleeping cars will be run daily, without change, between St. Louis and Eureka Springs." Regular service to Seligman included an afternoon daily passenger train leaving at 3:50 p.m., carrying the St. Louis sleeper, and a daily morning mixed train leaving at about 8:30 a.m., which carried no freight on Sunday mornings. For the return to Eureka there was the morning passenger, with sleeper, arriving at 11:30 a.m. and the afternoon mixed arriving at 6:30 p.m. Running time was about an hour.

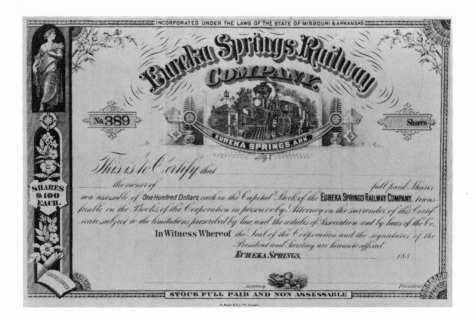

There was a total of 5000 shares of $100-par capital stock. First locomotive on the Eureka Springs Railway was the low-drivered consolidation, below. It is shown at the north end of the Eureka Springs yards. *(Above: C. E. Hull collection; below: Zoe Harp collection, courtesy P. A. Wobus)*

The railroad had procured a coach and a combination baggage-passenger car, and schedules were constrained not only by times of connecting Frisco trains but also by the availability of these cars and the single locomotive. For example, the afternoon passenger to Seligman would return as a mixed train, having exexchanged its sleeper for whatever freight cars had been set out for it. The Frisco did make available additional passenger cars to meet special demands.

Amidst all the gaiety at Eureka Springs over this new and lofty standard of transportation there was little concern over ominous events occurring some 150 miles east at Batesville, Arkansas. On February 10, the St. Louis, Iron Mountain and Southern branch line from Newport, on the St. Louis-Little Rock main line, was completed to Batesville. This 28-mile branch was built ostensibly as a feeder line, but Iron Mountain officials had in mind extending it further west, possibly to Harrison and Eureka, to tap mineral resources recently discovered in northern Arkansas. In a sense, the Frisco and the Iron Mountain had each sent a precursor toward the Ozark interior, and time would unfold parallels of thought and rivalry as the two lines pursued their individual interests.

The plan to extend the Eureka Springs east to Harrison has been mentioned, and the matter was considered seriously by the railroad officers. While construction was in progress in 1882, Chief Engineer Martin and his party conducted preliminary surveys for the extension and established a route that was to be followed 18 years later. The extension would be 49 miles long, would have 1.5% maximum grade and 8° maximum curves with one exception of a 9° curve at Kings River, and would cost $750,000, or about $15,000 per mile. Powell Clayton worked closely with Martin and agreed with him that the proposed route and cost estimate were entirely feasible. The line would provide service for Harrison, thriving seat of Boone County and adjacent to the rich zinc and lead deposits of Marion County on the east.

Little Rock, the capital city, was the ultimate objective. Extension to that place would give the Frisco a decided advantage over the Iron Mountain in handling traffic from Kansas and Western Missouri that was destined for Little Rock and points south to the Gulf of Mexico. The Frisco had previously announced a plan to build from Springfield, Missouri, south through Harrison to Little Rock, and actually constructed some of the mileage in 1882 as the "White River Branch" to Chadwick, 33 miles. Presumably this plan was still alive in 1883 and if so might dissuade the Frisco from immediate interest in the Eureka-Harrison extension.

As 1883 wore on, events of the railroad became more or less routine. Summer freshets dislocated some trestles near the White River; they had been built in the preceding winter and the contract employees had avoided spending enough time below the cold water level, securing the bents to bed rock. The contractor made the corrections. A number of excursion trains and special Pullmans were brought in during the summer.

In September, Engine No. 2 arrived from the Rogers Locomotive Works. This was a handsome American type especially suited for the passenger runs. It weighed 32 tons, had 66-inch drivers, and exerted a tractive effort of 12,500 pounds. As was the case for No. 1, it had a diamond stack and burned wood for fuel. It was christened THE POWELL CLAYTON and steamed proudly out of the Eureka Springs station with combination car, coach, and sleeper and could be heard for miles down Leatherwood Valley by the Eureka residents.

On November 3 there was an extensive fire in Eureka that destroyed a good portion of the business district. This gave Powell Clayton his chance to improve construction standards and the general appearance of the city. The rapid and unplanned growth had resulted in a chaotic array of shacks and frame stores. Clayton undertook an urban renewal program and, working through the city fathers, established condemnation procedures. Stone buildings began to rise in the business section and civic pride abounded.

At the end of 1883 the Eureka Springs Railway showed a neat profit. Total revenues were $88,246.97 and total expenses $22,-283.90. The large funded debt was there, of course, and it consumed $55,000 of the gross earnings. The balance of $10,963.07 went to the surplus account and things were looking decidedly good. It might be noted that aside from the $200,000 securities issued to the Frisco, the remaining $1,300,000 stocks and bonds probably represented a cash outlay of no more than $500,000, and

The station building at Eureka Springs, above, was photographed just before a train arrived from Seligman. The several horsedrawn conveyances will take passengers to the various hostelries up the hill side. In 1913 this frame depot was replaced by a stone structure. At the left immaculate engine No. 2, a Rogers 4-4-0, leads the afternoon passenger train toward Seligman. The time is summer 1883, and the flags suggest that this may be No. 2's maiden run. The location is about a mile west of the Narrows. Behind the locomotive are a combination car and a coach, plus the Pullman Palace Car making its over-night run to St. Louis. (*Above: Zoe Harp collection, courtesy of P. A. Wobus; left: Association of American Railroads, courtesy J. & W. Seligman Co.*)

there are indications that the common stockholders were also the bondholders. Thus, the cash investment returned about 10% the first year. The promoters had reason to be in good spirits.

A description of the completed railroad facility was now possible. The main line was 18.5 miles long and was laid with 56-pound steel on white oak crossties, 2800 to the mile. It was fully ballasted with creek gravel and crushed stone. There were 7.9 miles of curved track comprising 63 curves of 9° maximum. And there were only 1.1 miles of level track!

Turntables of 50-foot length were provided at Seligman and Eureka. There was a 250-foot two-span through-truss iron bridge at White River, set on piers of stone cut from a quarry nearby. (This quarry was to provide stone for several later bridgings and for numerous Eureka buildings.) Water supplies were provided at Seligman, Pender, and Eureka. Repair facilities at Eureka included an engine shed, backshop, sheds, and complete spring-fed water system.

The completed passenger depot at Eureka was indeed attractive. The main section was of two stories with offices on the second floor and passenger waiting rooms, ticket office and operators' office on the first floor. Extending from this main section were platform sheds connecting a lunch room at one end and a baggage room at the other. There was a separate freight depot. Opposite the trackside of the station was the area at which horse-drawn taxis and other conveyances would pull up to load and unload passengers. Typically, the Eureka Springs Transfer Co. placed an agent on all inbound trains to line up customers for transfer to the Southern Hotel, The Perry House, or other spots. The cost was 25 cents per bag or person.

The rolling stock of the line at the end of 1883 comprised engines Nos. 1 and 2, combination car, coach, and 6 flatcars. Of the 22,085 tons of freight hauled, principal items were lumber, fence posts, cotton, flour, and general merchandise. During the 11 months an average of 70 passengers per day were carried.

The most important event in 1884, at least for this chronicle, was the formation of the Eureka Improvement Co. This company was headed by Clayton, and its board of directors included Capt. C. W. Rogers of the Frisco as well as Kerens, Roots, and other investors in the Eureka railroad. The initial undertaking of this firm was to be the erection of a handsome stone hotel atop West Mountain, at an elevation of 2000 feet, that would compete with the best at the other important spas of the country. At the time, the Perry house, located near the Basin Spring, was the leading hotel at Eureka. It was built in 1882, had four stories, and 100 rooms, all connected to the office by "electric annunciator." The Southern Hotel had 50 rooms, and there were countless others that were smaller. A large, new hotel was sorely needed to handle the crowds of visitors; the Eureka Improvement Co. proceeded with building plans to fill that need, and named the hotel The Crescent.

The year 1884 saw the gross earnings drop to $40,777.99. After paying $30,000 on the first mortgage bonds it was possible to pay only $15,000 on the second mortgage bonds. The net was thus a deficit of $4,222.01. Better performance would be necessary if the road was to promote successfully the extension eastward.

The hope was that the Frisco would take over and extend the road. Captain Rogers was very much in favor of this plan, and did not extend the Frisco line further southward from Springfield. But the Frisco was having a difficult time financially, and advances to the Eureka line were not likely.

In 1885 the railroad performance was about the same as the year before, with the oversize funded debt being a problem. There were still reports in the news that the line would be extended to Little Rock. In the meantime passengers and freight were shuttled between Seligman and Eureka Springs, with regularity and without mishap.

The news of 1886 was centered around the Crescent Hotel, which was completed in April and had a gala opening on May 20. A quotation in the *Arkansas Gazette* of September 18, 1959, taken from an 1888 brochure describing the Crescent, reads in part as follows:

> . . . under the personal supervision of General Powell Clayton the hotel was built and furnished in the most substantial and elegant manner at a cost, including the grounds, of over $250,000.

The Crescent Hotel symbolized the "good life" to visitors and townspeople alike. The Frisco railroad's financial interest in the enterprise is proclaimed by the emblem above. The early view below appeared in *Harper's Weekly* for December 18, 1886. *(Three pictures: National Museum of Transport)*

The tranquil scene above is on a terrace of the Crescent Hotel's gardens more than 100 feet above the street at the foot of the precipitous slope at the right. Eureka Springs Railway schedules were closely tied to those of the Frisco connection at Seligman. *(Below: E. R. Braswell collection)*

# ·EUREKA SPRINGS RAILWAY·

## TIME TABLE, No. 16

### FOR THE GOVERNMENT AND INFORMATION OF EMPLOYEES.

In Effect *Monday March 1st*, 1886, at 6 O'clock, A.M.

| West-Bound Trains. | | | | Stations and Sidings. | | East-Bound Trains. | | |
|---|---|---|---|---|---|---|---|---|
| No. 1 *Sunday* *Leave A.M.* | No. 1. MIXED. Leave A.M. | No. 3. PASSENGER. Leave P.M. | DISTANCES. | | DISTANCES. | No. 2. PASSENGER. Arrive A.M. | No. 4. MIXED. Arrive P.M. | |
| 8.42 | 8.09 | 3.50 | 0 | EUREKA SPRINGS. | 18½ | 11.24 | 6.45 | |
| 8.54 | 8.24 | 3.59 | 3 | GASKINS. | 15½ | 11.15 | 6.31 | |
| 8.58 | 8.30 | • 4.02 | 4½ | † SKELTON. | 14½ | • 11.10 | 6.25 | |
| 9.00 | 8.34 | • 4.05 | 5 | † LEATHERWOOD. | 13½ | • 11.08 | 6.21 | |
| 9.03 | 8.38 | 4.08 | 5¾ | THE NARROWS. | 12¾ | 11.06 | 6.17 | |
| 9.12 | 8.54 | • 4.18 | 8 | † WALDEN. | 10½ | • 10.56 | 6.07 | |
| 9.36 | 9.34 | • 4.40 | 15¾ | PENDER. | 2¾ | • 10.34 | 5.36 | |
| 9.46 | 9.46 | 4.57 | 18½ | SELIGMAN. | 0 | 10.21 | 5.23 | |
| | Arrive A.M | Arrive P.M. | | | | Leave A.M. | Leave P.M. | |

Conductors and Engineers are ESPECIALLY CAUTIONED against too rapid running; and are required to adhere to the Running Time given in the Table as closely as possible, taking care to lose no time unnecessarily, to be made up by exceeding the prescribed speed. START PROMPTLY and RUN REGULARLY, and remember the rule that requires you to in all cases of doubt to take the side of safety.

All trains will run daily.

Work trains must not exceed 12 miles per hour.

Working hours for construction trains will be from 6 A.M. to 7 P.M.

†Trains stop only on signal.

*Trains do not stop for passengers.

All delayed time-table, construction, or irregular trains must whistle curves and keep a sharp look-out for hand cars and section men.

The speed of passenger trains must not exceed 12 miles, and other trains 10 miles per hour, when crossing the White River Bridge.

The use of intoxicating liquors, while on duty, is strictly prohibited, and will be considered cause for dismissal.

Use the signal bell to start passenger trains—two strokes to start, one to stop, and three to back up.

Engineers will answer Conductor's and Flagman's signals to stop with two short blasts of the whistle.

Engineers will whistle when track cannot be seen by reason of curves around projecting points.

Engineers will not allow any person to ride on their engine or tender, without permission from the General Manager, except the Road Master or Conductor.

> The house is five stories high and is built of a very
> handsome and valuable white stone, taken from the quar-
> ries at White River . . . It is lighted with gas, furnished
> with electric bells, heated with steam and open grates, has
> an hydraulic elevator, and all other modern improvements.
> The rooms are large, well-lighted and nearly all ensuite,
> many with private baths. The furnishing corresponds with
> the elegance of the structure.

> The house is supplied . . . with water from the Con-
> gress Spring, and the guests are furnished at their rooms,
> morning and night, with water from any spring desired.

The Crescent could accommodate 250 guests in its 100 rooms. It
was provided with a spacious lobby with oversized fireplace,
well-appointed dining room, billiard room, bowling alley, and
many other attractive features. It was set in a pleasant 27-acre
park with an unobstructed view for miles in all directions. At the
rear entrance were stationed the outsized "tallyho" wagons that
would take groups of guests on sightseeing or picnic rides.

The hotel was opened on May 1, 1886, and had a "formal"
opening on May 20. A great many prominent businessmen from
St. Louis and Little Rock were present for the latter occasion.
There were spectacular fireworks displays, gun salutes, band
concerts, a parade, and all the other events normally associated
with dedicatory celebrations of the times. It did appear that
Eureka Springs had a hostelry that could compete with the best
in the nation, and in its advertising literature the Frisco lost no
time in extolling that fact.

Sadder news in 1886 was the death of Captain Charles W.
Rogers, first vice president of the Frisco, on February 21. Rogers
was a close friend of Clayton and a strong supporter of Eureka
Springs and its railroad. Apparently he had convinced his management that the Harrison extension should be undertaken
promptly, and that the ultimate objective should be Little Rock.
(The story goes that a construction contract was actually negotiated.) However, after an extended illness he passed away in
Pasadena, California. Rogers did not live to see his Crescent Hotel
project completed and his death appeared to scuttle the Harrison

extension project; the others of Frisco top management were cool to the idea.

The late years of the nineteenth century rolled on without especial incident for the Eureka Springs Railway. There was no change in locomotives or rolling stock, little variation in schedules, and earnings were such that interest paid on income bonds averaged about 3%. Eureka Springs continued its development, but with a setback in 1888 when a fire destroyed 480 houses and the business section along Spring Street. In 1891 a street railway was built to connect the depot with the Crescent, Southern and other hotels (the Perry was destroyed by the 1888 fire), as well as the various springs and homes along Hillside Avenue, Spring Street, and Prospect Avenue. The cars were originally mule-drawn, but were electrified in 1898. Total length was three miles, and grades were heavy.

Summertime in Eureka Springs was the time for lighthearted gaiety. Tourists brought in revenue, and the weather was conducive to outdoor sport. A major summer event was the July Fourth celebration down at the Narrows, and the railroad played a major part in making it a festive one. Early on the holiday morning, locomotive No. 2, the POWELL CLAYTON, would back a string of flatcars up to the depot and collect a full load of excited picnickers. The cars were equipped with benches and railings. Once loaded, the train would steam off and down the hill to the Narrows Cut. At that point a crude platform had been constructed to accommodate the crowd, one car at a time; from the platform a stairway led up to the north part of the bluff. Planks had also been placed between the rails so that the excursionists could walk over the White River bridge to a rocky beach and to the little town of Beaver. This expanded the opportunities for locating choice picnic spots.

All through the day the train shuttled back and forth between the Eureka depot and the Narrows, making way of course for the regularly-scheduled trains to and from Seligman. The climactic event of the day came just after dark, when the fireworks were set off high atop the bluff. As the holiday crowd was pushed back up the hill late in the evening, its joy was supreme.

Private cars were often seen at Eureka Springs. The one in the upper view, opposite, is from the Burlington. Richard Kerens' car, the *Katharyne*, was a frequent visitor after it was delivered from Pullman in 1894. Through the Narrows cut, left, can be seen the White River bridge with locomotive No. 2 approaching across it. This cut was the scene of many excursions, especially on the Fourth of July when fireworks were set off from the top of the bluff. Engine No. 1 brings the morning train across the White River bridge, above. The sleeping car from St. Louis is at the rear. This bridge was replaced by a sturdier structure in 1907. *(Opposite above: W. A. Spalding; left: Arkansas History Commission; above: Eureka Springs Carnegie Library)*

Other events, external to the Eureka Springs locale, had their influence during the 1887-1899 era. One was the study of the zinc and lead region in 1890-1892 by Dr. John C. Branner, state geologist of Arkansas. This study was centered around Boone, Marion and Searcy Counties in the north central part of the state. One of the area's richest in high grade zinc ore was located on Rush Creek south of Yellville in Marion County and some 30 miles east of Harrison. Travel to this location in 1889 was described in an 1890 issue of the *Transactions of the American Institute of Mining Engineers* as follows:

> One hundred and twenty miles of hard travel over steep ridges almost due east from Fayetteville, . . . about 100 miles from Eureka Hot Springs [sic], or 75 miles northwest from Batesville, will bring the traveller to the waters of the Buffalo Fork of the White River, in a wild, thinly-settled, heavily-timbered country, now being prospected quite actively for zinc, and known as the Buffalo or Rush Creek district . . .
>
> What little ore has been shipped from this district was hauled to White River, 6 or 8 miles, floated in flats down to opposite Batesville, 60 or 70 miles (the flats being then poled back by hand), and then hauled 4 or 5 miles to the shipping point on the railroad; thence by rail to St. Louis. The ore shipped was hand-cobbed or hand-jigged, and the lean ore necessarily went to the dump . . .
>
> The advantage this district possesses in having deposits located in the hills above water level is evident. If they prove as extensive and as rich as the prospects indicate, zinc can be made here at very low cost.

Clearly, rail transportation of the ore would be required – a need not unknown to Iron Mountain management as well as to Eureka Springs Railway management. The Harrison extension, plus feeder lines to Yellville, Rush, and other mining centers should produce a great deal of revenue tonnage. Branner, in his 1892 annual report, urged that railways be built into the mining region. By 1897 a mining boom in Marion County burst forth, and stagecoaches served Yellville and Rush both from West Plains,

Missouri (on the Kansas City, Fort Scott and Memphis railroad) and from Eureka Springs.

Another external event influencing the railroad was the purchase of the Frisco by the Atchison, Topeka and Santa Fe Railroad on May 23, 1890. At the time the Frisco had 1329 miles of main line and owned 50% of the Atlantic & Pacific Railroad. The Santa Fe owned the other half. At the March 16, 1890 stockholders meeting of the Eureka Springs Railway a resolution to extend the line to Harrison had been passed, but with the new Frisco management this hope was again thwarted. The Santa Fe-Frisco system went into receivership during the national depression of 1893, and it was not until December 12, 1895 that it was reorganized and the Frisco again became a separate company.

Still another external event was the announcement by the Iron Mountain that a "White River branch" would be extended to the zinc region northwest of Batesville. Rumblings of this plan had gone on since an 1882 announcement of a projected Iron Mountain line from Newport to Eureka Springs. By 1888 Iron Mountain maps showed a proposed line from Batesville (on the branch line completed in 1883) northwest to Carthage, Missouri, a rail point near Joplin. The Eureka Springs management had St. Louis connections to keep it informed on Iron Mountain thinking. Some sort of action, if taken at all, would have to be taken soon.

As the century closed, the earnings record for the Eureka Springs Railway began to taper off. Freight business had not expanded much beyond the needs of Eureka Springs. Passenger travel to the springs was down, but after 1896 this was offset by travelers going on to the zinc fields. Daily stages between Harrison and Eureka Springs were operated through Berryville, Green Forest, and Carollton and their traffic was indication enough that the Eureka Springs Railway needed to extend into additional revenue-producing areas. Accordingly, Kerens and Powell decided to depend on the Frisco no longer, and to promote the extension themselves among St. Louis capitalists.

In 1898 Kerens and Powell went to work in earnest. They hired John Hinckley, well-known civil engineer and advisor to railroad magnate B. F. Yoakum, to review the Martin survey and to develop cost estimates for extending the line into the zinc region.

This idyllic scene is on the line west of the Narrows, near the confluence of
Butler Creek and the White River. The considerable amount of rockwork in
the original construction is evident in the picture.

*(Arkansas Geological Survey)*

Hinckley and his party went into the field and extrapolated the Martin survey beyond Harrison to Dodd City, 23½ miles, and with a 35½-mile branch line to Yellville and Rush.

The Hinckley estimate for the 74-mile line to Dodd City was as follows:

| | |
|---|---:|
| Grading, bridging and masonry | $ 660,698 |
| Tunnel, 1100 ft. | 85,800 |
| Track and switches (60-lb. rail) | 345,600 |
| Buildings | 37,000 |
| General expenses | 60,000 |
| Total Cost | $1,189,098 |
| Cost per mile | $ 15,961 |

If the branch line were to be built, it was estimated to cost $14,000 per mile or $497,000. This cost per mile was not greatly different from that estimated in 1883 by S. C. Martin. To the total cost of $1,686,098 was added a contingency to give a requirement of $2,029,000. This was the kind of money that Kerens and Powell would have to raise.

The success of these two men is evidenced by their incorporation of a new organization, the St. Louis & North Arkansas Railroad Co., on May 25, 1899 under the general laws of the state of Arkansas. On this date also the property, rights, and franchises of the Eureka Springs Railway Co. were conveyed by deed to the St. Louis & North Arkansas. Directors of the new company were John Scullin, C. H. Smith, and F. J. Wade of St. Louis; O. W. Watkins and George West of Eureka Springs; J. W. Freeman of Berryville; and G. J. Crump of Harrison. Officers were: Watkins, president; Smith, vice president; West, secretary; and a James Madill of St. Louis, treasurer.

According to Interstate Commerce Commission reports, the directors were authorized to "purchase and acquire from the Eureka Springs Railway Co. all of its assets of every kind and character, including its property, rights, and franchises, excepting its cash, bills receivable, and the revenue accruing from operation of its railroad up to and including January 31, 1900, and to pay therefor $500,000 in first mortgage bonds and $600,000 in common stock of the St. Louis & North Arkansas Railroad Co."

The first mortgage bonds of the Eureka Springs, amounting to $500,000, were exchanged directly. The income bonds were exchanged for like par value in common stock of the new company. Eureka Springs common, at $500,000 par value, was exchanged for $100,000 par value of St. Louis & North Arkansas common. Thus, Kerens and Clayton were still very much involved with the new company, although they elected to be represented by others on the board and among the officers.

As the year 1900 approached there was excitement a-plenty, not only along the streets and in the homes of towns like Berryville, Green Forest and Harrison, but also in the headquarters of Eureka Springs' railroad. There may not have been gold in "them hills," but there was zinc and lead, vast regions of hardwood timber, and the chance of building through them to reach Little Rock. The Eureka Springs Railway reached its corporate end amidst waves of optimism.

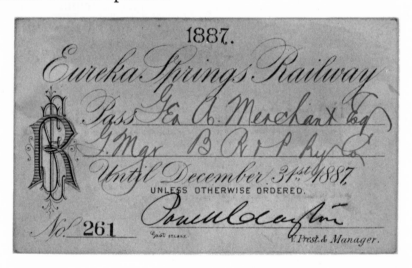

A few months after the Crescent Hotel opened, it was given a page of pictures (opposite) in *Harper's Weekly*, and a feature article. Both stressed the contrast between the hotel's gleaming elegance and the "primitive frontier town." Among the "many rare sights to be found among the Ozark Mountains" was the home of the "Modern Cliff Dwellers," a family of six, perhaps old-time hippies, who lived a mile and a half up the valley "under the

BASIN SPRING.

PIVOT ROCK.

OLD AND NEW.

EUREKA SPRINGS.

AT THE CRESCENT.

A RELIC.

MODERN CLIFF DWELLERS.

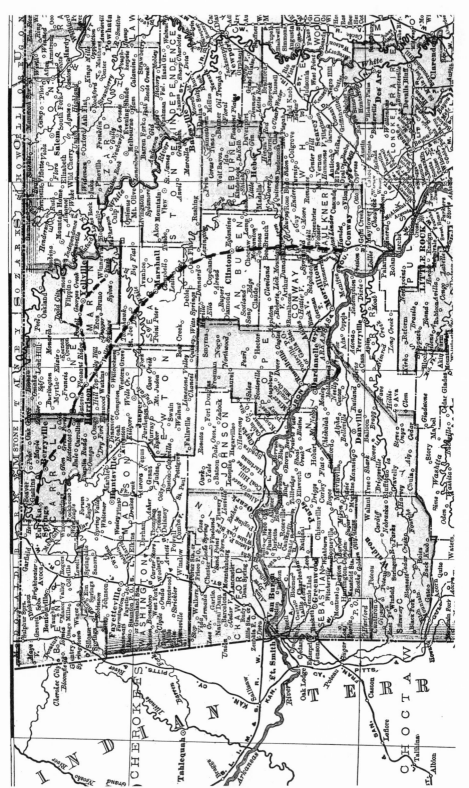

On this contemporary map of northwestern Arkansas have been superimposed the ex-

# Extension Eastward
## The St. Louis & North Arkansas

Eureka Springs in 1900 was a first-class city, and by today's standards was set amidst very rural surroundings. It had electricity, gas, waterworks, and a sewerage system — things which many important county seats of the Arkansas Ozarks did not have until the 1930s. Its street railway system was one of only a half-dozen ever to be built in the state. There was mail twice a day, telegraph and express service, and, not to be forgotten, the 42 springs whose water would cure kidney ailments, scrofula, liver complaint, eczema, catarrh of the bladder, etc. It was known as "The Gem of the Ozarks, where pure air blows and pure water flows, and where sleepless nights, mosquitoes and malaria are unknown."

The Frisco Line, in a 1900 brochure titled "The Top of the Ozarks" described the journey into Eureka by a typical traveler from St. Louis ($12.50 round trip fare):

> Seligman . . . illustrates the suddenness of the entrance into the Ozark Range . . . A neat little passenger train stands there, which the tourist takes to go to Eureka Springs. Immediately upon starting, this little train darts into a ravine, apparently on a downgrade, and stays in this gulch for about 19 miles. Then the impression deepens that the Ozark Mountains are not entirely make-believe, and as they are seen from this little train they do not convey the idea that one ought to attempt to walk all over them . . .

Because of its hillside homes, winding streets (never intersecting at right angles), and broad vistas, Eureka was, and still

The 45-mile stage run from Eureka Springs to Harrison had a scheduled running time of about eleven hours. Major stops were at Carrollton, Green Forest and Berryville, where the coach above is shown at the LaBelle House. Construction of the Harrison extension started from the point below, two miles north of Eureka Springs depot. The old road drops downhill to the Narrows. The new road curves to the right and follows a 1.75% grade to the tunnel. This wye was later given the simple name, "Junction."

*(Above: O. Klute Braswell; below: W. A. Spalding)*

is, called "America's Little Switzerland." Summer visitors included the gentility from St. Louis, Chicago and Little Rock, some of whom came by private railroad car and occupied choice suites at The Cresent. Things were going so well for the city that it did not seem possible that the brightness would ever fade.

The promoters of the railroad could well take credit for many of the conveniences of Eureka Springs. Powell Clayton himself had seen to the installation of the electrical power, water, and sewerage systems and provided an auditorium seating 3,000. The promoters had not done badly in their railroad venture, either. For the 17 years of operation up to the transfer of assets to the St. Louis & North Arkansas there had been operating income of $1,286,415 and expenses of $550,308. A total of $692,500 interest had been paid on the funded debt, leaving a surplus (after taxes and improvements) of $17,131. For an actual original cash outlay of around $500,000 the investors had been returned $692,500 in 17 years and they were now owners of St. Louis & North Arkansas securities.

In its subscription agreement dated June 27, 1899, the St. Louis & North Arkansas described the transfer of Eureka Springs securities and also stated that the traffic agreement with the Frisco would continue to contribute materially to the first mortgage bond interest. In fact, the percentage on freight went from 10% to 15% if the freight were minerals.

Details of issuing new securities were also disclosed in the subscription agreement. Capital stock would be issued on the basis of $25,000 per mile for the entire mileage from Seligman to the terminus of the extension and first mortgage 5% gold bonds would be issued also on the basis of $25,000 per mile from Seligman. Thus, if the 110-mile extension were made, total capitalization for the 129-mile system would be $6,450,000. Of this amount $1,100,000 would be transferred to the owners of the Eureka Springs Railway.

Harrison was the immediate objective. This city of 1,000 began as the post office of Crooked Creek in 1836, the name being changed in 1870. When Carroll County was subdivided in 1873, Harrison became the county seat of that portion named Boone County. Until the railroad to Eureka Springs was built, connections with the outside world were over mountain trails to Springfield, Missouri. After 1882, the stage, "fast hack," to Eureka, provided new travel convenience. But, quite naturally, Harrison wanted a railroad.

To extend to Harrison would require an actual outlay of some $800,000 to $1,000,000 for building and equipping the line. To accomplish this, new investors entered the picture, and one of the most prominent was John Scullin.

Scullin was a New Yorker who had entered the railroad construction business at an early age. He built 40 miles of the original Union Pacific and handled other construction contracts which gave him reputation enough to be selected to construct a major portion of the Missouri, Kansas & Texas line, the "Katy" from 1869 to 1874. During his work on the Katy he won from the Government the privilege of building through Indian Territory by laying 26.5 miles of track in 11 days, reaching the territorial boundary June 6, 1870. Scullin moved his headquarters to St. Louis in 1875 and prospered in railroad construction, street railway systems, and the manufacture of iron and steel. When he was persuaded to take an interest in the St. Louis & North Arkansas he was 62 years old but still vigorous and enthusiastic for new challenges.

Although he was also concerned with the building of the Arkansas & Choctaw line in southern Arkansas, Scullin gave full attention to the problems of constructing the line to Harrison. In July 1899 he selected Samuel W. Lee as chief engineer of the line. Lee, a Britisher, had worked for Scullin during the building of the Katy and had recently been chief engineer of the Wiggins Ferry Company, a large railroad terminal and ferry operation in the St. Louis area and which was headed by Scullin.

In August 1899 Lee began assembling men and equipment for final surveys. He also began negotiations with landowners and townspeople for the granting of right of way and cash bonuses to the railroad. This was common practice in those days, and if a town didn't come through with a reasonable contribution, the railroad might just miss it! Lee and the railroad officials were successful in getting most of the land donated and in getting the bonuses. The most important of the latter was $40,000 from Harrison if the railroad reached that point by April 1901.

Lee arranged for complete camp equipment, including wagons and draft horses, to be shipped to Eureka Springs, and with his party started surveying the new route in late August. Soon to join the party as a graduate civil engineer was young W. A. Spalding, who recorded much of the details of the survey and later construction, and whose name appears on the credit line of many of the photographs in this chapter. When Spalding joined the party he rounded out its full complement of eighteen, including the cook and his helper.

The survey progressed well and the party reached Harrison in late November. The new line was to connect with the old one about two miles north of the Eureka depot at Livingston Hollow. It would run up the hollow on a 1.75% grade and tunnel under the divide between the White and Kings Rivers. It would then drop to the Kings River crossing at Grandview, pass near Berryville, and cross a succession of ridges before bridging Long Creek near Alpena Pass. From Alpena there was a major divide to cross before the rails dropped downhill to Harrison in the Crooked Creek valley. The location of Berryville presented a problem, and to the consternation of the city fathers it was necessary to miss it by about three miles; a branch line would be built into town to provide direct service.

In order to run a line across the Ozarks without paralleling a major stream it was necessary to follow creeks to their headwaters and cut across the intervening ridge to connect with another creek. Because of this there were five 1.75% grades eastbound and six 1.75% grades westbound between Eureka and Harrison — and, to be sure, many other grades in the 1.0 to 1.75% range. And these stream courses were not very straight. The final location called for about 40% of the line to be on curves. Three major stream crossings required steel bridges, Kings River, Dry Creek near Green Forest, and Long Creek at Alpena.

When the property of the Eureka Springs Railway was transferred to the North Arkansas on July 31, 1900, action on the new undertaking proceeded rapidly. General contractor for construction was to be the Allegheny Improvement Company (John Scul-

A major undertaking of the Harrison extension was the excavation for and boring of the

lin, president) and the North Arkansas securities amounting to
$50,000 per mile would be issued to it. The agreement with Alle-
gheny was made February 7 and on the same date the contract for
clearing, grubbing, grading and bridge masonry was let by Allegheny to J. B. Colt & Son of Clinton, Missouri. Colt was well
known in railroad construction circles and among his jobs was
that of grading the Newport-Batesville branch of the Iron Mountain in 1882-1883. He also had worked for John Scullin on the
construction of the Katy through the Indian Territory. Colt immediately got forces and equipment into the field, and in March his
subcontractors were at work on both sides of the tunnel location.
Only about two miles from the start of the new line, this obstruc-
tion hindered movement of materials needed throughout the new
line location.

The initial stages of construction activity were described in a
Eureka Springs dispatch that was printed in the *Harrison Daily
Times* of March 3, 1900:

> This has been a rather hard week for those working on the
> new railroad, but work is progressing. Every train that
> comes from Seligman brings as many cars with construc-
> tion materials as can be safely hauled down the grade. This
> material is being unloaded at the switch put in at Living-
> ston Hollow where the new road begins. To one not accus-
> tomed to seeing such sights there seems to be enough on the
> ground to build a good long railroad, but it continues to
> come until the Eureka Road is forced to put a new force on
> its line to handle it . . .

The same article noted that the construction work force in Eureka
Springs had swollen in size while waiting for work to begin beyond the tunnel, and that the city people had generously provided
them with food while they waited.

A 1900 event of no little importance was the arrival in August
of Engine No. 3 from the Dickson Locomotive Works. (Eureka
Springs Nos. 1 and 2 had become St. Louis & North Arkansas
Nos. 1 and 2). This new engine was a ten-wheel (4-6-0) type,
useful both for passenger and freight service. It was a coal-burner
with straight stack, had 56-inch drivers, weighed 58 tons, and
exerted 20,900 pounds tractive effort. It was placed into service

shuttling construction materials from Seligman to the job site and later, after tunnel breakthrough, handled the tracklaying train. Two additional ten-wheel locomotives, heavier and more powerful than No. 3, were placed on order for early 1901 delivery.

By mid-1900 the North Arkansas management had decided to push on from Harrison to Little Rock, and not concern itself with branch lines into the zinc fields. The next segment of line would be built to the village of Leslie on Cove Creek, near the headwaters of the Little Red River. Leslie was only a few miles beyond the larger community of Marshall, county seat of Searcy County, but separated from it by a rather difficult mountain pass. Why Leslie was chosen is not quite clear, unless it was because of adequate level ground for terminal facilities and the proximity of dense growths of hardwood timber.

Parties were sent into the Harrison-Leslie area to establish preliminary surveys, and two alternate routes were selected. One would follow a circuitous but low-level route along Clear and Hampton Creeks to St. Joe and thence to Marshall and Leslie. The other would go directly to St. Joe through Valley Springs. Other studies took the surveyors as far east and north as Lead Hill and Yellville. After this preliminary work the parties returned to Eureka Springs in late 1900.

As 1900 wore on, progress on the tunnel was not at all satisfactory to Chief Engineer Lee. The tunnel was to be about 700 feet long and was a major undertaking when the extensive cuts on both ends were also considered. (At the time there was only one longer tunnel in Arkansas, that at Winslow on the Frisco between Seligman and Fort Smith; it was 1750 feet long and had been completed in June 1882.) Lee was concerned about losing bonuses and also felt that the contractor's boring equipment was inadequate. In October he took the tunnel out of the regular account and put it on a "cost-plus" basis. At the same time he installed a larger boiler, air compressor, and air piping. The work force ran 300 to 400 men and all efforts were redoubled. The final breakthrough came on Monday, January 7, 1901 at 2:00 p.m.

During the latter half of 1900 most of the grading to Harrison was completed; pile-driving and trestle-building progressed well and the masonry piers for the bridges were installed. Even the steel bridges were erected without benefit of the train, the steel members being hauled out from Eureka on wagons. The Wisconsin Bridge and Iron Company had the contract for the bridges and erection was under the supervision of a Swede named Ole Loken. He was especially proud of the handsome deck-truss spans at Kings River and Long Creek. Everything was in readiness for the tracklaying train when it could get through the tunnel.

During the last weeks of tunnel driving a tracklaying machine was constructed on a flatcar and by February 1901 it was through the tunnel and at work on the race to Harrison for the bonus. Engine No. 3 pushed six flatcars containing the laying machine, rail, and ties. The tracklaying gang was housed in bunk cars rented from the Frisco and moved along each day. Rails were curved at a material yard at Beaver, the current name of the station at the White River crossing by the Narrows, and brought forward each day as needed. Some local color associated with the tracklaying has been recounted by W. A. Spalding, the civil engineer mentioned previously:

> When the tracklaying had gotten opposite Berryville, I was ahead one day setting line stakes for the track when Mr. Lee rode up hurriedly and advised me that the tracklayers had struck on account of poor food. He instructed me to go back immediately and take charge of the boarding outfit, saying, 'keep them satisfied. I don't give a damn what it costs!'

> He was evidently again afraid of losing the Harrison bonus. Obeying his instructions, I sent for our old camp cook, Frank Bentley . . . [and] placed heavy orders for food, including California canned goods and Kansas City meats.

> The change pleased the 'hobos' and the tracklaying progressed satisfactorily . . .

> While laying track up the hill east of Long Creek, we had a small race riot. Snow was on the ground and the tracklayers had built a fire and were huddled around it, when a negro tie bucker pushed into a white man who pushed him away . . . The negro shot him in the leg and fled. He was easily tracked in the snow, captured and sent to jail in Harrison.

The tracklaying approached Harrison in mid-March and it was a favorite pastime of the local residents to go out to the right of way and watch the gang work. Fortunately the weather was dry and progress was rapid. Often only every other crosstie was put in place. Lynn Brown of Harrison reports that in March 1901 the patrons of Wiley Conley's Store in Harrison were invited to submit guesses as to when the track would be laid across the east line of a farmer's field at the city limits, winner to receive a ten-dollar gold piece.

An interesting aspect of the tracklaying was the insistence by Chief Engineer Lee that all the rail joints, on both curves and tangents, would be exactly opposite each other. Common practice then, as now, was to stagger the joints. This funny idea of Lee's may have come from his British background, but he certainly left his mark on the line. Opposed joints would be used throughout, until the North Arkansas was completed.

Finally, at the close of the day's work on March 21 the rails had reached a point just outside the Harrison city limits and the welcoming celebration was set for the next day. The train had backed up to Capps for more supplies (a supply train powered by a rented Frisco locomotive regularly shuttled materials from Beaver and Eureka Springs) and to spend the night.

The next morning at 9:15 a.m. the tracklaying team crossed the city limits. Bill Tarr, engineer, and Wesley Clayton, fireman, were probably the most important men in northern Arkansas in the view of numerous small boys present. The *Harrison Daily Times* recorded the event:

> It has been the intention of the people of Harrison to with-hold their enthusiasm for the arrival of the big excursion which will constitute the first passenger train to arrive in Harrison. But yesterday morning when the locomotive whistled for the corporate limits and the triumphant march of 200 spikers and others progressed toward the depot grounds, our people could hold their delight no longer, and the demonstration began which included everybody and lasted throughout the day. The construction train was decorated with bunting and the Harrison Coronet Band played for the enjoyment of everyone.

Brand-new engine No. 3 brings a construction train with a Frisco flatcar across the equally new Kings River bridge near Grandview. The first train into Harrison crosses the city limits at 9:15 a.m. on March 22, 1901, below. This was a tracklaying train, but the bunting suggests that some planning went into the occasion. *(Two pictures: W. A. Spalding)*

The Harrison people had, as Ralph Rea wrote, "dreamed of this day, ever since the railroad came to Eureka Springs twenty years before. Now two shining threads of steel winding through the hills stood as a symbol of hope."

During the next three weeks the entire line was surfaced, fully tied, and better aligned. Work into Berryville was completed and the tracklaying gang was disbanded. Some of the construction people moved back to the Seligman-Eureka Springs segment for rehabilitation work scheduled there. Regular train service on the Harrison extension began April 15, 1901.

Harrison had its formal celebration on April 15th. President Watkins, General Manager George West, and others were present. The special train was pulled by No. 2, which was brightly polished for the occasion. In his *Boone County and Its People*, Ralph Rea records the occasion as follows:

> . . . the people swarmed to [the station at] the end of the line to see the first train come in. The band played and local notables together with railroad officials spoke. Farmers crowded in close, craning their necks at the black steaming monster, and their womenfolk stood a little further back with babies in their arms and children clinging to their skirts.
>
> This was one of Harrison's greatest days, and the people were enthralled by the promises that they would someday be a great and prosperous city. Then the program was over, and the engineer leaned from the cab window and shouted: 'Give us room down there — we've got to turn around!'
>
> There was a mad scramble as men, women and children rushed away from the tracks.

Berryville had its formal inauguration of train service on June 15, and John Scullin was present for that occasion. A beautiful flower parade preceded the speech-making at the public square, and some 2,000 people attended. There was a break for lunch served in the courthouse by Berryville women and the proceeds from the lunch went to the "depot building fund." It was not unusual for a town to provide a depot building as well as the site for it.

A crowd gathered at the Harrison depot, above, for the arrival of the first passenger train. The location is Crooked Creek Valley, and the future site of the Harrison shops can be seen in the right background. On its return trip to Eureka Springs, the first train stopped at Freeman, below, where the depot was still under construction. (*Two pictures: W. A. Spalding*)

The completed line from the Eureka Springs connection (now a station with the unimaginative name, Junction) was 49.5 miles long and was laid with 65-pound steel rails on white oak ties. There were some 184 curves on the main line, with maximum curvature of 9°, except for a 10° curve near Grandview. Bridges were rated for Cooper E-40, more than adequate for the 31,000-pound axle loading of No. 3. Stations were of a standard wooden construction and were equipped with wooden platforms. As previously noted, maximum grades were 1.75%, compensated for curves. On such grades, No. 3 was rated at 396 tons hauling capacity.

April marked the arrival of engines Nos. 4 and 5, ten-wheel 4-6-0 types from Cooke Locomotive Works. Somewhat heavier than No. 3, these engines weighed 65 tons and exerted 25,600 pounds tractive effort. They were rated for 472 tons on the 1.75% grades. This gave the North Arkansas four serviceable engines, No. 1 having been retired in 1900 and its boiler used for steam generation at the Eureka shops.

Regular service from Seligman to Harrison included a daily passenger train, making the run of 66 miles in about four hours, and a daily freight that hauled passengers. Rolling stock was tight, and the arrival of a new baggage-express car late in the year freed the combination car for the freight, or mixed train. Prior to that, equipment was rented from the Frisco. A significant event in the traffic situation was the shipment on April 7 of the first car of zinc ore on the line, from the Almy mine near Alpena to a smelter at Granby, Missouri. Other carloads of ore followed, and the general development of freight business was promising.

Eureka residents were almost as excited over the new line as were the Harrison residents. Otto Rayburn reports that Eureka people hired rigs to drive them to Harrison in order to ride the first train back. During the celebration this verse was sung:

> A rubber-tired surrey
> A rubber-tired hack
> We're going down to Harrison
> to ride the Booger back

How widespread was the use of the term "Booger" is not known, but one may be sure that it was used with an endearing attitude. From the broad verandas of the Crescent its whistle could be heard beyond the tunnel as it approached Eureka and the sounds never failed to arouse the emotions of the listeners.

On a lower note the upsetting news came from the East that construction of the White River Railroad was about to begin. This subsidiary of the St. Louis, Iron Mountain and Southern was granted a charter on February 8, 1901, to build from Batesville generally northwestward to a connection with the Lexington and Southern Division of the Missouri Pacific at Carthage, Missouri — about 250 miles. Contracts were let and grading and rockwork begun near Batesville in May, the construction forces not far behind the parties making final location surveys. (An interesting account of the White River Railroad surveying work has been given by Tom Shiras, early newspaperman of Mountain Home, Arkansas, in *The History of Baxter County*.) With the resources of the Gould empire behind it, there was little doubt that this Iron Mountain project would be completed.

Of interest also to North Arkansas management was the news of a charter granted to the Morning Star Railroad Company on February 18, 1901. Named for the Morning Star mine, most famous in the Rush Creek mining district, this line was proposed to run from Rush or Yellville southeastward to Newport, about 100 miles. At Newport it would connect with the White and Black River Railroad (later Rock Island) for service to Brinkley and Memphis. The line was surveyed through a rugged mountain terrain under the direction of Major S. L. Shellenberger, a prominent civil engineer who had earlier been associated with Lee and Scullin on the Katy Railroad. The Morning Star survey called for maximum grades of 1%, but curves up to 15 degrees. Capitalization was $25,000 per mile. The Morning Star would be a direct competitor of the White River Railroad and both would be competitors of the North Arkansas for the zinc ore business.

The boom was on in the mining region, and a number of railroads had been chartered to serve it. But there were factors working against the commitment of outside capital. First, there was the variability of the zinc and lead market — there seemed to be a rapid succession of feasts and famines for the mining people. Second, the ore presented some difficulties of separation before smelting; the desirable zinc carbonate (smithsonite) was often admixed with zinc sulfide and zinc silicate. The required refining called for reduced values of the raw ore. Third, no one could be sure how extensive the deposits really were. The Morning Star interests apparently felt that the mines could support a 100-mile line. The North Arkansas management decided to "wait and see" before sending a feeder line into the Rush district. On the other hand, the projected line to Leslie penetrated directly an active district around St. Joe.

A survey party returned to the Harrison-Leslie area in the summer of 1901 in order to develop final location plans. This party was under the direction of B. J. Dawley, who had been operating the material yard at Beaver. Revisions made by this party called for bypassing Valley Springs by running from Harrison through Bellefonte and cutting across several ridges to reach St. Joe. From St. Joe, Dry Creek would be followed to the Buffalo River.

This location crew had its troubles working around the contours of the Ozarks. One member of the crew was a young engineer named Carlos Kirkpatrick, who later would rise to one of the top engineering jobs on the Missouri Pacific system. In a letter to W. A. Spalding, Kirkpatrick related:

> We spent weeks trying to get a line from the Buffalo River crossing . . . to the top of the Boston Mountains south of Marshall. We ran back lines down every hill and draw in that country. Finally we tried Brushy Creek, which runs into Buffalo River just below the proposed crossing, and were able to secure 1.75% maximum grade with compensation for curvature. The preliminary line had already been run ahead of us and somebody had made a ten foot mistake in the wrong direction on the levels. This caused the cut below Marshall to be deeper than planned.

Surveying mistakes were likely to generate the full wrath of Chief Engineer Lee. In this area he had made too low an estimate of the cost, and it was not unusual for him to shout to a transitman, "You run that transit like a small boy — or a jackass!"

At length, the line from the Buffalo to Leslie was established. It ran on a continuous heavy grade for about 12 miles to a summit at a point east of Marshall called by the early settlers "Gap of the Mountain." Then it dropped on an easy grade to Leslie. The length of the line from Harrison to Leslie would be about 60 miles. By the end of the summer the North Arkansas management had given Lee the "highball" to start construction.

Another 1901 activity of note was the complete rehabilitation of the original Seligman-Eureka Springs line. New 65-pound rails replaced the worn 56-pound rails. New ties and ballast were added. New piling went into trestles. There was some concern that the White River bridge might not be strong enough for planned heavier motive power, but a decision to strengthen it was held in abeyance. In general, the original line was brought up to the standard of the new line.

The contract for clearing, grading and bridging for the Leslie extension was let in October by Allegheny Improvement. There had been trouble in obtaining bidders, and the firm of Frank McGonigle finally agreed to do the job on a cost-plus basis. Active work got under way in November.

By mid-January about ten miles of the extension had been graded. Masonry piers for a two-span deck girder bridge across Crooked Creek at the Harrison outskirts had been set and were awaiting steel. (Wisconsin Bridge and Iron had been given the contract for all steel bridges between Harrison and Leslie.) Clearing was in progress at many points, and most of the land had been procured.

To the east, the first spike on the White River Railroad was driven on January 21, 1902. The ceremony was held at White River Junction, about two miles west of Batesville, Arkansas, on the Cushman branch. A large and enthusiastic audience watched Colonel J. C. Yancey, master of ceremonies and prominent Batesville lawyer, drive the spike and send this North Arkansas competitor on its way. The survey for the road was now fairly well established, and the route would pass only about 10 miles north of Harrison. Whether the Goulds would send a branch line to Harrison was a point of some concern by the North Arkansas management.

Celebrants at the formal opening of service to Berryville can be seen at the partly constructed depot, where the train stands with at least one coach from the Santa Fe. Engine No. 4 is pictured at the Eureka Springs shops, along with some of the shop crew, about 1906.

*(Above: O. Klute Braswell; below: E. G. Baker)*

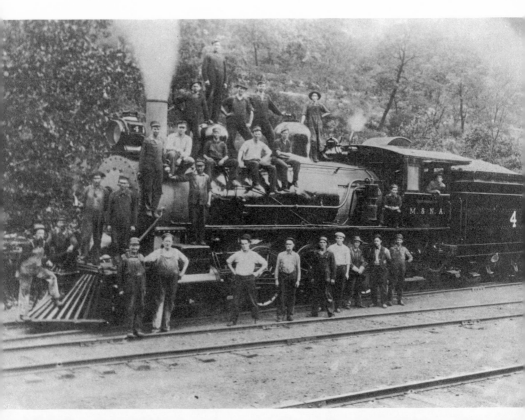

Tracklaying on the Leslie extension began Thursday, March 13, with the completion of the Crooked Creek bridge. Ten cars of steel rails had been received in Harrison earlier in the week, and 250 more carloads were on order. John Scullin was present when tracklaying began, but there was no ceremony. The gang just went to work.

By June grading was completed to St. Joe, 29 miles, and track had been laid to Olvey, 10 miles. The big undertaking of constructing concrete piers for the Buffalo River bridge was under way, using materials hauled by wagon to the site. On July 15 track was complete and train service started to Everton, 14.5 miles from Harrison.

As 1902 wore on, construction proceeded well until the Buffalo River was reached. Service was opened to St. Joe on September 15 and to the newly-created town of Gilbert on December 1. This new town was named for Charles W. Gilbert, Secretary-Treasurer of Allegheny Improvement Company and "confidential man" for Scullin. He had many other railroad affiliations and in later years would become president of the North Arkansas. The town was located on the north bank of the Buffalo, and considering the status of the bridge job it was apparent that Gilbert would serve as a terminus for some time. A wye was installed to turn the locomotives.

St. Louis & North Arkansas Time Table No. 17, effective November 30, 1902, showed the new service to Gilbert. A morning daily passenger train from Seligman arrived at 1:30 p.m., turned, and departed again at 2:30 p.m. A daily freight left Eureka Springs in the morning and arrived at Gilbert at 6:30 p.m. After a short layover it returned to Eureka during the night. Motive power availability was still tight, what with only four engines, but the passenger car shortage was alleviated a bit by the delivery from American Car and Foundry of a new combination car and a new baggage-mail express car.

The citizens of Marshall had raised $2,000 for the "depot fund" and had made right of way contributions to the railroad; now they were eager to see the rails reach their town. But the delay in completing the bridge seemed interminable. This was a large structure with curved approaches and comprised three 150-foot through-

The St. Louis & North Arkansas ordered some handsome rolling stock from the American Car & Foundry Co. Shown above is 12-wheel baggage car No. B7, later No. 60; below is combination car No. C9, later No. 51.

*(American Car & Foundry Co.)*

truss spans plus a 90-foot deck plate girder span. There were problems of alignment, high water, and cold winter weather. The Buffalo waters were extremely treacherous at this point, and there had been problems of securing the foundations adequately. The delay in completion lasted until mid-1903.

The *Harrison Daily Times* of August 8, 1903, contained a dispatch from Marshall, apparently dated Friday, August 3:

> Marshall is now a railroad town. Let those who doubt it come to town and take a look at the cars. The construction train reached the city limits on Thursday afternoon and track will be laid to the depot today. A great crowd watched the first approach of the locomotive into Marshall. Work on the depot is progressing rapidly. It is thought that Marshall will have regular service by the tenth or fifteenth of August.

The tracklayers continued through Marshall, up the 1.75% grade over "Gap of the Mountain," and then moved rapidly along the next seven miles to Leslie. This latter stretch contained two of the three straight sections of a mile or more between Harrison and Leslie. There is no record of a celebration of the arrival of the tracks at Leslie, but regular train service was started on September 11, 1903. Leslie had until a few years before been known as the village of Wiley's Cove, but had incorporated in 1902 and could now look forward to becoming an important point on the railroad. It was with keen interest that the townspeople observed the erection of an engine shed, shop building, yard tracks and wye.

Additional motive power for the North Arkansas arrived in 1903. In January Nos. 6 and 7 were shipped from Baldwin Locomotive Works. These engines were of the mogul type and at 68 tons they were the heaviest on the line. Their axle loadings of 38,000 pounds took them close to the E-40 bridge limit that had been used east of Junction and caused further concern over the old White River bridge which was limited to loadings of about 30,000 pounds per axle. Later in the year, probably around October, No. 8 — another 2-6-0 — arrived. This was the first second-hand engine to be used by the railroad; it was built by Baldwin in 1887 and had been in service on the Cincinnati, New Orleans &

Texas Pacific line. At 50 tons, it was considerably lighter than the other moguls.

The White River Railroad, now officially a branch of the Iron Mountain, was completed to the newly-established river town of Cotter, Arkansas in September. The line had followed the north bank of the river some 95 miles from Batesville, and now must leave the valley and cut across a rugged section of the Ozarks. Work in this area would move slowly. There were five long tunnels and many high trestles and this would give the North Arkansas some time to look toward its sources of competitive bridge traffic. It was clear that the Frisco traffic agreement would have to be sacrificed. The competition of the Morning Star line was of no great concern; that line had applied for a year's extension of time (in which to construct 10% of its route) in December 1902, and in mid-1903 was having no success in selling a $3,500,000 bond issue through the New York trustee.

It was significant that on December 18, 1902, a charter in the State of Arkansas was granted to the Leslie & Southern Railway to construct a line between Leslie and Little Rock. The North Arkansas was behind the venture, with Charles Gilbert and George Sands listed among the directors. Sands was a veteran railroad man who had become associated with Scullin in the St. Louis, Kansas City, & Colorado line from St. Louis toward Kansas City. When that line was sold to the Rock Island, Sands joined the North Arkansas (in August 1902) as a vice president. The Leslie & Southern was to be about 120 miles long and would pass through Stone, Van Buren, Cleburne, White, Faulkner, and Pulaski Counties. Capitalization was to be $3,000,000.

There was much speculation regarding the location of the line. The listing of counties gave a clue that the route to Little Rock would be somewhat circuitous. Contemporary newspaper reports from Heber Springs, Quitman, and Conway indicated that those towns would be served by the new line. Chief Engineer Lee and his party were known to have covered the corresponding areas, but when questioned Lee would not give out details. The reason for this was that North Arkansas management had not yet decided that Little Rock should be the objective.

The town of Alpena developed when the railroad missed the more stable nearby community of Carrollton. The view above, looking east, shows water tank, depot and new stores as they were in 1901. The Long Creek bridge, below, was picturesquely situated in the middle of an S-curve. This scene, looking toward Alpena, indicates that construction standards for the line were quite good. (*Two pictures: W. A. Spalding*)

The actual route proposed was as follows: from Leslie the line would follow the Little Red River Valley to a point near Heber Springs and then cross the divide to the valley of Cadron Creek, passing near the town of Quitman. It would then run south to Conway where it would connect with the Iron Mountain line for access to Little Rock. There would be relatively few heavy grades and by swinging to the east the important community of Heber Springs would be served, at least by a short branch line.

During 1903 there were conflicting reports about the pursuit of this effort. In July it was announced that the extension to Little Rock would begin shortly. In August, as the rails were nearing Leslie, it was reported that the construction contract had been let. Then, in September, North Arkansas officials denied letting the contract. In November, the intention to build to Little Rock was reiterated, and final location surveys were scheduled for spring 1904.

The year 1903 closed with Seligman-Leslie operations of the St. Louis & North Arkansas firmly established. For the year ending June 30, 1902 there had been gross earnings of $107,871 which did not quite cover the $121,042 interest payments on the funded debt, but there had not been full operation of the line. Daily passenger and freight trains moved in and out of Leslie, discharging merchandise and machinery, and collecting carloads of wood products such as staves, spokes, hubs, and handles. The new line from Harrison was complete with station buildings at Bellefonte, Olvey, Everton, Kilburn (later Pindall), St. Joe, Gilbert, Marshall, and Leslie. Water tanks were provided at Everton, Leslie, and just north of Gilbert. There were more of those ubiquitous 1.75% grades — six eastbound and four westbound — and 14 stream crossings requiring one or more steel spans. Curves were generally limited to six degrees, but a few of them sharpened up to the 7 to 10-degree range. Construction had been fairly expensive, averaging some $20,000 to $25,000 per mile.

Evidently North Arkansas management wanted to take a "breather" on construction and study their railroad resource. They may well have mused over such questions as: "Will the Iron Mountain build a branch into Harrison?" "Will the Searcy & Des Arc (Rock Island) extend north from Searcy to Heber Springs?"

"Will one of the many chartered railroads actually build into the Rush Creek zinc field?" Perhaps the most important question to be answered was the continuing one: "How can a large railroad be induced into purchasing the North Arkansas?"

The year 1904 came and went without particular incident for the North Arkansas. Just to the north, the gap in the Iron Mountain's White River railroad had closed to less than 100 miles, but construction progress was exceedingly slow. Gross earnings in 1904 for the North Arkansas were $131,838 but bond interest payments were $153,543. Business was good, but the overcapitalization at $3,065,500 common stock and $3,065,500 first mortgage bonds was clearly too much for a railroad of this type. The investors were getting a good profit on their cash outlay of less than $3,000,000 but were bleeding the company too heavily.

In 1905 Eureka Springs celebrated its 25th anniversary of incorporation, and the April 24, 1905 special edition of the *Daily Times-Echo* was filled with photographs and stories about Eureka Springs people and their activities. There was a section dealing with the railroad and the towns it served. For example, St. Joe was noted as being surrounded by the greatest deposit of zinc ore to be found on the North Arkansas. Gilbert was described as "a pretty little point . . . where the hacks meet the train to carry prospectors and investors over to the rich Rush Creek mining district." Leslie was noted as destined to be an important division point on the railroad "when [it] is extended on to Little Rock or Memphis, wherever its destination may be." It was also noted that the large H. D. Williams Cooperage Co., of which more will be said later, was moving to Leslie from Poplar Bluff, Missouri.

The newspaper item gives the first indication that Little Rock might not be the eastern destination of the railroad. It was definite, however, that the line would go at least as far down the Little Red River as the community of Settlement, 25 miles. Chief Engineer Lee made final location surveys for this segment in early 1905, and then continued preliminary surveys on down the river valley to Heber Springs, another 27 miles. Then, in May or June, the North Arkansas management made the fateful decision not to build directly to Little Rock, but rather to head directly toward some point on the Mississippi River.

Clearly, this was not a decision arrived at lightly. Many factors had been at play. Taking the line to Little Rock from Leslie would mean constructing about 45 miles of route across rough terrain and acquiring 30 miles of trackage rights over the Iron Mountain from Conway to Little Rock. And this would be the completion of the undertaking — there would be no place to go from Little Rock. On the other side of the coin (and one may have been flipped!), taking the line to the Mississippi could be a step in the direction of building on to Mobile or Pensacola on the Gulf. Construction in Arkansas would be across comparatively level land at modest cost.

The favored initial terminus was Helena, Arkansas. This Mississippi River town was founded about 1820 and had enjoyed an interesting history associated with river activities and with the Civil War. Situated at the southern end of Crowley's Ridge (a chain of hills extending north into Missouri), and about 50 crowline miles southwest of Memphis, it had a population of about 7,500 in 1905. Helena had adequate port facilities for barges and river steamers, and was served by the Illinois Central (by ferry from Trotter's Point, Mississippi) as well as by the Iron Mountain and the Arkansas Midland railroads. There was good reason to believe that on an interim basis it would be an entirely acceptable southern anchor for the line.

From Helena, further extension of the North Arkansas would carry it through Meridian, Mississippi, to Pensacola, Florida, or Mobile, Alabama, some 360 to 380 miles. Scullin and Sands made several trips to those Gulf ports, and reportedly took options on acreage for terminal facilities. These far-reaching plans even included a branch line to be constructed to Little Rock from some appropriate point on the main line.

To implement the plan for building to the Mississippi, the Southeastern Railroad Co. was incorporated on July 17, 1905, for the stated purpose of extending the line from Leslie "southeasterly, an estimated distance of 144 miles." Capital stock of $3,500,-000 was subscribed almost entirely by St. Louisans. North Arkansas management was prominent among the officers of the new company: George Sands was president, John Scullin was vice president, and Charles Gilbert was treasurer.

Washouts were always a problem on the North Arkansas. Above is shown one of the early ones which occurred near Pender, about five miles east of Seligman, in the spring of 1901. The depot platform scene below was at Alpena in April 1902. The camera was pointed toward Eureka Springs. The chair in the foreground was on a flatcar used for observation by a group arbitrating between the railroad and the construction contractor over payments. (*Two pictures: W. A. Spalding*)

Notable among the directors of the Southeastern Company was David R. Francis, a very prominent St. Louisan who had these credits: Mayor of St. Louis, 1885-1889; Governor of Missouri, 1889-1893; Secretary of the Interior, 1896-1897; and President of the Louisiana Purchase Exposition (St. Louis World's Fair of 1904) Corporation. He was also a successful businessman and had collaborated with Scullin in the profitable purchase and re-sale of the St. Louis, Kansas City, and Colorado line. Francis would continue to have a close interest in the North Arkansas until well after his appointment as Ambassador to Russia in 1917.

Management was not completely preoccupied with expansion to the south. The northern terminus at Seligman was unsatisfactory in its complete dependence on the Frisco. Several other railroads could be reached at nearby Joplin, a thriving Southwest Missouri city of 30,000 and adjacent to rich lead mining areas. Chief Engineer Lee went into the Seligman-Joplin region to locate a northward extension. His early surveys called for bypassing the 2.6% Seligman Hill by departing northward from the main line at Beaver, climbing gradually to the Ozark Plateau at Cassville, through what is now Roaring River State Park and then cutting across the Plateau through Granby to Joplin, a distance of about 60 miles.

But a less expensive extension location was ultimately selected, with new construction of only 30 miles. The rigors of Seligman Hill would be retained, and trackage rights would be required over the Frisco for about 10 miles north of Seligman, and over the Kansas City Southern for the final 20 miles to Joplin. Agreements with those railroads were duly obtained and the northward extension route was fixed.

Concurrent with expansion optimism was a pessimistic development. It was necessary to default on the July 1 bond interest payment of $76,625. The fiscal year ending at that time showed a $47,186 loss which wiped out the small surplus carried forward a year earlier. Frisco interchange payments and other sources would permit later payment of $106,357 interest during the 1906 fiscal year, but the bondholders clearly wanted a reorganization, and asked the mortgage trustee, St. Louis Union Trust to arrange for foreclosure.

Thus, the year 1905 was one of confrontation for Scullin and his colleagues. The line had to be extended, and the Frisco traffic agreement had to be sacrificed. The southern terminus was to be Helena, with its important rail and barge traffic connections. The northern terminus was to be Joplin, with its many rail connections. And last, but not least, the company had to be reorganized. Whether all these decisions were founded on complete objectivity is not clear. Retrospection shows that a great deal of subjectivity must have been involved. At any rate, a turning point had been reached and 1906 would open an important new expansion era for the North Arkansas.

Seligman is shown above, looking northwest toward the Frisco main line and the joint depot. North Arkansas trains from the south climbed a 2.6% grade in a cut just behind the stores and connected with the Frisco just beyond the picture to the left. They then backed to the depot on North Arkansas tracks to the rear of the building and tank. The photograph was taken about 1906. In the 1906 scene below, the train is headed toward the high bridge across the Buffalo River just downstream from the town of Gilbert.
*(Above: Bennie McCann; below: Eureka Springs Carnegie Library)*

# Completion of the Missouri & North Arkansas

---

The decision not to build the North Arkansas directly into Little Rock was indeed a fateful one. In retrospect, one is reminded of the words by Whittier:

> For all sad words of tongue or pen,
> The saddest are these: 'It might have been!'

Yes, it might have been that the North Arkansas would be running today if the management had elected to build a good bridge road from Joplin to Little Rock, giving a Kansas City-Little Rock distance of about 450 miles. This would be some 75 miles shorter than the present Missouri Pacific line through Coffeyville, Kansas, and Fort Smith, Arkansas (the old Central Division), where most of the traffic rolls, and about 55 miles shorter than the present Missouri Pacific line through Carthage, Missouri, and Newport, Arkansas (the old White River Division). At Little Rock, bridge connections with the Rock Island would have provided through service to Memphis or Louisiana. As noted earlier, sale of the road was prominent in the minds of Scullin and Francis; a Joplin-Little Rock line would probably have been quite salable to the Frisco.

The actual reaction of North Arkansas management to the pressure of the times can only be guessed. It seemed clear that help from the Frisco was not to be expected, what with that road's economic problems. But the national financial climate was good, and the idea of building on beyond Helena seemed reasonable. Any portents of the upcoming 1907 financial panic were apparently unnoticed.

Curiously, management made statements to the press that the Joplin-Helena line would "shorten the Kansas City- New Orleans haul by at least 100 miles"; such thinking must have been misguided. The total distance from Kansas City to New Orleans, via Kansas City Southern-North Arkansas-Illinois Central, was 922 miles. (Had the line gone through Little Rock, the distance would have been almost the same — 918 miles, using Rock Island plus Louisiana Railway & Navigation south of Little Rock.) This compared with existing routes as follows:

|                                                  | miles |
|--------------------------------------------------|-------|
| Kansas City Southern-La. Rwy. & Navigation       | 868   |
| Frisco-Illinois Central (via Memphis)            | 878   |
| Missouri Pacific (via Little Rock)               | 1012  |

One wonders whether the thinking regarding extension plans was not as misguided. But the die was cast in favor of Helena and points southeast, and that was that!

By 1906 the North Arkansas had become an "institution" to the hill folk from Seligman to Leslie. This was not just because of the endearing cars and engines meandering through the Ozarks. These people had contributed hard-won cash and real estate at the time of construction. They felt a proprietary interest in the road, an interest that would be manifested many times during the serious struggles that lay ahead for the North Arkansas. Still at the moment there was much visible activity in operations along the line, and the people must have felt that their railroad was indeed a prosperous one.

At the St. Louis headquarters there was anything but that serenity that is bred by prosperity. The St. Louis Union Trust Co. proceeded with arrangements for dissolution of the St. Louis & North Arkansas, and a "Committee of Reorganization" was given broad powers to foreclose the mortgage, form a new corporation to acquire the property, control operations of the existing railroad, and arrange for financing construction of the northern and southern extensions. This was a big assignment, but the committee was an able one: Scullin, Clayton, Kerens, Francis, plus the very prominent businessman and Washington University benefactor Robert S. Brookings.

A Principals' Agreement dated February 15, 1906, reveals the plan of the Committee:

1. On behalf of the bondholders, the Committee would make a reasonable bid for the property when it was sold.
2. The charter of the Southeastern Railroad would be amended to show a southern terminus at Helena.
3. It would be necessary to spend about $5,000,000 new money on the extensions.
4. Securities would be issued at the rate of $25,000 each of common stock and 4% gold bonds for each mile of new line constructed.

Allegheny Improvement Co., or another construction firm, would take the securities in payment for constructing and equipping the line. Finally, subscribers would be guaranteed that arrangements would be completed and construction under way by March 1907.

The St. Louis & North Arkansas was sold at Harrison on May 29, 1906 to the Committee for $2,000,000, and on June 16 the property, rights, and franchises were duly conveyed. The company was then reorganized as the Missouri & North Arkansas Railroad Company, with articles of incorporation filed in the Arkansas Secretary of State office on August 6, 1906. John Scullin was the president, George Sands was vice president, and David Francis was chairman of the board. Thus, the first half of 1906 was given over to creating a new organization and planning for its immediate growth.

Meanwhile, the last spike on the Iron Mountain's parallel White River line had been driven home on December 29, 1905 and regular train service established on January 21 following. (The first passenger trains starting from each end of the line never made it through — one was halted by a landslide and the other encountered impassable snowdrifts!) The 240 miles of new line between Carthage, Missouri and Batesville, Arkansas, had taken almost five years and $10,000,000 to build, but one could not argue over its being anything short of a first-class line in all respects. A 1906 company brochure exaggerated very little in proclaiming that in building the line the Iron Mountain had ". . . surmounted difficulties that, to the layman, are apalling: blasting, bridging and tunneling, until today, from Newport to Carthage

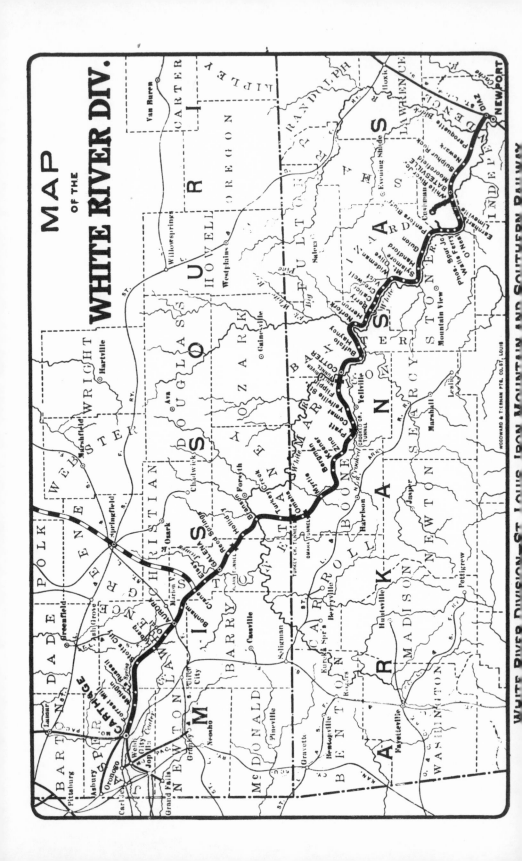

# MAP

OF THE

# WHITE RIVER DIV.

WHITE RIVER DIVISION—ST. LOUIS, IRON MOUNTAIN AND SOUTHERN RAILWAY

WOODWARD & TIERNAN PTG. CO. ST. LOUIS

266 miles of shining rails, on a roadbed a marvel of mechanical perfection, testify to its foresight and enterprise." The line was divided into three distinct segments topographically, with the center section of 97 miles between Crane, Missouri and Cotter, Arkansas, being the mountainous (and thus traffic-controlling) section.

In view of announced expansion plans, the same topographical division could be made of the North Arkansas. The line north of Seligman would be in the Ozark uplands and would have relatively minor grades;the line south of Leslie would follow the Little Red River before cutting across flat delta country and likewise would give minor hauling difficulties. In the center would be the mountain section of 121 miles, the characteristics of which could be compared with the equivalent section of the White River line as shown in the following table.

*Characteristics of Mountain Sections*
*North Arkansas vs. White River*

|  | North Ark. | White River |
|---|---|---|
| Route miles | 121 | 97 |
| Ruling grade, per cent | 1.75 | 1.00 |
| Max. curve, degrees | 10 | 6 |
| Avg. total curvature, degrees/mile | 120 | 82 |
| Wt. of rail, lbs./yd. | 65 | 85 |
| Bridge rating, Cooper | E-40 | E-50 |
| No. tunnels | 1 | 5 |
| Total tunnel length, ft. | 670 | 10,525 |

These data for January 1906 demonstrate the very high standards imposed on White River engineers by Iron Mountain President George Gould (son of the famous railroad tycoon Jay Gould), and they account for construction costs soaring as high as $100,000 per mile in the mountains. The numerous high trestles, deep cuts, and long tunnels gave the line a distinction that was discussed widely in civil engineering circles. But in North Arkansas circles these feats only meant a greater competitive position for this line that ran 10 to 40 miles north and which gave Gould his connecting link between Midwest and Southeast. And now it

The publicity view of No. 3 and a short mixed train emerging from the east portal of the tunnel near Eureka Springs dates from about 1908. The view from highway 7 south of Jasper, Arkansas, below, was taken in the 1960s, but it is still typical of the Ozarks' scenery through which the North Arkansas line was built (*Above: Louis Goodwin; below: Arkansas Publicity & Parks Commission*)

would be possible for Gould to send a branch line in from Bergman to Harrison, 10 miles, such as was already contemplated from Crane to Springfield in Missouri. Also contemplated by the Iron Mountain was a spur into the Rush Creek zinc region, already incorporated as the Marion County Railroad.

With such a formidable competitor just to the north, the expansion-minded resolve of the North Arkansas promoters must be admired if not condoned. On August 15 an agreement with Allegheny Improvement Co. was signed; Allegheny would construct and fully equip the line in consideration for $50,000 per mile in securities. The next step was to raise the money for payment.

The earnings record of the St. Louis & North Arkansas had not been bad, considering that no through traffic could be handled and that the region served was naturally slow in developing on-line traffic. For its corporate life from February 1, 1900 to June 16, 1906, performance was as follows:

| | |
|---|---:|
| Total revenue | $1,525,426 |
| Expenses | 937,324 |
| Gross earnings | 588,102 |
| Tax accruals | 56,279 |
| Interest on debt | 606,423 |
| Deficit | $ 74,600 |

The operating ratio (expenses to operating revenue) of 67% was in a good range. And the incremental cost of building from Eureka Springs to Leslie, somewhat less than $2,000,000, had received a $600,000-plus return in about six years. If the extensions could produce as much on-line revenue and, in addition, benefit from through routings, the venture could be profitable. This was the story taken to the potential new investors, many of them St. Louisans. And it worked.

The southern extension called for some 178 new route-miles that would cost about $4,000,000. The northern extension, now surveyed at 32 miles, would take another $750,000. History would show that the actual cost would exceed these estimates, but for the moment it was necessary to secure about $3,000,000 in subscriptions from people who had not previously invested in the

The group of men above are track laborers for the North Arkansas, just arrived in Searcy via the Rock Island. The building is the first Rock Island depot there, which was later replaced by a handsome brick structure. The date is early 1908. The pastoral scene below is at Cross Mountain, near Diamond Cave in the Jasper area of the Ozarks. *(Above: Oran Vaughan; below: Arkansas Publicity and Parks Commission)*

enterprise. And this took a bit of time and effort. It was not until October 20, 1906, that bids were opened for construction of the extension south as far as Searcy (92 miles); Burke and Joseph, a Cape Girardeau, Missouri firm, obtained the contract for clearing, grading, pile trestles and bridge masonry. Wisconsin Bridge and Iron won the contract for steel bridges. Right of way acquisition proceeded, and on November 19 it was announced that the contractor was moving into Leslie, that 10 miles of 65-pound rail were on hand, and that another 60 miles of the same weight rail would be delivered by February. Initial plans called for working primarily from the north end, with the North Arkansas covering a good portion of the hauling of materials and people.

On November 23 stockholders of the Southeastern Railroad voted to transfer their property (the assets were the usable surveys from Leslie to Pangburn) to the M. & N. A., and on December 17 the North Arkansas charter was amended to permit building to Helena. As a final official move in 1906, a contract was signed on December 27 with Scott and Dalhoff, a combination of St. Louis and Little Rock construction firms, for clearing, grading, and trestle installation on the northern extension. It would appear that all legal and financial arrangements were under control, and Allegheny could move ahead with final right of way arrangements and actual construction through the various subcontractors.

As indicated earlier, the initial southern objective was the city of Searcy, thriving seat of White County, 50 miles northeast of Little Rock and just four miles west of Kensett on the Iron Mountain main line from St. Louis to Little Rock. Searcy was at the end of a branch of the Rock Island system, and a shortline connection from Kensett and nearby Doniphan was under construction. These rail connections would permit construction to proceed northward from Searcy as it seemed desirable.

The Leslie-Searcy route as surveyed by S. W. Lee and party, generally followed the Little Red River Valley and traversed a thickly-timbered and thinly-settled section of the Ozarks. The only towns already established along the route were Settlement, Miller's Point, Heber Springs, and Pangburn. The survey called for 0.6% maximum grades, six degree maximum curves, and some

The view of men laying track into Shirley, above, was taken in April 1908, looking west, with the Little Red River in front of the bluffs in the background. Pushing the cars of ties and rails plus the tracklaying machines is locomotive No. 2, the old POWELL CLAYTON. Just below Shirley was a cut 43 feet deep, below. When completed in June 1908 it permitted tracklaying to continue south to Heber Springs. View is to the southeast with the Little Red on the right. (*Two pictures: W. DeWoody Dickinson*)

98 bridges. For miles the line would follow every twist and turn of the river and would pass through a scenic "Collonades of the Little Red" 20 miles south of Leslie, where heights of 500 feet above the roadbed were only a half mile apart. The line was far from straight; between Leslie and Heber Springs, 61 miles, some 160 curves would account for 50% of the total mileage!

Location of the northern extension offered few problems to the engineers. It would begin at Woodruff (later called Wayne), 9.2 miles north of Seligman on the Frisco, and would run generally west and north to Neosho. Although there were no established towns along the route, the area traversed was well populated and was considered one of the best farming areas in Missouri. The maximum grade would be 1%, the maximum curve four degrees, and over 80% of the line would be straight — something very unusual for the North Arkansas! Only one bridge with steel spans would be needed. Construction should move rapidly and inexpensively.

As 1907 opened, construction activity south of Leslie was picking up. Several hundred men were hired and put to work cutting timber and clearing a right of way. The first major construction camp down the road would be at Settlement, an old river town some 33 miles from Leslie. By the end of January dynamite charges were being set off to fashion a track shelf from the bluffs along Trace Creek, the tributary followed by the line from Leslie to the Middle Fork of the Little Red. By mid-February manpower shortages had been overcome, and there were more than 2000 men distributed over the entire Leslie-Searcy route. In addition to Leslie and Settlement, field offices were set up at Heber Springs and Searcy.

A very significant event of January 1907 was the placing of large orders for locomotives and rolling stock. If the North Arkansas was to expand to prominence, it would need the equipment to handle the volume of business. Arrangements were made for the purchase of a mogul (2-6-0) type locomotive secondhand from the Illinois Terminal Railroad at St. Louis. This engine was built by Baldwin in 1903 and thus was not overly-worn. It was given Number 9 and was assigned to the Searcy end of construction work.

One of the new consolidations, No. 10 to No. 14, heads a short consist toward Alpena on the Long Creek bridge, circa 1908. (*Grace Faulkner, courtesy O. Klute Braswell*)

On January 21 five consolidation (2-8-0) type freight locomotives were ordered from Baldwin for about $75,000. Although
basically standard 10-38 E Baldwin units, their specifications were
carefully developed to serve North Arkansas needs. The 167,000
pounds on the drivers represented a maximum axle loading for
65-pound rail and for the E-40 bridge ratings north of Leslie.
(Bridges on the extensions were upgraded to an E-50 rating.)
The 37,000-pound tractive effort permitted a 750-ton rating on
the 1.75% grades. They would nearly revolutionize freight hauling
practices on the North Arkansas. Given Numbers 10 through 14,
they would bring the total locomotives on the system to 13.

Also ordered in January were 100 all-wood boxcars and two
wooden coaches from American Car and Foundry, plus four
wooden coaches and a wooden baggage-express car from Pullman.
At the time the per diem rate on freight cars was only 25 cents,
but in July it was scheduled to go up to 50 cents. The higher figure
still didn't support the investment of about $600 per freight car,
but the North Arkansas needed leverage to get the cars that it
required, now that the Frisco interchange agreement had been
broken. In early February 100 wood stock cars and 100 wood flatcars were ordered from American Car, and by mid-1907 when
deliveries were in, the North Arkansas could boast a sizable
rolling stock, 354 cars, to be exact.

By March some 15 miles of "dump" were ready for rails, but
were broken by a gap where 190 feet of deck-plate girders would
span the Little Red. Some work was under way on the south end,
and Searcy had just announced a $6,500 bonus for the road plus
the usual donation of land for the route through the city.

As spring moved into summer, work progressed slowly. Steel
laying at Leslie started in mid-July. Glen Hackett, in his *History
of Shirley, Arkansas*, describes activities farther down the line
near Shirley, the name of the proposed station across the Little
Red from Settlement. He quotes his father, Will Hackett, a construction worker, as follows:

> We started above Shirley in March. Ten to fifteen men
> started to work. That was one of the hottest March months
> I had ever seen. Many men quit the first week. We chopped
> the trees down with axes. We were told to cut the large

Mogul No. 9 brought the first regular train from Searcy to Heber Springs. Standing in front of the engine are, left to right, fireman Feaman, engineer W. E. Tucker, conductor S. A. Mearns, brakeman Harry Clark and Heber Springs agent George W. Musick. The old photo below shows the locating crew for the extension south from Leslie in May 1907. The men are not identified but the scene is near Shirley and the Little Red River is below. *(Above: Fred Johnston)*

trees into lengths for crossties to use for building the railroad. The going was better when we passed through the
fields. Then we hit the big trees below Shirley. By the last
of August we reached the Van Buren County line below
Shirley. They wanted us to work with a crew on south, but
the mosquitoes got bad. We heard about workers needed in
the 'cut' below Shirley, so we got a job there.

According to Hackett, the cut below Shirley was a major undertaking for the construction forces. It took 50 mules and 75 men
several months to complete the job. Natives from Austria and
Bulgaria were imported and assigned to pick-and-shovel work
while others drove the mule teams hitched to Fresno buckets for
moving the earth. When crops were laid by, farmers from all over
Van Buren County put in brief terms as mule skinners. The Hackett history underscores the excitement wrought by the railroad's
plan and by the outsiders imported to help build it.

Clearing and grading for the northern extension got under way
in April 1907. John Scullin proceeded with arrangements for terminal property in Joplin, and on April 8 told the press that the
M. & N. A. would spend some $450,000 in that city. He also stated
that the North Arkansas would eventually build its own line in
from Neosho, paralleling the Kansas City Southern. In May,
Scullin turned his attention to the other end of the line, and
awarded to John Scott and Sons, of St. Louis, the contract for
clearing, grading, and bridging the 43 miles between Helena and
Wheatley, where the line was to cross the Little Rock-Memphis
main line of the Rock Island.

During the summer there was construction activity at one of
the older sections of the system. The original truss bridge at
Beaver, near Eureka Springs, was built in 1882-1883 to support
axle loadings of the day. The new consolidations and their succes-
sor locomotives would be too heavy for it, and it was not prac-
tical to strengthen it. So Wisconsin Bridge and Iron was called in
to construct and quickly move into place a heavier bridge with an
E-50 rating. This completed the rehabilitation of the original
Eureka Springs Railway as planned back in 1901.

Surveys south of Searcy had started northward from Helena
in March. In his "A Civil Engineer's Reminiscences" Ray Parme-

Shirley was a new town spawned by the North Arkansas. The view above shows its elements: school up on the hill, depot and water tank to the right, hotel near the depot, store buildings and lumber mill as they appeared about 1910. Another new town that came with the building of the railroad was Wheaton, Missouri. The lower view, circa 1910, shows civic effort in setting land aside for a park by the railroad station.

*(Above: William Ham; below: Olin Cartwright)*

lee, a member of the locating party, describes some of their tribulations:

> The year 1907 was a rainy one. Through water in creeks and bayous we waded and swam all during March and April, and finally reached Cotton Plant about the first of May, at least three weeks behind our schedule. Here we were delayed another two weeks waiting for the water to recede out of the White [River] and Cache River bottoms. . . . Because of malaria we came out of the bottoms with a debilitated crew. Two men died . . .

In charge of the locating party was John R. Wilbanks, who reported directly to Chief Engineer S. W. Lee. In April, Lee, then a man in his seventies, was replaced by W. S. Dawley and became a consultant to the railroad. Dawley had been Chief Engineer of the Chicago & Eastern Illinois line and, according to Parmelee, "His character and ability among railroad men of that era was outstanding."

The North Arkansas directors met on September 28 to approve final surveys for the 38-mile Kensett-Wheatley gap (the Dalhoff-Scott contract had been extended from Searcy to Kensett, four miles), and during the week of November 30 five separate contracts were made for preparing the right of way in that territory. The line from Searcy to Helena was almost a straight one. Totally different in character from the route north of Searcy, it involved only 10 curves in 86 miles and essentially no grades except near Helena where slopes of Crowley's Ridge gave one grade of 0.5%. Such an arrow-straight line across level country would appear to offer few obstacles for construction, but obstacles there were!

The problems lay in the Kensett-Wheatley section, where eight miles of line traversed wooded bottom land between the White and Cache Rivers. This was a habitually-flooded area, and to prepare a track elevation above flood level would require extensive embankments with riprap (stone) supports. The fill dirt would have to come from adjacent borrow pits. Neither river had levees, and whether these might have afforded real protection was questionable. It was this section that would later prove to be the Achilles heel of the North Arkansas.

Chief Engineer Dawley entertained bids for these eight miles on the basis of 650,000 cubic yards of side-borrow for embankments and 8,300 feet of pile trestle. Also, it would be necessary to cross the White River on a steel drawbridge 706 feet long. Because of the special enquipment and skills required, the short distance was divided and two contractors were used; each would employ revolving derricks with Page (drag-line) buckets in addition to the common mule-powered drag buckets and Fresno scrapers. Because of heavy stands of hardwood timber, it would be no little task to clear and grub areas for the railroad and for the borrow pits.

By October 1907 a financial panic was upon the nation. The stock market had started a decline in March, and by autumn a serious depression was threatening. Muir and White, in their book *Over The Long Term* describe how the country's financial leaders were called to Washington by President Roosevelt, and by a mighty collaborative effort staved off disaster. Inevitably, this turn of events delayed work on the North Arkansas, and an interested outsider would hear of relatively-slow progress. Yet there was the continued monotony of blast, scrape, and carry. Supplies for men and mules came in from the surrounding hills and from the railheads near Leslie and Searcy. Whether due to a shortage of men or money (or both) is not clear, but without question there was not a great deal of progress made during 1907 and 1908. Tracklaying inched forward behind bridge crews and excavation teams; at the end of 1908 a scant 20 miles of unsurfaced "65 pound" were down south of Leslie, and a heavy cut at Backbone Ridge had limited tracklaying to only six miles out of Searcy. On the northern extension progress was more rapid, and 20 miles of track had been put down during the last two months of the year.

Vice President George Sands took an active interest in construction, and employed an interesting conveyance for shuttling back and forth between Eureka Springs and the railheads north and south. Outwardly, the conveyance appeared to be caboose 305, outshopped by American Car and Foundry in September 1907, and resplendent in a coat of virulent red paint. But the interior was much less conventional: it was fitted out as a private car for Sands. There was a stateroom, beautifully furnished in light hardwood paneling and fitted with an iron half-bed, a toilet and lavatory, a kitchen and a combination lounge-smoker-guest room. Further, it had a feature few other private cars could boast, a special "vistadome" (the cupola) for broader viewing. When the car had served Sands' purpose, it was converted to a regular "hack" and it served the line well for many years. Executive comfort without extravagance . . .

On January 25, 1908, tracklaying on the northern extension was completed with a final tie-in to Kansas City Southern trackage at Neosho. John Scullin's plans for a Joplin terminal began to change as he discussed with the Santa Fe and the Kansas City Southern the possibility of pooling resources and constructing modern joint facilities for freight and passengers. For the present, the North Arkansas would use the K.C.S. facilities at Joplin.

Another January event of note was a meeting in Eureka Springs between Richard Kerens, Powell Clayton, and other Crescent Hotel directors and a Professor A. S. Maddox from Little Rock. Maddox had been operating a girls' boarding school in Little Rock, and was interested in transferring operations to Eureka Springs. The idea was to use the Crescent during the school year, at which time the hotel was normally closed. It so happened that there had been a disturbing decline in summer patronage of the hotel, and Maddox' idea fell on receptive ears indeed. Accordingly, Maddox Seminary, with its view from a bluff overlooking the Arkansas River, was transformed into Crescent College and Conservatory, with a much more impressive view from the heights overlooking Leatherwood Valley. Effective mid-September 1908 the school would, according to advertisements, be available for

> Those seeking a select boarding school which is both healthful and healthy, where thorough and standard high school work is offered . . . and those especially who are interested in the cultural development of the daughter should write . . . the College direct and a catalog containing full details will be furnished.

Construction work on the North Arkansas struggled along despite the nationwide economic recession. The railroads were particularly hard hit. On February 6, Baldwin Locomotive Works announced a layoff of 10,000 of its 19,000 workers at Philadelphia;

weekly production of locomotives was down from 60 to 20, and a further drop was imminent because new orders were not coming in. (One locomotive turned out by Baldwin in February was North Arkansas No. 15, a ten-wheel [4-6-0] passenger locomotive.) Railroads cut salaries and work-weeks, and closed entire shops and station facilities. The Santa Fe announced that it had $10,-000,000 tied up in idle equipment. The Gould lines struggled with some desperation, and tonnage along the White River line dropped nearly to nothing.

These widespread economic factors had their effect on Scullin and company. They kept a large construction force in the field, but they had to face reality in the plan for extending the line beyond Helena to the southeast. For the moment, they would settle for a Joplin-Helena route. Preparations for the opening of the north end went forward, and regular service to Neosho was established on March 1.

The idea of the North Arkansas running into Little Rock was fanned to a faint glimmer when, in early March, the Board of Trade in that city approached the railroad management on the subject of a connecting branch line. Chief Engineer Dawley had a preliminary survey put together hurriedly for a 53-mile connection that would run from Negro Hill (where the main line crossed the White River, and which in December 1908 would be given the name Georgetown) to Little Rock. The line would parallel the Iron Mountain to the south, and would encounter neither serious grades nor swampy terrain. At a Little Rock meeting on April 4, North Arkansas officials agreed to consider the line favorably if the city would provide local right of way plus terminal facilities. Because of the awkward location of the branch line and because of the expense to both parties, there was little further development of the plan, and again an entry of the North Arkansas into Little Rock was thwarted as it had been three years earlier.

The problem of adequate interchange and terminal facilities at Joplin remained. Scullin decided to join forces with other lines and on June 23 announced the incorporation of the Joplin Union Depot Co., jointly sponsored by the North Arkansas and the Santa Fe. Shortly afterward the Katy and the Kansas City Southern joined the venture, and planning went forward for the construc-

No. 12 was one of five consolidation-type engines received in mid-1907. Mogul No. 8 brought the first train through the new Edgemont cut. The picture below was taken just north of Higden. The trestle in the background crosses South Fork of the Little Red River; soon afterward it was partially replaced by a two-span through-truss steel bridge.
*(Above: H. L. Broadbelt; below: Oran Vaughan)*

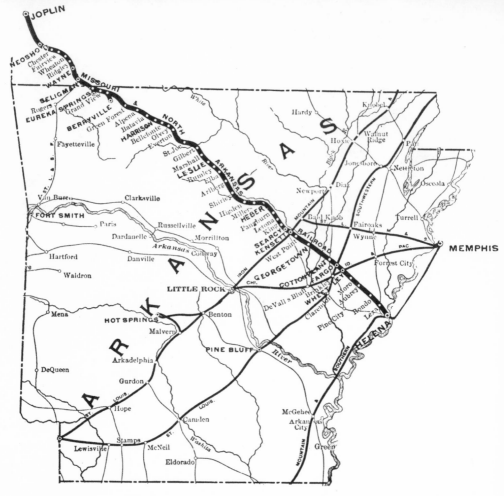

The route of the newly completed line from Joplin to Helena included trackage rights over the Kansas City Southern from Joplin to Neosho and over the Frisco from Wayne to Seligman. The picture below was taken during the 1960s near Fayetteville and shows the Frisco line. (*Map: Arkansas History Commission; below: Arkansas Publicity and Parks Commission*)

tion of modern joint facilities. It would be March 1910 before final plans were set, and mid-1911 before the new freight station, passenger depot, and shops were in full operation.

Meanwhile, construction work down in the Ozarks progressed steadily and on June 15, 1908, regular service between Leslie and Shirley (Settlement) began with a daily mixed train. At this time the grade between Shirley and Searcy was complete except for gaps near Shirley and Edgemont, where obstinate rock formations interferred, and at the crossing of the South Fork of the Little Red at Higden, where 265 feet of steel spans were missing.

The cut at Shirley was broken through in early summer, and tracklaying south proceeded rapidly. The cut at Edgemont was another matter. This incision was through a narrow arm of land between forks of the Little Red, and involved the removal of 125,000 cubic yards of rock. Blasting was carried out continuously, and a steam shovel plus special dump cars were brought in to remove the rubble. By July it was apparent that completion of this cut would involve an interminable delay, and Engineer Dawley elected to build a temporary shoo-fly that would involve 4% grades in by-passing the cut. Furthermore, he elected to install a temporary pile trestle across the South Fork, which was to be located just south of the big cut. Counting proposed fill, the temporary trestle was 1700 feet long. The *Arkansas Gazette* of August 15, 1908, commented that construction costs for the road were among the highest ever in Arkansas, approaching those of the White River line. Certainly, in this region they exceeded the $50,000 per mile covered by the securities issues.

With the Edgemont cut taken care of, on a temporary basis at least, the other pieces of construction began to fall into place. Service between Searcy and Heber Springs was inaugurated in July over track not completely surfaced. Allegheny Improvement Company operated the trains, and would do so for several months. With little ceremony the rails from north and south were joined at Higden in late August and, with a helper boost, through work trains crawled over the shoo-fly at Edgemont.

On the south end, tracklaying started at Helena on September 9. As far as Cotton Plant, 43 miles, grading was complete and all bridges were in; the tracklayers averaged better than a mile per day in reaching Cotton Plant on October 12. Almost immediately a scheduled freight run was set up between Cotton Plant and Helena, partly to fulfill a contract with the latter city and partly to gain revenue from hauling the fall cotton crop. There was a bit of celebrating at Cotton Plant, and those local residents who had contributed to the M.&N.A. project were given a free excursion trip to Helena and back.

For the next six months there was general completion and cleanup of construction along the way, and train service by the North Arkansas was gradually extended. The line from Shirley to Higden was turned over to the railroad on October 1. Scheduled trains between Higden and Kensett began October 19, although that section was not conveyed to the North Arkansas until December 1. On November 25th Clayton and Scullin returned from a five-day inspection of the property and reported to the press that only the eight-mile gap between the White and Cache Rivers remained to be completed, with the major holdup being installation of the large drawbridge at Georgetown (Negro Hill). They also stated that over 1000 carloads of logs, mostly from right-of-way clearing, were ready for shipment once the gap was closed.

On December 1 all of the line except the Kensett-Cotton Plant section was in the hands of the M.&N.A., and regular schedules were announced. The December 1, 1908 timetable showed daily local passenger trains between Leslie and Kensett, and daily-except-Sunday passenger trains from Cotton Plant to Helena and return. Passenger service into Joplin had not yet been established, but freight trains were running through.

The year 1908 ended with 308.6 miles of road in operation. Fiscal years ending June 30 showed the following results:

|  | 1907 | 1908 |
|---|---|---|
| Total revenue | $326,753 | $357,173 |
| Expenses | 269,906 | 347,743 |
| Gross earnings | 56,847 | 9,430 |
| Taxes and joint facilities | 13,268 | 17,283 |
| Income | $ 43,579 | $( −7,853) |

The 1908 figures reflected the business recession as well as increased cost of maintaining equipment and right of way. The

stress of pushing construction had left little latitude for developing traffic along the way, but with growth to a full-fledged road
in 1909 this would be taken care of. The patience and forebear-
ance of the St. Louis sponsors must be admired; thus far they had
received no dividends or interest on their investments. There had
been no choice but to complete the road as soon as possible and
*then* make it pay, hopefully under an improved business climate.

In early 1909 work was concluded on the south end. The
White River bridge went into place, Wisconsin Bridge and Iron
forces erecting two 125-foot through-truss fixed spans; a 300-foot
through-truss turn span, and a 60-foot deck plate girder approach
span. The Cache River was crossed by 530 feet of pile trestle,
including approaches (in later years, a deck-plate girder crossing
would be used at this point). The embankment was carefully
positioned and, barring serious floods, should be sufficient. By
February all was in place and rails were down. On March 1,
through service between Neosho and Helena was established
amidst many sighs of relief.

And so the North Arkansas was finally completed when it
reached its full Joplin-Helena length of 359.3 miles. But like a
stringbean adolescent schoolboy, it would need a lot of filling-out
and a lot of maturing. This was planned through betterments that
would cost perhaps a half-million dollars: shops for Helena, completion of the Edgemont cut, replacement of pile trestles with dirt
fill or steel spans, additional buildings such as berry sheds, cotton
platforms, and freight depots, application of rock riprap and
ballast on the south end, and so on. The maturing process would
have to go along with time, the development of Arkansas, and
high-quality management of the railroad.

A contemporary editorial in the February 15, 1909 issue of the
*St. Louis Globe-Democrat* praised the builders of the North Arkansas and projected a bright future for the road:

> John Scullin, David R. Francis and Richard C. Kerens are
> the three St. Louis cloud-pushers who have put their shoul-
> ders, and $6,000,000 in money, to the wheels. . . . Appar-
> ently they have never been able to understand there was a
> panic in the land. . . They kept on spending money with

that confidence which many wealthy men were urging
everybody else to have. . .

This line will aid the development of Arkansas and the development of Arkansas will aid the development of St.
Louis. The rich mineral deposits hid in the hill country of
Northwestern Arkansas, from where it begins near Seligman
to where it breaks down to a new level east of Searcy, have
long been an open secret to men who know the Southwest.
. . . East of the hills it traverses one of the most productive
parts of the cotton belt, and at Helena, on the Mississippi
River, it gets in touch with the heavily and finely timbered
region of Southeastern Arkansas. When St. Louis booms the
Southwest, the Southwest will boom St. Louis. . .

Yes, the construction work had cost more than six million
dollars in cash outlay and the bottom of the money barrel was
being scraped. The fiscal year ending June 30, 1909, showed a
deficit of $17,150 on total earnings of $486,371, with no charge for
interest on the funded debt. However, the gross was up and, with
national conditions improved, should double itself during the next
year. The time was now at hand for the North Arkansas to carve
out a proper niche at its assigned spot on the earth's face. The next
few years would prove to be the crucial ones in its relatively
short life.

The Basin Park Hotel opened July 1, 1906, and became the second most prominent hotel (after the Crescent) in Eureka Springs. This picture was taken in 1906 and shows a car of the Citizens' Electric Co., a three-mile street railway that climbed around the mountains of Eureka Springs. The Basin Park was nationally known for its eight floors all being "ground floors" with connections to the hillside behind. *(Little Rock Public Library)*

HOMESEEKERS' EDITION 1912

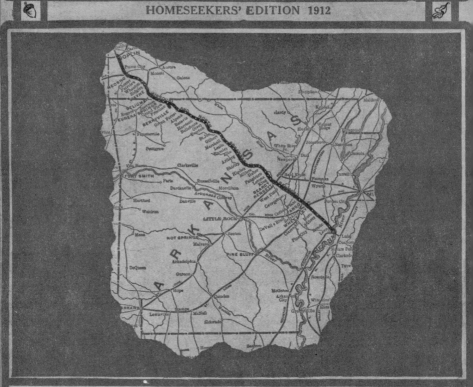

# Missouri and North Arkansas Railroad

From the Mining Districts and Grain Fields of Missouri, through the
Fruit Belt of the Ozarks and Timber Regions of Northern Arkansas
To the Cotton and Rice Districts of Eastern Arkansas and the Mississippi Valley,
where Climate and Water Excel and Live Stock and Poultry
are Raised at a Profit

# *Motor Cars and Through Sleepers*

With trains running up and down the line on regular schedules moving logs, crossties, wood products, cotton, zinc concentrates and general merchandise, as well as farmers, merchants,
drummers and tourists, it was imperative that North Arkansas
management chart a careful course for the profitable development
of the business. The word had come through that George Gould's
White River Line to the north was not doing well; it was known
to be "long on scenery but short on revenue" and was thwarted
continuously with rock slides, tunnel cave-ins, and other costly
maintenance problems. Scullin and Francis set out to work with
the Santa Fe, Illinois Central, and other connecting lines in order
to get through freight routed via the North Arkansas. Commercial
agents were stationed at Kansas City, Memphis, and New Orleans.
Industrial and agricultural development offices were set up. Attention was given to printed publicity; an attractive system timetable folder was issued on August 1, 1909, and at the end of the
year there appeared the first issue of an illustrated, slick paper
magazine called *Oak Leaves*.

This publication venture was designed to tell outsiders about
living opportunities in the region served by the railroad, as well
as to impress potential shippers that this newest railroad in Arkansas was indeed among the finest and most modern to be found.
The map of the system emphasized the solidity of this connecting
link between midwestern and southeastern America. The intro-
ductory editorial stated that

> *Oak Leaves* has been launched and we intend to make it a
> magazine of high grade; we will not allow its influence to
> be used for any purpose other than to advance the interests
> of its patrons and the Missouri & North Arkansas Railroad.

George Sands, vice president of the company since 1902, was
Scullin's man on location. He functioned as general manager,
calling on talents developed through many years in the railroad
business. He enjoyed a favorable reputation among the operating
employees, as evidenced by his aiding of blacklisted strikers from
the great American Railway Union strike of 1894. Quoting from
Freeman Hubbard's book *Railroad Avenue,*

> In those distressing days that followed the . . . strike and
> blacklist, the benevolent old gent who owned the Missouri
> & North Arkansas railway was a tower of strength for the
> boomer. I wish I could remember his name, for he deserves
> a monument. His pike was called the 'Clickety-Bang.' A
> man could brake for a month or two on the M & N A and
> get himself a service letter that would cover the 1894 strike.
> As late as 1912 I saw boomers hiring out on Clickety-Bang
> letters, and such references were always okayed by the
> friendly old gent who owned the streak o' rust . . .

Hubbard was actually quoting an oldtime "boomer" (a drifter
who stayed on each job but a short time) named Harry McClin-
tock, and clearly some license was taken regarding "ownership"
of the road. And, of course, the designation "Clickety-Bang" must
be taken lightly!

George Sands was, however, an "old gent." In 1910 he was in
his mid-sixties, and the challenge of the new road called for more
vigor than he might possess, hence he and Scullin began to look
around for a full time (and younger) general manager. From his
office in the Sanford Building at Eureka Springs, Sands very
likely took stock of what the new general manager would find. His
conclusions as to the railroad's condition would be as described
in the following paragraphs:

Physically, the line was complete and in fairly good condition.
That part from Seligman to Leslie was well broken-in and was
holding its own quite well. The newer sections were having the

Freshly painted No. 16 and its passenger train stop near Eureka Springs, probably in the late summer of 1909. The depot at Berryville is typical of the frame structures the railroad built north of Kensett. The banner-type train order signals were used exclusively by the North Arkansas. Although the depot was typical, its location was not: it was on a 1000-foot-diameter loop at the end of the branch from Freeman. Trains could head into Berryville, whereas they had to back into Eureka Springs. The picture below dates from 1910. *(Above: Eureka Springs Carnegie Library; below: O. Klute Braswell)*

normal "startup" problems of spongy roadbed, slides in new cuts, and insecure bridges, but section gangs were on top of most of these problems. The line was divided into two operating districts with Leslie as the division point. To the small shops at Eureka Springs and Leslie had been added a similar facility just west of Helena at a station designated "Outer Yard." Terminal properties at Joplin were under development as the Union Depot Co. At Helena, arrangements had been made with the Illinois Central to use that line's freight and passenger facilities in exchange for the use of valuable North Arkansas trackage serving industry on the west side of town. Plans had been made to install storage trackage at Outer Yard, but time would never see them materialize.

At Kensett, arrangements were made to share the Iron Mountain freight and passenger depot, and at North Arkansas expense it was moved some 250 yards to be adjacent to the crossover. At Wheatley, the shared Rock Island depot happened to be in the right place. At Fargo, where the line crossed the Cotton Belt, there was no established town, and it would be 1911 before the North Arkansas would erect a station for joint usage. In general, joint depots were desirable, to make train-to-train transfers convenient and to divide costs of operation.

Locomotives and rolling stock appeared adequate for the needs. In January 1910 two ten-wheel passenger locomotives, Nos. 17 and 18, were delivered from Baldwin along with the road's first mikado-type freight locomotives. These latter engines, Nos. 19 and 20 (later renumbered Nos. 30 and 31), were similar to the very successful consolidations (Nos. 10-14), the only significant differences being a slightly higher heating surface due to longer tubes, and a slightly lower weight on the drivers. In typical fashion, only about ten per cent of this $60,000 locomotive order was paid in cash, with equipment trusts executed to cover the remainder. By the end of January the company could boast of 9 passenger locomotives, 11 freight locomotives, 21 passenger cars, and 393 other items of rolling stock.

George Sands might well have viewed on-line business potential as problematical. The most important local industry was that based on hardwood timber; crossties (the Ozarks region was becoming known as the "crosstie capital of the world"), staves, furniture veneers, special shapes such as hubs and handles, building lumber, and so on. There were sawmills of assorted sizes strung all along the line, but the acknowledged centers of the timber goods manufacture were at Leslie and Helena.

The H. D. Williams Cooperage Co. had completed its move from Poplar Bluff, Missouri, to Leslie in 1908, and by 1910 was claimed to be the largest cooperage works in the world. It could produce up to 3,000 oil barrels daily, and regularly shipped several carloads per day of wine barrel shooks for export to France. It owned a number of specially-dimensioned freight cars for handling barrels. Over 500 people were employed in and around Leslie, and in a region where lamp-lighting was the rule, the Williams electrical power facility was indeed impressive.

The Williams company arranged timber leases on 85,000 acres to the west and south of Leslie, and built a 19-mile standard gauge railroad to reach them. This line was known locally as "The Dinkey Line" or as the "Leslie, Mountaintop & Southwestern." Because of the steep grades, Shay type geared locomotives were used and these strange looking engines were permitted to venture onto North Arkansas iron to pick up stave bolts deposited along the Leslie-Marshall right of way. As one would suspect, oldtimers in the Leslie area have many fond memories of The Dinkey.

The first locomotive of the Dinkey line had arrived on a North Arkansas flatcar on November 4, 1906, and the second one arrived two weeks later. The *Marshall Mountain Wave* noted this second event as follows:

> Another cogwheel engine for the Williams Cooperage Company at Leslie whizzed down the line Wednesday evening. It made a noise like a 400-pound man at his first effort on roller skates trying to keep his balance, [and] it woke up all the babies in town, scared all the dogs within a mile of the right of way, and caused consternation generally; but nevertheless that kind of engine is the one for grade climbing and power, and . . . is the kind the Williams Company needs.

Brand-new ten-wheeler No. 18 had been running on break-in with white flags denoting its "extra" status, in January 1910, when crew and officials climbed aboard at Junction for a picture. Shay No. 1 of the H. D. Williams Cooperage Co., below, stands at "Dinkey Town" on the northern outskirts of Leslie. The North Arkansas main line and water tank are behind the locomotive. This picture is dated 1910.

*(Above: E. G. Baker; below: Earl Saunders)*

A tale about the Dinkey was told by Lloyd Curtis in the *Arkansas Democrat* of September 1, 1963. The time was 1910. To quote Curtis,

Williams hired an engineer by the name of Wilhelm, who had been "fighting the extra board" on the Missouri and North Arkansas line and who claimed he had operated a side-rod engine in the mines at Pittsburg, Kansas.

On the morning Wilhelm reported for work he went out on the dinkey with a crew composed of Dave Nelson as engineer, George Binder as fireman and Clyde Boyd as brakeman. Nelson pulled the dinkey with six empty flats over the the mountain and out to the end of the line. The flats were switched off, six loaded cars were picked up and they started the return trip, with Wilhelm at the controls.

That was the beginning of a wild ride.

Wilhelm failed to stop at the summit siding so Boyd could set the hand brakes on the flatcars. He just sat back and let the dinkey roll down the mountain toward home. The little train picked up speed quickly on the steep grade. The flatcars were rocking, and Boyd was flung from the train. . . . Soon logs, too, were flying from one of the cars.

In the cab, Nelson and Binder were frantically trying to help Wilhelm with the steam jam and sand brakes. When they applied the steam jam, the engine wheels merely slid along the rails without checking speed. Nelson and Binder decided that it was time to jump, and warned Wilhelm that he better jump, too. This was sound advice, so the engineer tied down the whistle cord with a heavy wrench and jumped from the cab.

Down the mountain roared the crewless, runaway engine with whistle screeching, scattering logs along the way. An entire flatcar of logs was strewn from the summit to Dinkey Town, as the line's home base at Leslie was known. Four cars of stave bolts and a car of steel rails rode out the course to Barrel Plant No. 1, where the dinkey crashed against a barrier and overturned. . .

The 20-ton engine was a battered wreck. No one at the plant was injured, thanks to the tied-down whistle, which first brought the workmen running out of the plant to see the dinkey headed downhill, and then sent them scattering as they took stock of the situation.

The train crew came limping in, none of them seriously
hurt, but all looking somewhat sheepish. . .

The Dinkey Line continued to operate until 1927 when the
operation at Leslie, then known as Export Cooperage Co., closed
down.

Besides the Williams Cooperage Co. there were other on-line
industries based on forest products. At Searcy, the nearby Doniphan Lumber Co. was a large operation. The firm built its own
railroad, the Doniphan, Kensett & Searcy, to connect with and
operate over the North Arkansas in gaining access to timber properties. The D.K. & S. built logging railroads that connected with
the North Arkansas near Snell (26 miles from Searcy) and Letona
(13 miles from Searcy).

At Helena, several lumber companies set up business about six
miles west of Helena on the North Arkansas. This was undoubtedly due to the influence of Powell Clayton (who had married a
Helena girl), John Scullin, and other members of the railroad's
management. This gave the North Arkansas a valuable asset and,
because of the originating business of lumber products, explains
the apparently-generous Illinois Central swap arrangement for
downtown freight and passenger facilities. The town of West
Helena was quickly established in connection with this industrial
complex, and became a prominent suburb. It was soon joined with
Helena by an electric interurban line, one of only five ever to
be built in Arkansas.

The movement of mineral products continued to show more
promise than reality. The market price for zinc and lead concentrates was variable, and even when it was high it could hardly
cover the burden of expensive hauling to the railroad for shipment. Total production of concentrates from the northern Arkansas region did jump from 994 tons in 1909 to 1,985 tons in 1910
but most of the material was mined nearer to the Iron Mountain
line than to the M.&.N.A. The Rush Creek district was beginning
to stir, and there was talk of erecting a tramline to carry the concentrates across the mountains to Yellville or Buffalo City. If the
North Arkansas was to participate in whatever potential this mining region might possess, it would be necessary to build a branch

line to serve it (and this was under discussion) or discover important deposits of ore along the railroad's own right of way.

As the foregoing paragraphs indicate, local freight business prospects were fairly good, but in need of development. And as to passenger business, it was significant that on November 9, 1910, an agreement was signed with the Pullman Co., and on December 1 drawing room sleepers between Kansas City and Helena were placed in service on Trains 1 and 2. A through passenger would depart from Kansas City at 2:00 p.m., pass through Eureka Springs about midnight, awaken (if the curvaceous route had permitted sleep!) at Searcy, and arrive at Helena at noon, about 22 hours from Kansas City. The return schedules about matched, and thus in both directions the startling scenery of the Ozarks was passed in darkness. These new sleepers were in addition to those which had continued between Eureka Springs and St. Louis since the opening of the road in 1883.

Mention has been made of extra income derived by the North Arkansas from trackage rights for lumber and logging companies. In 1910 and 1911 similar arrangements were made for passenger movements. The Searcy-Kensett Transportation Co. contracted for the operation of a gasoline motor car (purchased from the Rock Island) between Kensett and Searcy, to meet the Iron Mountain trains. And the Southwestern Veneer Co. at Cotton Plant made a similar arrangement to transport employees between Cotton Plant and Georgetown. The income was slight but every little bit helped.

A ride on the North Arkansas was, of course, a thrilling experience for the regional people. The coaches were neatly painted and were fitted with Pintsch gas lamps, Baker stoves, and mahogany interior trim. The vendors of candy, gum, and tobacco were employed by Van-Noy Interstate Co. with the M.&N.A. getting 18 per cent of the gross receipts. When the sleepers were running, the first-class passengers could enjoy electric lights and fans as well as a full meal in the buffet section. The speed of the trains was not great, and Nos. 1 and 2 may very well have been the "slowest trains through Arkansas." Because of irregularity in meeting schedules it was at about this time that the M.&N.A. abbreviation was judged to stand for "May Never Arrive." One gets the

After the original station at Seligman, Missouri, burned in 1909 the depot shown in the 1915 picture above was constructed. The train stands on the Frisco tracks; the North Arkansas track is at the left. Passenger train No. 2 stands at Helena, below, prior to its 3:30 p.m. departure on a day in August 1911. The frame depot of the Illinois Central, used by the North Arkansas, can be seen at the left; the Solomon Building in the background stands today as the Helena National Bank Building. The engine is either No. 15 or No. 16. The end car is the Helena-Joplin Buffet Pullman Sleeper.

*(Above: Bennie McCann; below: Garland Case, courtesy* RAILROAD MAGAZINE*)*

# MISSOURI AND NORTH ARKANSAS RAILROAD
## "NORTH ARKANSAS LINE."

| | | SOUTHBOUND. | | | | Miles. | June 18, 1911. | | NORTHBOUND. | | | | | |
|---|---|---|---|---|---|---|---|---|---|---|---|---|---|---|
| No. 9 | No. 37 | No. 13 | No. 11 | No. 3 | No. 1 | | | No. 2 | No. 4 | No. 12 | No. 38 | No. 14 | No. 10 |
| | | | | | | | [LEAVE]          [ARRIVE] | | | | | | |
| | | | | *6 20 A M | *8 20 P M | 0 | ....Joplin,[1] Mo.... | 8 50 A M | 11 00 P M | | | | |
| | | | | 7 00 " | 8 00 " | 19.30 | .....Neosho[2].....δ | 8 10 " | 10 17 " | | | | |
| | | | | 7 20 " | 9 14 " | 25.78 | .....Aroma....... | 7 45 " | 10 02 " | | | | |
| | | | | 7 35 " | 9 23 " | 30.00 | .....Chester....δ | 7 35 " | 9 52 " | | | | |
| | | | | 7 50 " | 9 37 " | 36.70 | ....Fairview....δ | 7 19 " | 9 37 " | | | | |
| | | | | 7 59 " | 9 45 " | 40.90 | ....Wheaton....δ | 7 09 " | 9 28 " | | | | |
| | | | | 8 09 " | 9 58 " | 45.90 | ....Ridgley,....δ | 6 59 " | 9 19 " | | | | |
| | | Mixed. | Mixed. | 8 20 " | 10 10 " | 51.40 | ....Wayne[3].....δ | 6 47 " | 9 05 " | Mixed. | | Mixed. | |
| | | *7 00 P M | *12 15 A M | 8 40 " | 10 37 " | 60.60 | ...Seligman[4]....δ | 6 29 " | - - | 9 50 A M | | 6 00 P M | |
| | | - - | - - | - - | - - | 63.35 | ....Pender...... | - - | - - | | | | |
| | | - - | - - | - - | - - | 70.85 | ..Walden, Ark.... | - - | - - | | | | |
| | | 7 38 " | 11 50 A M | 9 10 " | 11 07 " | 73.35 | ....Beaver.....δ | 5 44 " | 8 09 " | 9 10 " | | 5 09 " | |
| | | - - | - - | - - | - - | 73.60 | ...Leatherwood.... | - - | - - | | | | |
| | | - - | - - | - - | - - | 74.85 | ....Skelton...... | - - | - - | | | | |
| | | 7 47 " | 12 01 Noon | 9 17 " | 11 16 " | 76.19 | ....Gaskins.....δ | 5 38 " | 8 03 " | 8 59 " | | 4 59 " | |
| | | 8 10 P M | 12 15 Noon | 9 30 A M | 11 29 P M | 79.10 | ar.Eureka Springs δ lv. | 5 30 A M | 7 55 P M | *8 50 A M | | *4 50 P M | |
| | | | | 9 40 A M | 11 35 P M | 79.10 | lv..Eureka Springs.ar. | 5 18 A M | 7 45 P M | | | | |
| | | | | 10 02 " | a - | 88.43 | ...Grand View...δ | 4 43 " | 7 13 " | | | | |
| | | | | 10 25 " | a - | 95.24 | ....Berryville...δ | 4 25 " | 6 55 " | | | | |
| | | | | 10 32 " | 12 10 Night | 97.81 | ....Freeman.....δ | 4 13 " | 6 43 " | | | | |
| | | | | 10 39 " | - - | 101.10 | ...Urbanette.....δ | 4 04 " | 6 35 " | | | | |
| | | | | 10 48 " | - - | 105.16 | .....Cisco......δ | - - | 6 25 " | | | | |
| | | | | 11 00 " | 12 40 Night | 109.99 | ..Green Forest..δ | 3 41 " | 6 14 " | | | | |
| | | | | 11 14 " | - - | 115.72 | .....Coin......δ | - - | 5 58 " | | | | |
| | | | | 11 25 " | a - | 120.45 | ....Alpena.....δ | 3 13 " | 5 45 " | | | | |
| | | | | 11 41 " | a - | 126.84 | ....Batavia.....δ | 2 55 " | 5 27 " | | | | |
| | | | | 11 48 A M | - - | 130.10 | .....Capps.....δ | - - | 5 17 " | | | | |
| | | | | 12 05 Noon | 1 39 A M | 136.59 | ...Harrison.....δ | 2 28 " | 5 00 " | | | | |
| | | | | 12 16 " | a - | 140.44 | ...Bellefonte...δ | 2 16 " | 4 48 " | | | | |
| | | | | 12 30 " | 2 01 " | 145.03 | .....Olvey.....δ | 2 01 " | 4 34 " | | | | |
| | | | | 12 42 Noon | a - | 150.07 | ....Everton.....δ | 1 48 " | 4 22 " | | | | |
| | | | | 1 00 P M | a - | 157.72 | ....Pindall.....δ | 1 31 " | 4 03 " | | | | |
| | | | | 1 19 " | a - | 164.83 | ....St. Joe.....δ | 1 10 A M | 3 43 " | | | | |
| | | | | 1 37 " | a - | 171.30 | ....Gilbert.....δ | 12 53 Night | 3 25 " | | | | |
| | | | | 1 52 " | - - | 177.10 | .....Zack...... | - - | 3 09 " | | | | |
| | | | | 2 06 " | 3 25 " | 182.30 | ...Marshall....δ | 12 24 " | 2 55 " | | | | |
| | | | | 2 17 " | - - | 184.80 | .....Baker..... | - - | 2 47 " | | | | |
| | | | | 2 30 P M | 3 47 A M | 190.93 | arr...Leslie δ ...lve. | 12 01 Night | 2 30 P M | | | | |
| | | | | 2 35 P M | 3 56 A M | 190.93 | lve...Leslie.....arr. | 11 50 P M | 2 20 P M | | | | |
| | | | | 2 45 " | 4 06 " | 196.02 | ....Rumley.....δ | 11 36 " | 2 09 " | | | | |
| | | | | 2 58 " | 4 16 " | 201.42 | .....Elba.....δ | 11 22 " | 1 55 " | | | | |
| | | | | 3 18 " | 4 34 " | 210.42 | ....Arlberg....δ | 11 00 " | 1 35 " | | | | |
| | | | | 3 50 " | 5 05 " | 224.64 | ....Shirley....δ | 10 25 " | 1 01 P M | | | | |
| | | | | 4 18 " | 5 30 " | 237.30 | ...Edgemont...δ | 9 51 " | 12 31 Noon | | | | |
| | | | | 4 24 " | 5 36 " | 239.30 | ....Higden.....δ | 9 45 " | 12 25 " | | | | |
| | | | | 4 41 " | 5 56 " | 246.52 | .....Miller....δ | 9 24 " | 12 06 Noon | | | | |
| | | | | 4 54 " | 6 12 " | 252.95 | ..Heber Springs..δ | 9 06 " | 11 50 A M | | | | |
| | | | | 5 12 " | 6 29 " | 260.97 | .....Snell.....δ | 8 46 " | 11 11 " | | | | |
| | | | | 5 25 " | 6 42 " | 266.00 | ...Pangburn....δ | 8 34 " | 11 00 " | | | | |
| | | | | 5 36 " | 6 54 " | 271.02 | ....Letona.....δ | 8 21 " | 10 46 " | | | | |
| | | | | 5 49 " | 7 08 " | 276.45 | ...Crosby[5]....δ | 8 06 " | 10 33 " | | | | |
| | | Mixed. | | 6 05 " | 7 25 " | 283.46 | lve...Searcy[6] δ ..lve. | 7 46 " | 10 15 " | Mixed. | | Mixed. | |
| *7 05 P M | †7 30 A M | | | 6 05 " | 7 25 " | 283.46 | lve...Searcy....arr. | 7 46 " | 10 15 " | | 4 00 P M | | 9 55 A M |
| 7 15 " | 7 50 " | | | 6 20 P M | 7 45 " | 287.30 | ...Kensett[6]...δ | 7 31 " | *1000 A M | | 3 45 " | | 9 44 " |
| 7 52 " | 8 12 " | | | | 7 55 " | 290.89 | ...West Point..δ | 7 19 " | | | 3 15 " | | 9 10 " |
| 8 30 " | 9 15 " | lve.Monett. | | | 8 24 " | 301.50 | Georgetown(Negro Hill) " | 6 48 " | | | 2 15 " | | 9 10 " |
| 8 45 " | 10 45 " | | | | 8 58 " | 315.59 | ...Cotton Plant[7]..δ | 6 11 " | | | 1 00 P M | | 8 28 " |
| 8 58 " | 11 30 " | | | | 9 12 " | 321.29 | .....Fargo[8]....δ | 5 64 " | | | 12 15 Noon | | 8 12 " |
| 8 59 " | 11 50 " | | | | 9 26 " | 326.02 | lve..Wheatley[9] δ .arr. | 5 58 " | | | 11 50 A M | | 8 00 " |
| 9 28 " | 12 50 Noon | lve.Seligman. | | | 9 26 " | 326.02 | lve..Wheatley....arr. | 5 38 " | | | 11 50 " | | 8 00 " |
| 9 50 " | 1 35 P M | | | | 9 55 " | 336.55 | .....Moro.....δ | 5 05 " | | | 10 55 " | | 7 31 " |
| 10 05 " | 2 15 " | | | | 10 15 " | 344.09 | ....Aubrey.....δ | 4 43 " | | | 10 15 " | | 7 10 " |
| 10 18 " | 2 45 " | | | | 10 31 " | 349.90 | ....Rondo.....δ | 4 26 " | | | 9 30 " | | 6 55 " |
| 10 42 " | 3 52 " | | | | 10 44 " | 354.72 | ..North Lexa[10].. | 4 12 " | | | 9 00 " | | 6 44 " |
| 11 05 P M | 4 30 P M | | | | 11 05 " | 362.71 | ..West Helena..δ | 3 52 " | | | 8 20 " | | 6 22 " |
| | | | | | 11 25 A M | 368.95 | ....Helena[11]...δ | *3 30 P M | | | †7 30 A M | | †6 00 A M |
| | | | | | | | [ARRIVE]          [LEAVE] | | | | | | |

## THROUGH SLEEPING CAR SERVICE.

### ST. LOUIS AND EUREKA SPRINGS.

| No. 3 | STATIONS. | | No. 22 | |
|---|---|---|---|---|
| *9 00 P M | lve.St. Louis......... (St. L. & S. F.) arr. | | 7 00 A M | |
| 7 25 A M | lve.Springfield.................. " arr. | | 8 50 P M | |
| 9 45 A M | lve.Monett.................. " arr. | | 7 40 P M | |
| 11 05 A M | arr.Seligman.................. " lve. | | 6 10 P M | |
| 11 15 A M | lve.Seligman.......(M. & N. A.) arr. | | 6 00 P M | |
| 12 15 Noon | arr.Eureka Springs......... " lve. | | *4 50 P M | |

### JOPLIN AND HELENA.

| No. 1 | STATIONS. | | No. 2 |
|---|---|---|---|
| *8 20 P M | lve.Joplin......(M. & N. A.) arr. | | 8 50 A M |
| 11 29 P M | arr.Eureka Springs " lve. | | 5 30 A M |
| 7 25 A M | arr.Searcy.......... " lve. | | 7 46 P M |
| 11 25 A M | arr.Helena.......... " lve. | | *3 30 P M |

‖ Meals.     δ Telegraph stations.

* Daily ; † daily, except Sunday ; § Sunday only ; a stops to leave passengers from Joplin and points beyond Joplin, Neosho and Seligman on connecting lines.

## CONNECTIONS.

[1] With Kansas City Southern Ry., St. Louis & San Francisco R.R., Missouri Pacific Ry. and Missouri, Kansas & Texas Ry.
[2] With Kansas City Southern Ry. and St. Louis & San Francisco R.R.
[3] With St. Louis & San Francisco R.R.
[4] With Chicago, Rock Island & Pacific Ry.
[5] With St. Louis, Iron Mountain & Southern Ry.
[7] With Chicago, Rock Island & Pacific Ry.
[8] With St. Louis South-western Ry. (Cotton Belt).
[9] With Chicago, Rock Island & Pacific Ry.
[10] With St. Louis, Iron Mountain & Southern Ry.
[11] With Arkansas Midland R.R., St. Louis, Iron Mountain & Southern Ry., Yazoo & Mississippi Valley R.R. (Illinois Central System), Arkansas River Packet Co., The Lee Line and Memphis & Arkansas City Packet Co.

Write C. D. WHITNEY, Traffic Manager, Eureka Springs. Ark., for "Oak Leaves," a handsomely illustrated magazine.

These three prominent St. Louis businessmen were influential in the North Arkansas management during the 1910-1920 period. David R. Francis, upper left, was an ex-governor of Missouri. Festus J. Wade, president of the Mercantile Trust Co. in St. Louis became receiver in 1916. John Scullin, bottom, had many business interests in St. Louis but was perhaps fondest of the North Arkansas; he was its president from 1899 until his death in 1920.

feel of slow and deliberate movement of the trains from these
lines by Mrs. Josephine Crump, inspired by a trip from Harrison
to Marshall about 1911:

> Through mountain passes winding down
> The ponderous train like living thing,
> Crept in and out from Nature's haunts,
> As if it sensed the pulse of Spring,
> While from the window of the car,
> The flush of life now felt and seen,
> Thrilled, stirred, and startled hill and dale,
> Where winter barriers long had been.

Taken from Mrs. Crump's book, *Echoes from the Ozarks*, the lines
also imply that the traveler on the North Arkansas had time to
enjoy the scenic wonders as he moved along.

Train operation on the North Arkansas may have been slow and
deliberate, but it had its share of excitement and surprises. One
exciting event was a pre-arranged record-breaking freight run
that took place in 1911. It was designed to break the "slow train"
image, and was described in the 1912 Homeseekers' Edition of
*Oak Leaves*. Ten cars of export packing house products were handled expeditiously from Joplin to Helena:

> This train was from Kansas City and was received from
> a connecting line at Joplin and destined to New Orleans,
> La. Was received at Joplin at 7:50 a.m., handled by Con-
> ductor Cobb, Engine 20, Engineer Dobbins as far as Leslie
> and from Leslie to Helena Conductor Dignan, Engine 14,
> with Engineer Beer at the throttle, arriving at Helena at
> 1:50 a.m. — 18 hours and 20 minutes. The 20 minutes were
> consumed at Leslie changing engines, crews, etc., making
> the actual running time 18 hours; an average of 30 miles
> an hour over the entire line. The train was delivered at con-
> nection at Helena and made a good run to New Orleans,
> making the entire run from Kansas City to New Orleans in
> 70 hours.

> The new route through Arkansas, i.e., the 'North Arkansas
> Line,' is fast coming to the front as a through freight line
> and is becoming an important factor in the business be-
> tween the Northwest and Southeast.

Engine 20 was the mikado type that was later renumbered No. 31. Without question the above train had a lot of special handling; in the better days of the line the schedule for the manifest, or "Red Ball," between Joplin and Helena was 31-33 hours.

A surprise developed in 1911 when a train seemed to disappear from the line — a ghost train. The description comes from an old issue of *Railroad Magazine:*

> Phantom trains have long been subjects for the most exciting fiction, but it is seldom that a well-authenticated instance of such apparitions occurs. A story from Eureka Springs, Arkansas, seems to fill the bill in this particular, however.
>
> The engineer of a passenger train was about to slow up for the water tank at Gaskins, as was his custom, when he saw just ahead a caboose with the signal lights burning. He also saw the conductor come out of the cupola with his lantern and noted the burning fusee on the track.
>
> He yelled to his fireman. The fireman glanced out of the window, saw the caboose, grasped the reverse lever, and helped his chief to throw it over; then both men dropped down to jump. But before they could go over, the caboose vanished, and the only thing left was the charred fusee on the track.
>
> Fireman Harrelson had such a fright that he refused to go out next morning; and although Engineer Dobbins went out under protest, he recommended Master Mechanic Dolan to have everything in readiness, as there was sure to be a wreck somewhere.
>
> But trains ran as usual, and if there was any object in the visit of the ghost train it has not been made clear yet. The account is supplemented by the statement that Agent Braswell, of Gaskins, also saw the phantom caboose and lights from his home.

E. R. "Ernie" Braswell remained with the North Arkansas until it stopped operating in 1946. He could make no further comment on the phantom train.

To return to the developmental events of the railroad, early 1811 found George Sands seriously seeking a younger and more vigorous man to take over the general management of the line.

Concurrently, a gentleman named Edward M. Wise, vice president and general manager of the newly-built 285-mile Pan-American Railroad in Oaxaca, Mexico, was adversely affected by an organizational shakeup of the parent National Railways of Mexico. Somehow he and Scullin got together and in May he accepted an offer to become general manager of the M.&N.A. By June, Mr. Wise was on the job at Eureka Springs.

Wise was an Alabaman who had been railroading for 21 years, the last 11 of them in Mexico. Before going to the Pan-American, he was general superintendent of the Mexican Railway. When he joined the North Arkansas he was 40 years of age. The idea was to give Wise a free hand in developing the property into a paying proposition. The fiscal years ending on June 30 in 1910 and 1911 had not been good:

|                   | 1910      | 1911      |
|-------------------|-----------|-----------|
| Total revenue     | $826,693  | $884,839  |
| Expenses          | 745,060   | 806,071   |
| Gross earnings    | 81,633    | 78,768    |
| Taxes and other   | 95,290    | 109,951   |
| Deficit           | $ 13,657  | $ 31,183  |

Mr. Wise faced a difficult situation. A deficit had been run for each year, and the cash surplus had about run out. No bond interest had been paid. He could see that planned (and needed) betterments had not been made. After taking a close look at the property and traffic conditions, he decided that a rather large sum of money would be needed. The best way to get the money appeared to be through a reorganization of the company.

The total allowable first mortgage bonds of $8,340,000 had been pledged to secure $6,000,000 in Allegheny Improvement Company notes. During final construction of the line, Allegheny had failed to settle with some subcontractors, and they brought suit against Allegheny. The subcontractors won a judgment of $139,820, and this amount was declared a lien against the North Arkansas. This pressure, plus the need for more capital, caused the mortgage trustee, St. Louis Union Trust, again to apply to the government for receivership action.

One of the new gasoline-electric motor cars purchased as part of general manager E. M. Wise's revitalization program, No. 103 is shown above at Helena. The drawings below show dimensions and seating arrangements of the cars. *(Max Moore; author's collection)*

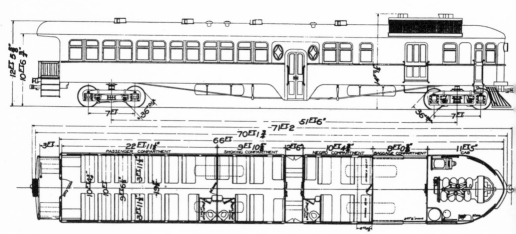

Gas-Electric Car—Elevation and Plan

Thus, the road went into receivership on April 1, 1912. Receivers appointed by Jacob Trieber, Federal Judge of the Eastern District of Arkansas, were George Sands, Jesse McDonald, St. Louis lawyer and former Circuit Court Judge, and William S. Holt, Little Rock businessman who had retired as City Postmaster in February 1910. The Receivers were authorized to issue up to $2,500,000 in Receivers' Certificates that would take absolute first lien on the property. These Certificates were due May 1, 1915, and carried six per cent interest. The Mercantile Trust Co., through President Festus J. Wade, proceeded to sell the Certificates, and General Manager Wise was able to proceed with extensive improvement plans.

First, Wise ordered two gasoline-electric motor cars from General Electric. One car would be used in Joplin-Eureka Springs service, the other between Heber Springs and Helena. These were heavy (47 tons), all-steel cars that were engagingly handsome in every way. Their exteriors were Pullman green with gold lettering; there was a brass railed observation platform on the rear; there were drop level side doors; and the cars had a curved nose that was suggestive of the competitive McKeen motor cars. The interiors were finished in mahogany, and upholstery was frizette plush in the two passenger compartments (one of them for negroes) and Spanish leather in the smoking compartment. The seats were unusually long and each could accommodate three persons when necessary. In this way the normal seating capacity of 62 could be expanded to 85. The cars were powered by two 100-horsepower motors mounted on each of the two front axles. Such gasoline-electric cars had become popular during the preceding decade, and promised a combination of luxury and economy that was attractive to Wise. The cars were to be delivered in October, and cost $26,000 each.

Wise also reactivated the through Pullmans, which had been suspended in September 1911 after ten months of service. This time he specified observation-buffet-sleepers and scheduled them for daylight hours through the Ozarks. In *Oak Leaves* and in attractive brochures he noted that:

This picture of excursionists on the observation platform of one of the new motor cars appeared on the November 1, 1913 timetable, and may have been taken in June of that year. The young ladies wearing the mortar boards were perhaps new graduates of the Crescent College and Conservatory at Eureka Springs. (*Louis Goodwin*)

These cars are electric lighted throughout, are equipped with electric fans and all modern conveniences. The menu in the buffet section is first class, and meals are served at all hours of the day. The observation end is provided with comfortable chairs for accommodation of passengers who do not desire berths, and the charge for which is about one-half cent per mile, with minimum of 25 cents. A writing desk and several of the latest magazines are provided for use of passengers. The Ozark Mountain scenery along the M. & N. A. R. R. is beautiful beyond description, and will be thoroughly enjoyed from the observation cars.

Wise also planned a number of right-of-way improvements. Several pile trestles would be filled, to reduce maintenance and fire hazard, and a few would be replaced by steel bridges. Extensive ballasting, bank widening, and grade straightening would be carried out. There would be new frame depots for Ridgely, Wayne, and Urbanette. And, including an order placed in March, 150 flat and 50 furniture cars would be added to the rolling stock.

Finally, Wise faced up to a problem that had been recognized for several years — that of inadequate shops for maintaining the sizable quantity of rolling stock. For example, it was necessary to send the locomotives away for major (Class 1) repairs. Limited space in Leatherwood Valley had previously prevented expansion of the Eureka Springs shops, and furthermore they were not well located to serve the entire line. The two-stall roundhouse shop at Helena (Outer Yard) was never intended for more than light running repairs. This left the small shops at Leslie as the possibility for expansion.

Operating practice for through trains was to change engines and crews at Leslie. This extended to freights, since Wise had inaugurated through freight service between Joplin and Helena, with a running time southbound of 29 hours. The districts were then 182 and 177 miles — about as even a split as could be found. But with the recent move toward the basic eight-hour day coupled with the basic 100-mile run, such district lengths were too long for crews as well as engines. Wise decided that a three-district operation was to be preferred, with Harrison and Heber Springs as division points which gave district lengths of 127, 116 and 116 miles. This made Harrison a contender for a shops location, and in truly shrewd business fashion the North Arkansas permitted Leslie and Harrison to bid against each other for such a juicy plum. On September 16, 1912, Wise met with the officers in St. Louis and then announced that Harrison was the winner not only of the new shops, but also of new general offices. The *Eureka Springs Times* commented as follows:

> . . . The Leslie people were game to the last, and their committee had a larger guarantee than Harrison. As soon as possible, construction at Harrison will start and will occupy all of the valley in which the depot is now located. The citizens raised $25,000 and also provided a site for [an office] building.

Later accounts indicate that the bonus by Harrison may have been as high as $35,000, but this may have included the value of donated land. By the end of September final negotiations had been concluded with owners of the 60-acre shops site in Crooked Creek Valley, and North Arkansas surveyors were at work.

This move was, of course, a blow to Eureka Springs and Leslie. On a consolidated basis, the monthly payroll for the North Arkansas at Harrison would be in the range of $30,000. The offices in the Sanford Building and at the depot in Eureka Springs would be closed and the occupants relocated to Harrison. The shops facilities at both Eureka and Leslie would be dismantled. Both towns would show a resulting decline in population, especially Eureka Springs.

The depot at Eureka had been about the busiest place on the entire North Arkansas property. In making reference to "the old red depot," W. T. Tarkington recollects (in *Unique Eureka* by B. L. Crump) that:

> The depot was a large, two-story building with offices of Master Mechanic and Superintendent of Bridges and Buildings on the second floor. The first floor constituted a railroad eating house in the south end, a large passenger waiting room, then the large ticket office, with the baggage room north of the ticket office in which three to five men were employed daily.

In 1913 there were eight passenger trains arriving and departing each day: the Joplin-Helena through trains, the Joplin-Eureka motor car, and two Seligman-Eureka steam trains that handled Frisco connections. One of the agents was E. R. Braswell, mentioned earlier in connection with the phantom train. Braswell described the schedules of these trains as follows:

Missouri and North Arkansas is the name of the road
    Always on time and our connections are good,
First train in the morning leaves at eight forty-five,
    With fifteen minutes at Seligman after you arrive
To get a train to St. Louis unless they are late
    But for Ft. Smith and Paris you have a two hours' wait.

The next train arrives at ten fifty-three
    Brings visitors from St. Louis, Dallas and K. C.
Leaves Eureka Springs promptly at eleven o'clock
    Makes connection at Kensett for Memphis and Little Rock
The Iron Mountain South leaves Kensett nine five
    And at eleven o'clock in Little Rock you arrive
Then at one ten A.M. the Memphis train will be due
    And gets you to Memphis about five fifty-two.

Twelve fifty-five is the Motor Car time
    Brings visitors from Lebanon and south on that line
Then leaves Eureka Springs promptly at two P.M.
    Takes you to Elk Ranch and Beaver and right back again
Arrives at Eureka at fifteen past four,
    And leaves at five o'clock for Seligman once more
Ten minutes wait at Seligman for the local train north
    One hour for the train for Dallas and Ft. Worth
Then the train from St. Louis is just pulling in,
    We get all their passengers and hike out again
Arrive at Eureka about seven forty-five
    Just before the passengers from the south will arrive.

Number two is the last and will leave eight o'clock
    Brought our passengers from Kensett, Memphis and Little Rock
It takes you to Seligman where you make connections north
    But you stay there all night if for Dallas or Ft. Worth

But passengers for Joplin go right through you see
    To make connection for Wichita and K. C.
And various points too numerous to mention,
    But for all these places we make good connection.
If there's any other information, rates, e-t-c,
    Just write, phone, or ask the agent: E. R. B.

Now, with the changes planned by General Manager Wise, much of this activity would be dispersed.

The plans for the new Harrison facilities were impressive. There would be a $15,000 brick office building downtown on the city square; it would have a fireproof vault and rooms to accommodate 40 people. Out in Crooked Creek Valley some $175,000 would be spent on five miles of trackage; a 70 x 238-foot machine shop attached to a six-stall roundhouse with 80-foot turntable; a stores building; a coach shop and other structures. A new and more convenient passenger depot would be erected near the business district, and the old depot would be converted to an operations office. There would be a 100,000-gallon spring-fed water reservoir up on the hillside, supplying the various shops' needs. And electricity and steam would be provided from a new powerhouse. There was no question but that the North Arkansas was going "big time." With all this, it was natural for the *Harrison Times* to make reference to:

> . . . that untiring hustler, that prince of good fellows, E. M. Wise. He is jerking the kinks out of the road, even though it has taken a trip to the United States Court to get the money.

The people of Leslie received another blow on the evening of November 26, 1912. At about 8:00 p.m. fire was discovered in the Williams Cooperage Co. plant. Although the company fire crew fought well, the fire roared through the plant and consumed most of it, including the electric light facility. Only the company office building and the boiler house survived. President Williams stated that the plant was "fully insured," but this was evidently not the case, and in 1913 only a portion of the plant was rebuilt.

Ground was broken for the Harrison shops construction on March 15, 1913, and by the end of the year all was in readiness.

No. 16 pulls the southbound passenger train across the White River bridge at Beaver in 1911. These spans represented a sturdy replacement for the original bridge shown on page 21. The new ten-wheel engine No. 20, in the builder's photo below, proved the most versatile and long-lived of all the locomotives on the railroad's roster. *(Below: H. L. Broadbelt)*

The relocation of people from Eureka Springs to Harrison began in the summer. With the new schedule of January 11, 1914, Harrison officially became a division point and the G.E. motor car run was extended to operate between Joplin and Harrison. Heber Springs, the other new division point, could also boast of new facilities, costing $15,000: engine shed and small shops building, coaling platform, 50,000-gallon water tank and 5,000 feet of new track. The second G.E. car continued in Heber Springs-Helena service, laying over at the former town each evening. And, possibly as peace offerings for their deprivations, the people of Eureka Springs and Leslie were provided with handsome new stone depots at a total cost of about $20,000.

The *Oak Leaves* issue of January 1914 was indeed optimistic. One could read that every station on the line represented a "live-wire town." New limestone and marble quarries had opened up near St. Joe. After a recovery in prices of zinc concentrates, 1914 promised to be a good year at the mines. As an example of business for the railroad, the city of Harrison reported shipping in 1913:

|                             | Cars |
| --------------------------- | ---- |
| Hogs                        | 50   |
| Mules and horses            | 20   |
| Cattle                      | 75   |
| Tight barrel cooperage      | 200  |
| Zinc and lead ore           | 20   |
| Poultry, wool, fruit, etc.  | 250  |
| Total                       | 615  |

The Williams Cooperage plant was back in operation, and contemplated a 15-mile extension of its railroad, in order to reach 50,000 additional acres of white oak timber. In February four additional locomotives were ordered which, when delivered, would give the road 27 serviceable engines.

General Manager Wise had been operating on the principle, "Spend money to make money," and this general approach was supported by the Receivers. By mid-1914 he had put the road in first-class condition, and it was available for large tonnage movements. Yes, he had spent money and now it was time to make it. His three year showing was as follows (June 30 basis):

|                          | 1912       | 1913        | 1914        |
|--------------------------|-----------|-------------|-------------|
| Total revenue            | $ 956,454 | $1,236,145  | $1,293,618  |
| Expenses                 | 945,814   | 1,200,129   | 1,225,154   |
| Gross earnings           | 10,640    | 36,016      | 68,464      |
| Taxes and other (net)    | 121,718   | 132,268     | 132,205     |
| Interest                 | 177,820   | 62,733      | 69,866      |
| Deficit                  | $ 288,893 | $ 158,985   | $ 133,607   |

The combined deficit for these three years, plus the cost of capital improvements, meant that Wise had already run through well over half of the allowed Receiver's Certificates. The total revenues had passed the million dollar mark, and on July 1, 1912, the road had been given the Interstate Commerce Commission grade of a Class 1 carrier. Wise had spent heavily on maintenance of way:

| 1911 | $243,078 |
|------|----------|
| 1912 | 343,157  |
| 1913 | 413,294  |
| 1914 | 337,444  |

It would appear that this expense could be cut back, but Wise resisted such an idea; he would only settle for a greater volume of traffic. There was growing friction between the Receivers and Wise, and for George Sands it was too much. Now almost 69, he requested retirement and on March 6, 1914, was replaced by John Scullin as one of the three Receivers.

By August, war in Europe was under way and there were signs of a pickup in the economy. Along the North Arkansas spirits were good and the resort town of Eureka Springs was having a good season. This was very much in evidence on the afternoon of Wednesday, August 5, at the handsome new Joplin Union Depot. A large crowd was gathered on one of the platforms when North Arkansas motor car No. 103 rolled into position for the start of its regular evening run to Harrison. Many in the crowd were headed for Eureka Springs to enjoy a cool and relaxing respite from the summer heat; in routine fashion they moved in through the side door and filled the car well.

The train was under the supervision of Conductor S. A. Nicholas, who had been with the North Arkansas since 1901 and whose record with the railroad had been excellent. His train would operate as No. 209 over Kansas City Southern tracks to Neosho, 19 miles, and would become M.&N.A. train No. 5 for the run into Harrison. Scheduled departure was 5:30 p.m.; scheduled arrival at Harrison was 11:59 p.m.

Just before scheduled departure, Nicholas picked up orders from operator William M. Hadley, who was a relatively new employee of the Joplin Union Depot Co. One order was routine, it called for the motor to leave Joplin one hour 15 minutes late by the now-outdated K. C. S. timecard. Then there was a "slow order" for track maintenance activity. The third order was a bit out of the ordinary:

> 1st No. 56 meet No. 209 at Tipton Ford and wait at Tipton Ford until 5:30 PM Saginaw 6:00 PM for extra No. 563 south.

Thus, the motor car was to take a siding at Tipton Ford, a "signpost" station 10.8 miles south of the Joplin depot, to accommodate a northbound train. The train was actually K. C. S. passenger No. 2 which had been delayed almost eight hours by a freight train wreck south of Gravette, Arkansas. Its passengers and mail had been transferred to another train, and it was now running as the first section of time freight No. 56. Less than 15 passengers were on the train, all having boarded at Neosho.

The cited order came from K. C. S. dispatcher W. R. Sebring at Pittsburg, Kansas, and was acknowledged at Neosho by conductor Sisk of 1st No. 56. It was also acknowledged by conductor Nicholas of the motor car — at least, he is purported to have signed the receipt copy. And if he followed normal procedure he had it read and understood by motorman Ratliff.

Promptly at 5:30 Ratliff blasted the air horn, actuated the pneumatic bellringer, and notched current into the traction motors. The car clattered over the terminal switchpoints and soon picked up speed to about 35 miles per hour as it began its steady climb along Shoal Creek. Some 77 persons were aboard the train, counting the crew of three men in the baggage-mail compartment, and several people riding on passes. Returning home to Eureka Springs was Mrs. Ratliff, wife of the motorman. Because of crowded conditions, M. & N. A. line foreman J. J. Lauderback located a folding stool and sat out on the rear platform. Among the revenue passengers was W. M. Drury of Webb City, Missouri (near Joplin) who, with his wife and three children, had only been able to find seats at the very rear of the car, next to the door to the rear platform.

At about 5:55 p.m. the car rocked right on through Tipton Ford, Ratliff apparently oblivious of the order to take the siding. Approaching from the south was K. C. S. heavy Pacific-type loco-motive No. 805 (Alco 1912) with seven cars, also traveling at about 35 miles per hour. After passing the south switch the motor car rounded a curve to bring into view the approaching passenger train, some 450 feet away. The response of the motorman can only be imagined, but witnesses indicate that he did not brake the car violently. Engineer John Brennan applied emergency air and started toward the gangway just before the instant of impact.

The trains collided head-on with a terrific transfer of momen-tum. The locomotive telescoped some 20 feet of the motor car and drove it directly backward 650 feet. The impact caused a drawbar on the train to break, and the train parted by some 300 feet. Passengers, seats, and luggage in the motor car crashed into heaps — and were soon enveloped in flames burning on gasoline from the ruptured gasoline tank beneath the car. Those surviv-ing the initial impact were prevented from escaping because of jammed doors and walls of fire. Of the 14 men in the smoking compartment, only one was able to get free. Miraculously, Lauder-back and Drury were thrown clear and were able to help many to safety. Lauderback crawled through a window and brought nine persons from the car, having to fight one of them, a woman whose child was lost. Mr. Drury managed to rescue all the members of his family and then go back for three more people. After further rescue work was impossible, Lauderback went back to Tipton Ford to telephone the dispatcher and ask for emergency help. In the final analysis, 43 persons died, including all members of the M. & N. A. crew. No one on the passenger train was killed.

A Dr. H. F. Foster, of Neosho, happened to be in the vicinity and gave first aid to the injured. A relief train was dispatched from Joplin to convey the injured to hospitals. Some of the imme-diate survivors were badly burned and died later; local newspapers later estimated that the death toll would reach 50. On August 7, there was a public burial in Neosho for over 30 unidentified bodies. The community and the railroads were grief stricken; this was the first serious accident in the 15-year history of gasoline railcars.* And because no one in the passenger train was seriously injured, the safety aspects of the motor cars were open to serious question.

The North Arkansas crew died in the crash (Mrs. Ratliff, wife of the motorman, also died), and the mixup on orders could not be explained. The conductor was a long and honored employee of the North Arkansas, and always careful to tend to business details. There were allegations that operator Hadley failed to deliver the order (he was a "drifter" who had been discharged by the Santa Fe for such overtness) and then forged the name of Nicholas on the receipt copy. Yet, Nicholas was seen with what appeared to be a train order while standing at the register book. And, strangely, he did not register his train. It was clear that either the motorman had not been informed, or that he was incapable of slowing the train before the collision. Conductor Nicholas completed taking tickets at least three minutes before the collision and thus did not have that diversion to prevent him from pulling the emergency cord when (and if) he saw the Tipton Ford siding. It seemed immediately as if Nicholas and Ratliff were collaborators in some maniacal suicide attempt!

The Interstate Commerce Commission and the Missouri Public Service Commission began their investigations on August 8 at Neosho. Lineman Lauderback, operator Hadley, dispatcher Sebring, conductor Sisk, the K. C. S. fireman, and many others testified, but a real explanation for the accident could not be developed. Fault was not established. It was up to each railroad to pay for its own property damages and liability claims. And, of course, most of the cost fell to the North Arkansas.

The news of the crash was a shock to all those in the region and, of course, a serious financial jolt to the North Arkansas. The motor car was a complete loss and was hauled away as junk, but

*In his book on railroad accidents, *Down Brakes*, author R. B. Shaw noted that only one significant accident involving a motor car has occurred since — at Cuyahoga Falls, Ohio, on July 31, 1940, in which 41 were killed.

Motor car No. 103, shown on page 102, looked like this after its head-on collision near Tipton Ford, Missouri. After the collision parts of No. 103 were left clinging to the front of the Kansas City Southern Pacific-type engine No. 805. The picture below was taken at Neosho on August 6.

*(Above: Earl Saunders; below: Merritt McGaughey)*

management retained faith in the motor car concept and immediately ordered a replacement from General Electric. Attorney O. L. Cravens, of Neosho, proceeded with settlement of claims and by the end of the fiscal year would pay out almost $160,000. Counting the cost of the motor car and other expenses, the Tipton Ford affair would take almost $190,000 from the treasury. General Manager Wise was understandably shaken by this first consequential accident ever to have been experienced by the railroad, and the event may well have been the turning point in his tenure with the M. & N. A.

Later that month, on August 25, Powell Clayton died. He had been living in Washington after having served as ambassador to Mexico, and though not active in North Arkansas affairs had never dismissed "his railroad" from mind. He attempted to reply to the many charges against his mishandling of public office responsibilities in a book, *Aftermath of the Civil War,* but died a very controversial figure. He still owned a significant amount of North Arkansas stock, but no doubt had commiserated many times with his friends Scullin and Kerens over the rather sad state of their business venture.

As 1914 ended, the through sleepers were taken out of service, and would never again grace the rear end of the North Arkansas passenger trains. News of the war in Europe crowded almost all other news off the front pages of the newspapers, and the need for strategic metals touched the northern Arkansas zinc fields. The price of concentrates jumped over 100 per cent, and the Rush Creek district sprang to life. Scattered operations along the North Arkansas also opened up, and plans were developed for the construction of ore transfer platforms at Harrison, Everton, Pindall, St. Joe, Gilbert, and Marshall.

Early 1915 marked a significant pickup in business for the railroad, but the report for the fiscal year ending June 30 showed the largest deficit ever, over $350,000, aided materially by the cost of the Tipton Ford accident. Since arriving on the scene, E. M. Wise had increased the worth of the capital investment by $1,200,000 while at the same time incurring operating deficits totalling $932,-000. Most of this had come out of Receiver's Certificates that now totalled $2,062,750. This amount was close to the maximum allowed and was much more than the railroad could afford to pay for in interest. The cold fact was at hand, strict economy would be required if the line was to continue to operate.

The pressure on Wise was mounting. He had put the road in first-class physical condition: bridges were sound, tie replacements on a good schedule, rolling stock in good repair, and hardly a weed was to be found between the rails. The volume of business had plateaued at about $1,200,000 annually, but with the war in Europe Wise might expect an upturn in 1916. This was his hope, and he could count on the readiness of the facilities to handle such an upturn with dispatch.

As noted above, there were hopes that on-line business from hauling ore concentrates would increase. The September 19, 1915 timetable described the potential as follows:

> The rich zinc and lead mining district around Harrison, Ark., is fast bringing this city into prominence as the metropolis and center of the North Arkansas Mineral Belt. Within a very short time the Harrison District will be as widely known as the Joplin District.

> Within a radius of 25 miles of Harrison there are now located over 200 producing mines and new properties are being opened up daily. The cost of operation of these mines is small because of the fact that the ore literally crops out. Little machinery is being used and the zinc is taken almost from the surface of the ground. The ores are of a high grade and much of it is shipped with great profit without milling.

> Mining in this District is only in its infancy. The great possibilities of the zinc fields of this section are as yet, comparatively speaking, in a dormant condition compared to what they will be in a few weeks. There are thousands of acres in this District rich as 'Solomon's Mines,' practically untouched. There are yet open for leasing and for sale, great areas of mineral producing ground, that can be obtained on liberal terms.

In truth, the real center of mining was along Rush Creek, some 14 miles down the Buffalo River from the M. & N. A. bridge near Gilbert. The little town of Rush had mushroomed to a population of 2,000, with most of the people living in tents and crude shacks.

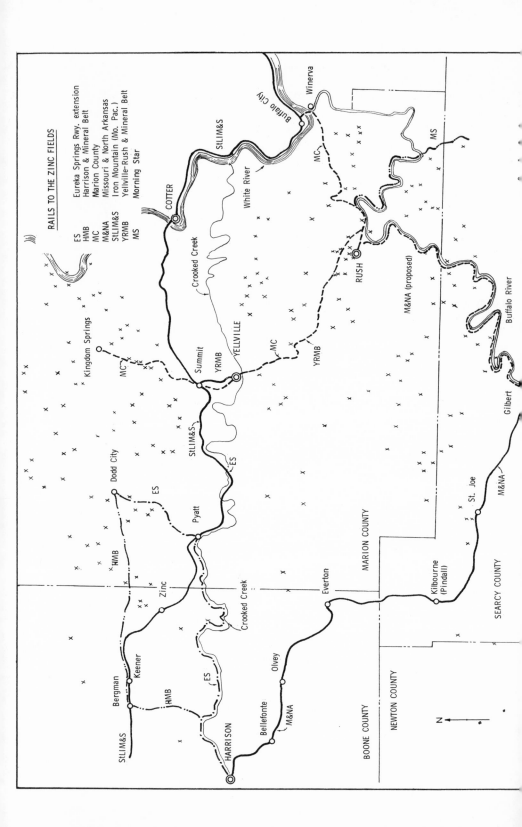

RAILS TO THE ZINC FIELDS

| | |
|---|---|
| ES | Eureka Springs Rwy. extension |
| HMB | Harrison & Mineral Belt |
| MC | Marion County |
| M&NA | Missouri & North Arkansas (Mo. Pac.) |
| StLIM&S | Iron Mountain |
| YRMB | Yellville-Rush & Mineral Belt |
| MS | Morning Star |

But the difficulty of hauling out ore by wagons may be imagined from this description by a correspondent of *The Engineering and Mining Journal*, occasioned by a 1915-1916 winter journey from the railroad at Yellville to the zinc fields:

> To get to Rush I crossed Rush Creek 43 times and when not in the creek was on the worst road ever, the ground being cut hub-deep and frozen. A storm on the ocean was not a circumstance to a ride in the stage. I walked three of the 12 miles and would have been pleased to have walked more, but the darned creek kept getting in the way. To add to my discomfort, the temperature was 16 above and the breeze brisk . . .

The *Harrison Times* of November 19, 1915 gave the news that the M. & N. A. was again considering the scheme to build from Gilbert to Rush. It was stated that the line would follow the Buffalo River for some 14 miles and would be inexpensive to construct; there would be no tunnels, bridges, or heavy cuts. And its last nine miles would be in direct contact with revenue-producing mines. Actually, such a line would not be cheap, to make it invulnerable to the periodic floods on the Buffalo would require a total outlay of at least $300,000. And where would such money come from, particularly in view of the ups and downs of mining activity?

During such deliberations it was announced on December 17 that a charter had been granted to the Yellville, Rush & Mineral Belt Railway that would connect the Rush Creek District with the Iron Mountain line. The venture appeared to be a live one, and in January 1916 surveys were under way. The line would be narrow gauge, 19 miles long with 42 bridges totalling 3100 feet, maximum grades of four per cent, and maximum curves of 16 degrees. Two Shay type locomotives and 20 ore cars were purchased from Pine Bluff, Arkansas, interests. Rail weight would be 35 pounds to the yard, and a third rail would be laid from the Yellville station (at Summit, Arkansas) to the downtown district, two miles, to provide standard gauge service. By spring work was active all along the route, and a mile of track had been laid. Such

No. 36 was one of seven 30-class mikado freight locomotives that served the road for many years. The handsome new Eureka Springs passenger station was built on the location of the original depot of the Eureka Springs Railway, shown on page 13. The camera view is northward toward Junction; the freight station may be seen to the rear and the original shops were to the right, just outside the picture.

*(Above: H. L. Broadbelt; below: E. R. Braswell)*

a development made the North Arkansas back away completely from the branch line down the Buffalo.

David R. Francis continued to be active in management affairs of the railroad until the exigencies of war called him to public duty. In early 1916 he was appointed ambassador to Russia, and while he was overseas his letters to his son, David, Jr., and to Festus Wade reveal many interesting incidents in the history of the North Arkansas.* While on his initial voyage to Petrograd, he wrote to his friend Charles Gleed, a Director of the Santa Fe line, regarding possible purchase of the North Arkansas by that railroad. The letter was dated April 25, 1916, and stated in part:

> I do not remember ever to have become so much interested in any enterprise that proved so altogether unsatisfactory . . . the St. Louis holders of the securities are very much discouraged, but John Scullin and R. C. Kerens and myself, who are the largest holders [of securities of the road] have never lost confidence in the outcome of the road.

And in the same letter, Francis made this interesting comment:

> The strained relations between the United States and Germany may result in war, but I cannot think that Germany will be so thoughtless.

If relations between the United States and Germany were strained, so were those between management and Wise. Only John Scullin did not share in the antagonism toward the general manager. Festus Wade, President of the Mercantile Trust Company, representing a number of noteholders, decided that if the property could not be sold immediately, Wise would have to go. The reply of Gleed to Francis was in the negative; the Santa Fe was not interested in taking over the North Arkansas. The next prospective purchaser contacted by Wade was the Illinois Central.

In late May, two private cars were coupled behind an M. & N. A. locomotive and deadhead car at the Joplin Union Depot. The first car was No. 100, business car of General Manager Wise. The other was the private car of Charles H. Markham, President of the Illinois Central. Included in the party were Scullin, Wade,

---

*These letters are contained in the D. R. Francis Collection at The Missouri Historical Society in St. Louis. They are quoted here by permission.

Charles Gilbert, David Francis, Jr. and, of course, E. M. Wise. Along with Markham was his Chief Engineer L. W. Baldwin (later President of the Missouri Pacific). The objective was to make a careful two-day inspection of the M. & N. A. property. There were the expected stopovers at Eureka Springs, Harrison, and Leslie; the night was spent at Heber Springs. On the next day the party proceeded to Helena.

President Markham's conclusion was to the point: the Illinois Central could not purchase the road. (The hope was that the note-holders could sell for 50 cents on the dollar, or $3,000,000 for the notes plus outstanding Receivers' Certificates, or $5,067,500 total.) But he did offer the following bits of encouragement: the road was in excellent physical shape, thanks to the efforts of E. M. Wise; the new Traffic Manager, J. C. "Jack" Murray, appeared to be very capable; and he would take action in getting traffic for the road. On the side he offered to provide a top-flight replacement for Wise, if Wade wanted a new general manager.

Festus Wade obtained permission from Judge Trieber to become the sole Receiver of the property, replacing Scullin, McDonald, and Holt. He took over in early June and on June 6th accepted the resignation of E. M. Wise. On June 9th, Wade, Scullin, and others interviewed C. A. Phelan, the man recommended by Charles Markham. Mr. Phelan was 36 years of age and had been with the Illinois Central for 18 years. He agreed to the same salary being paid to Wise, $5,000 annually, and was promised a bonus if he could get the railroad into the black. Phelan took office on June 15th, the same date that Wade officially became sole Receiver, and Wise remained until June 30th to effect a reasonable transition of office.

Edward Wise returned to his interests in Old Mexico. The Francis letters indicate that Scullin continued to support him because of his general reputation as a "good railroad man," but that the wishes of Wade and the "Committee of Noteholders" (George L. Edwards, David Francis, Jr., and G. H. Walker) prevailed to have him replaced. During his five years with the North Arkansas he had accomplished much in his desire to make the railroad first class; his difficulty seemed to be in compromising high standards in the face of an acute shortage of money and a limited potential for traffic.

Receiver Wade and General Manager Phelan took over quickly, and proceeded to institute severe economies of operation. Many workmen in the shops and along the way were laid off, and all possible maintenance was deferred indefinitely. Wade attempted to interest the Rock Island, the Kansas City Southern, and other lines in purchasing the property, but had no success. The city of Helena was pressuring Wade for improved passenger facilities; he responded by arranging for the Illinois Central to plan a new depot, with the M. & N. A. as a tenant.

An interesting maneuver by Wade concerned the Tipton Ford accident case. After consulting with L. F. Loree, Chairman of the Board of the Kansas City Southern, he felt that there might be a chance of getting back some of the money paid out in damages. The key issue was whether Operator Hadley had failed to deliver the order to the motor car conductor. If such could be proved, then the Kansas City Southern, because of its dispatching responsibility, would be liable for the damages. Now, the North Arkansas had never paid the $10,000 owed to the lawyers who had handled the claims settlements. In exchange for this amount Wade offered them half of any judgment that they could obtain from the Kansas City Southern. They accepted the challenge, and in due course entered suit against the Kansas City Southern, in the name of the M. & N. A.

In September 1916 Wade was able to report definite progress in his economy drive. Operations for the months of July and August showed $63,000 net earnings after interest charges on Receivers' Certificates, although there was essentially no maintenance done. Wade had prevailed on the State of Missouri to reduce taxes from $9,200 to $6,000 per mile of line, and had gotten the State of Arkansas down to $7,200 per mile of line. The only cloud at the time was a threatened nationwide railroad strike, and Phelan went directly to the men with these thoughts:

> If you fail us in this hour when we are under new management, making every effort to increase our business, it is simply going to add to the deficit now charged to the road,

and it is a very serious question whether or not it can continue to operate, as it has not paid operating expenses and taxes during the last five years.

We have in our service a class of men second to none in the country, with as high as twenty years service, having their own homes and property, and I sincerely hope they will consider these things before resorting to drastic action in an effort to get concessions which simply cannot be granted by a road in such deplorable financial condition as the Missouri & North Arkansas.*

The strike was averted, and as business continued to grow with the war effort, the road operated in the black. For the last six months of 1916 there were net earnings after interest of $147,-963.38, compared with a deficit of $59,695.57 during the same period of 1915. A large contributor to this apparent success was a $106,000 decrease in charges for maintenance of way. For the calendar year 1916 there was a net of $51,128, the first in years (although there was nothing for interest to the bondholders).

The gross revenue in January 1917 was up to $114,972 compared with $82,366 a year earlier. Things seemed to be going well, and Wade proceeded to buy up $117,000 of the Receiver's Certificates. The mining business was active, and competition from the new Yellville, Rush & Mineral Belt line disappeared when that line failed to finance completion of construction. The market for concentrates remained variable, and it was typical for the *Harrison Times* of February 10, 1917, to remark that 13 carloads of zinc ore were adjacent to the M. & N. A., but would not move until the price reached $50 per ton.

Threats of a nationwide strike had continued for several months, the basic issue being a shift from the basic ten-hour day to a basic eight-hour day for the railroad brotherhoods. The North Arkansas, along with other lines, had resisted legislation granting the shorter day. But on March 19, the U. S. Supreme Court upheld the eight-hour law and the railroads were required to increase wages by paying overtime rates for daily hours over eight. How-

---

*Delivered by C. A. Phelan at a meeting on the Courthouse lawn at Harrison on August 29, 1916. Also printed in a circular, a copy of which is in the files of the Missouri Historical Society.

ever, war demands were increasing traffic volume on the North Arkansas and this turn of events was not too upsetting to Wade and Phelan.

April 1917 was a noteworthy month for the railroad. On April 6th war with Germany was declared by the United States and, in a patriotic move, Phelan announced that the entire right of way would be offered free of charge for "victory gardens." On April 15th, Cafe-Parlor-Observation cars were placed in service on Trains 1 and 2 between Joplin and Helena. Two cars had been purchased secondhand* for $14,078 and were well equipped with "upholstered, roomy, revolving chairs; observation platform; dining compartment and all modern conveniences." And on April 16th work started on a new $75,000 passenger depot at Helena that would be opened formally on December 6th. (This terminated strained relations between the railroad and the Business Men's League of Helena. The citizens had originally subscribed over $100,000 for depot facilities and right of way, but the funds never came through. The League paid for the North Arkansas' share of the new depot.)

An April event of singular importance was the decision on the M. & N. A. suit against the Kansas City Southern over the Tipton Ford accident. The services of a nationally-prominent handwriting expert (a man named Carvahlo) had been engaged, and he had convinced the jury in the Circuit Court at Bentonville, Arkansas, that the train order signature was a forgery and that the M. & N. A. crew had never received the order to meet the K. C. S. passenger train. The jury rendered a verdict of $190,000 in favor of the M. & N. A.; but, as expected the K. C. S. appealed the case to the Arkansas Supreme Court. Later, in March 1918, that body would decide that the personal liability costs should be shared equally by the two railroads and that each should pay for its own property damages. And at the same time that court would deny a K. C. S. petition for a rehearing. Thus, after splitting with the lawyers, the M. & N. A. would recover about $40,000 of the Tipton

---

*The source of these cars, Nos. 3220 and 3221, is not known to the author. They were built by Pullman in 1890 and were of all-wood construction. Contemporary *Railway Equipment Register* issues indicate that they may have come from the Southern Pacific.

Ford collision costs and at the same time remove the $10,000 debt from the books. The court decisions represented a minor, but very important, victory for the North Arkansas.

As 1917 moved on, the wartime traffic intensified nationally and the railroads were plagued with shortages of equipment and people. The major lines attempted to work together without success, and there was talk of the government taking over the railroads. The North Arkansas continued with stable and profitable operation, and on September 29 Wade reported to Ambassador Francis that the railroad facilities were in excellent physical condition, despite the reduced maintenance; that vigorous efforts were being made to develop the agricultural capabilities of the region served; and that handsome new brick freight and passenger depots at Helena would soon be in service.

On December 1, in a special report to Congress, the Interstate Commerce Commission recommended that President Woodrow Wilson assume control of the railroads. Equipment shortages had become acute, and operating efficiencies had sagged significantly. President Wilson followed the recommendation, and acting under the authority of the Federal Possession and Control Act, on December 26, 1917, issued a proclamation providing for U. S. operation of the railroads. The effective time would be noon on December 28. William G. McAdoo, then Secretary of the Treasury, was appointed Director General of Railroads. In response to this action, Wade wrote to Francis that "the future of the M. & N. A. is very uncertain."

The railroad had shown a profit in calendar 1917 of $88,004. Comparisons of financial results for recent years were as follows:

|  | 1914 | 1915 | 1916 | 1916* | 1917* |
|---|---|---|---|---|---|
| Total revenue | $1,293,618 | $1,181,851 | $1,199,987 | $1,310,935 | $1,417,969 |
| Expenses | 1,225,154 | 1,333,045 | 1,115,090 | 1,027,497 | 1,122,310 |
| Gross earnings | 68,464 | −151,194 | 84,897 | 283,438 | 295,659 |
| Taxes and other | 132,205 | 115,257 | 117,663 | 109,715 | 94,788 |
| Interest | 69,866 | 86,165 | 123,765 | 122,595 | 112,867 |
| Earnings | $−133,607 | $−352,616 | $−156,531 | $ +51,128 | $ +88,004 |

*Calendar year basis; accounting systems changed from June 30 basis used prior to 1917.

With the railroad operating well, it was indeed unfortunate for the government to have to "rock the boat." The government would, of course, provide a guarantee to cover costs of operation and, hopefully, include some kind of a profit. The major concern was how the railroad would be operated, and in what condition it would be returned to the owners. As history would show, this governmental intervention was one of the worst things ever to happen to the North Arkansas during its hectic career.

The new $75,000 depot at Helena was photographed on December 5, 1917, just as finishing touches and landscaping were being applied. The view is toward the south, with the Mississippi River just beyond a levee to the left of the picture. For many years, North Arkansas passenger trains were the only ones to use the depot. The building was torn down in 1962.

*(Illinois Central Railroad)*

No. 19, one of the North Arkansas line's general-purpose ten-wheelers is shown at Joplin about 1920. The arrival of the train was always an important event in the lives of Ozark folk along the North Arkansas. At Shirley, below, on Sunday, June 10, 1917 a crowd awaits the arrival of northbound passenger No. 2, due to arrive about 2 p.m. The view is toward Heber Springs.

*(Above: John B. Allen collection; below: Mrs. Homer Brown)*

# CHAPTER FIVE

## *1918-1925*

# *Government Operation and the Big Strike*

The government takeover of the railroads was complete. All common carriers came under control of the United States Railroad Administration. But on January 1, 1918, the *modus operandi* of such a vast and cumbersome transportation system existed only as an ill-defined idea. All Director-General McAdoo could expect from the individual managements was, as he telegraphed them, "to make every possible effort to move traffic by the most convenient and expeditious route." The objectives of the U. S. R. A. were directed generally toward improving the effectiveness of the railroads in supporting the war effort. Measures such as the following would be taken: routings of traffic would be shortened, without regard for shipper preference; facilities of several roads would be consolidated; duplication of passenger service would be eliminated; demurrage rates would be increased, in order to alleviate car shortages; designs of new locomotives and freight cars would be standardized; and so on. But to implement these objectives through a national organization would take time and at least on the M. & N. A. business continued about as usual.

The road was operating well at the start of 1918. It had been in the black for about 18 months and General Manager C. A. Phelan had shown that he could run a tight ship, although his cutbacks in maintenance could be questioned by knowledgeable railroad men. The motive power and rolling stock were adequate, and freight was being interchanged without delay, in fact, much more rapidly than it could be transferred at such large terminal points as Kansas City, St. Louis, and Memphis. Of the 588,481 tons of freight hauled in 1917 about 18 per cent represented "bridge traffic," i.e., freight transferred to and then from the road. Freight originated and terminating on-line was at a stable level, but there were indications that the bridge traffic could be increased by emphasizing "rapid handling" at such points as Joplin, Seligman, Kensett, Wheatley, and Helena. Thus, in early 1918 Festus Wade and company were in no hurry for the U. S. R. A. to rock the boat. As a matter of fact, Wade busied himself with other U. S. R. A. matters; he accepted an appointment on the Advisory Committee, Financial Section, Division of Finance and Purchases.

On March 15th it was announced that Judge John B. Payne, General Counsel for the U. S. R. A., was ready to make contracts with the railroads. The railroads were to be guaranteed annual net incomes equivalent to their average for the three years ending June 30, 1917. Clearly, such a policy would not be satisfactory to the M. & N. A. or a great many other roads that had not been profitable during that period. By definition, interest on Receiver's Certificates would have to be paid out of the guarantee. If one followed the strict letter of the guarantee basis, the North Arkansas would have to pay the government money!

Of even more concern to management was the wage situation. For some months there had been widespread dissatisfaction among railroad employees because of low wages in relation to other industries and to the rising cost of living. There had been almost continuous threats of strikes, and to study the matter Director-General McAdoo appointed on January 18 the Railroad Wage Commission. And on April 30 the Commission made its report and recommended wage increases averaging 16 per cent retroactive to January 1, 1918. The increases were approved in less than a month, and the M. & N. A. was forced to go along with the other railroads of the country in paying them.

To compensate for the wage increases, the U. S. R. A. advanced freight rates by about 25 per cent, effective June 25, and passenger rates to about three cents a mile, effective June 10. But, of course, the retroactive wage increase amounts could not be covered by these increased rates. And long before the M. & N. A. could profit from the rate increases, the government had closed the commercial offices at Kansas City, Little Rock, and Chattanooga so solicitation for increased bridge traffic was made more difficult.

Meanwhile, Judge Payne proceeded to make guarantee contracts with all of the major trunk-line railroads. But dealing with the 1700 or so "short lines" (in which category the North Arkansas was included) was a different matter. Because of their basically unprofitable nature they didn't fit well into the government formula. And it was only natural for them to insist on compensation for the disruption of business imposed by government operation. The enabling law required that decisions regarding the short lines be made by July 1, and on June 29, Payne sent telegrams to all but 128 of the short lines, telling them that they were being returned to their owners for private operation. The M. & N. A. was included in the group being returned.

The action of the U. S. R. A. in returning the line was not exactly satisfying to the North Arkansas management. Government methods in increasing wages, closing off-line offices, and diverting traffic to other roads had cut heavily into the earnings efforts of Wade and Phelan. For the first half of 1918 net earnings (before interest payments) dropped $104,341 from the corresponding 1917 period and were barely in the black at $4,692. Moreover, the M. & N. A. had not gone along with a second round of wage increases granted nationally to railroad shopmen. As strike threats began circulating, Festus Wade began negotiations with the U. S. R. A. to acquire the road on a basis such as was worked out with the trunk-line roads. He wrote to David Francis that his hope was for an annual guarantee of $290,000, to extend for the duration of the war plus 21 months.

On September 18 the shopmen at Harrison walked off their jobs, and in deference to them the other union employees of the road also stopped work. Operations came to a dead halt, and a frantic plea was made to the U. S. R. A. Festus Wade was very happy to accept an annual guarantee basis of $175,000 and a term equal to that of the trunk-line roads. On September 24 the U. S. R. A. took over, the shopmen went back to work on the basis that the government would hear their case, and all operations were resumed.

The M. & N. A. was placed in the Southwestern Region of the U. S. R. A. and grouped with the Kansas City Southern, Texarkana & Fort Smith, Midland Valley, Houston East & West Texas, and Kansas City, Mexico & Orient under Federal Manager J. A. Edson, a capable administrator and on leave from the presidency of the Kansas City Southern line. As the U. S. R. A. moved in, top management of the M. & N. A. moved out. Some of the latter found jobs elsewhere in the U. S. R. A. organization; for example, C. A. Phelan moved to Philadelphia, Pennsylvania, to become Operating Assistant of the Allegheny Region. On November 24, Time Table No. 1 of the government-operated M. N. & A. was issued and it showed some cutbacks in service. A single freight train was operated, daily except Sunday; the through daily passenger run from Joplin to Helena was shortened to Joplin-Kensett; and the motor cars were used for the Joplin-Eureka Springs and Helena-Heber Springs turns. The parlor cars, which had operated unprofitably on-and-off during the year, were taken off for good. In turn, maintenance spending was increased — by illustration, monthly maintenance of way charges after August 24 averaged $50,000 compared with $27,000 earlier in the year.

The war effort was successfully prosecuted and victory came on November 11, with the 805 North Arkansas employees showing their loyalty by subscribing 100 per cent to Liberty Bond drives. On December 4th, Festus Wade and the U. S. R. A. executed their formal agreement, and Wade requested a $150,000 advance in order to meet year-end payments of interest on the Receiver's Certificates. Mr. Walker D. Hines, who succeeded Director-General McAdoo on January 1, 1919, announced that the first year of government operation of the railroads had been something less than profitable, the controlled lines had earned $250,000,000 less than their guaranteed payments! Including the prorated 1918 guarantee, the U. S. R. A. loss on the North Arkansas line, August 24 through December 31, was about $178,000.

In January 1919 Festus Wade and John Scullin, now 82 years of age and failing rapidly, toured the line in the latter's private car. They were able to report that the government was maintaining the roadway, equipment, and other facilities in beautiful condition. It seemed clear that the U. S. R. A. intended to keep the railroad workers fully occupied at good wages, and in April the general wage scale went up again. When President Woodrow Wilson announced that the railroads would be returned to their owners in early 1920 the M. & N. A. noteholders might well have been concerned: how could a "gold-plated" type operation be reconciled with the geographic and economic limitations of private operation in peacetime?

The year 1919 continued without particular incident. Mining operations around Harrison and St. Joe had essentially folded up, following a severe drop in ore prices in early 1918 and that ever-tempting traffic potential was gone. In trouble also was that portion of the timber business devoted to materials for whiskey and beer barrels; the 18th Amendment had received the necessary ratification and would go into law January 16, 1920. Having no concern for such portents, the U. S. R. A. continued first-class operations and ran a 1919 deficit of $633,557 plus the $175,000 guarantee. The corporate "residue" operation showed a modest $5,099 deficit after paying $118,434 interest and miscellaneous expenses of the Receiver.

An incident out on the line was an interesting, if not newsworthy, one. It occurred near the little town of Arlberg, Arkansas, where the line passed through the "Collonades of the Little Red." This is a particularly scenic part of the Ozarks, and it is unfortunate that no publicity photographs of trains running under the bluffs have been located. In fact, they may never have been taken. Mr. G. H. Morley, ex-roadmaster of the Missouri Pacific, described the incident in *Railroad Magazine:*

> For several years I was a rock gang and an extra gang foreman on the old Missouri & North Arkansas Railroad and was fascinated by a boulder which had been left hanging over the track south of Arlberg, Ark., when the roadbed was blasted out of the mountainside. The construction engineers probably thought it would add to the scenic interest to leave the huge rock balanced on the tip of the bluff.
>
> Maybe they just waited until it was convenient to send somebody the long way around to where the mountain could be climbed, to blast it off, but finally forgot to do so. And so the rock remained, and attracted much attention.

The road curved coming north, so passengers could look out of the train windows and see that landmark hanging exactly over the engine of the train they were on. I have heard many say, 'What if it should fall?' But there was always somebody to reply: 'It is too heavy for the wind to move. It can't fall.'

After returning from the World War, I went to work as section foreman at Arlberg. That boulder finally got on my nerves. I couldn't pass under the darned thing without believing it was a source of danger, although so far as the eye could detect it had not changed in all the years. I remarked to my crew, 'She's likely to fall ahead of a train some time.' An old man answered me: 'I been a workin' here since this road was built nigh onto twenty years. She ain't fell yet.' In April 1920, the first Sunday morning after my wife and I had started keeping house, I awoke with a feeling of dread. I was not given to nervousness, but I couldn't shake it off. I told Mrs. Morley at breakfast that I had dreamed the old boulder was falling on the track. She looked at me as if she wondered just what she had tied herself up to, and told me to snap out of it.

I wandered across town to the depot, but I couldn't get that premonition off of my mind. Two of the section men ambled up, and then I got busy. I told them to help me drag the motor car out and run over the south end with me, before the passenger train came. We were started all right and were going pretty fast when a farmer came up the track waving frantically for us to stop. He said the old landmark had crashed at last, right across the rails. We took him on the motor car for help and then I put on speed so that a flagman could get a safe distance out ahead of the passenger train.

I motioned for one of my men to grab the flags, and when we stopped right against the rock, he jumped and ran on ahead. I looked at the famous old boulder half buried in the dirt, gravel and broken ties. It had hit exactly between the rails, which were not damaged. The part above the ground was higher than my waist. Fortunately, nobody was hurt.

In early 1920 there were much more important developments on the national scene, developments that would influence the North Arkansas. First, the date for returning all railroads to their owners was set for March 1 with, in addition, a six-month guarantee period to soften the transition to private operation. Second, passage was imminent for the Transportation Act which would give the government broad control of railroad wages, rates, earnings, mergers, and so on through expanded powers of the Interstate Commerce Commission. Another development, mentioned previously, was the establishment of Prohibition.

C. A. Phelan resigned his U. S. R. A. job in January and returned to Harrison to resume his general manager duties. On February 28, the Transportation Act became effective and in addition to providing for the return of the railroads to their owners, established the Railroad Labor Board to deal with the difficult question of reasonable wages for railroad workers. After obtaining suitable permission from Judge Trieber, C. A. Phelan became Receiver and General Manager on March 6. Festus Wade elected to devote more of his "M. & N. A. time" to the problem of the longer-term future of the railroad.

As he took over the railroad, Phelan was faced with these facts:

1. The six months' guarantee of $87,500 would be available, and the government would cover losses during that period.
2. The payroll on the line was about 66 per cent greater than it was in 1917.
3. Further wage increases by the Railway Labor Board were likely.
4. The Interstate Commerce Commission was likely to increase freight and passenger rates.
5. The facilities of the M. & N. A. were in excellent condition.

On the surface, this didn't look bad. Phelan elected to operate on a "business as usual" basis until the transition was complete. True to form, on July 20 the Railroad Labor Board granted another

round of wage increases (this time averaging 22 per cent) and the
M. & N. A. payroll jumped to an annual rate of $1,410,000 com-
pared with $695,000 in 1917. These increases were retroactive to
May 1, 1920. In parallel action, the Interstate Commerce Commission on July 29 granted increases in freight rates of about 25 per
cent and passenger rate increases to five cents per mile.

In the midst of this transition, on May 28, the death of John
Scullin was noted. Although he still retained the title of President,
he had been relatively inactive in the administration of the M. &
N. A. since stepping aside from the Receiver position in 1916. It
was Scullin who was the real builder of the road, and to such a
capable and generally successful person the North Arkansas venture must have been a bitter pill to swallow. Of the $6,000,000
Allegheny Improvement notes, he owned over $1,000,000, in addi-
tion to Receiver's Certificates. In his last years he relied heavily
on his right-hand man, Charles Gilbert, to follow the detail of the
M. & N. A. And to Gilbert, as co-executor of Scullin's estate, fell
the responsibility of recouping the very large investment in the
road.

The guarantee period ended September 1, and the earnings
picture was then watched very closely. For the last four months
of the year, operations about broke even, a net loss of $209 after
deducting prorated interest. The dollar volume of business was
good, averaging over $200,000 a month because of the increased
rates. When the government settled finally with the road, the payment for losses plus guarantee amounted to $265,000. With this
input, the corporate deficit for 1920 totalled only $378.

Toward the end of 1920 there were definite signs of an im-
pending postwar recession of business. Phelan was certain that he
could not continue with an annual payroll of $1,410,000, and he
did not feel that a significant cut in work force was practicable.
After much study, and with the permission of Judge Trieber, he
notified the railroad union representatives that he would be forced
to reduce the monthly payroll by $25,000, as of February 1, 1921.
This would shift wages back to their level during the first part of
1920. At the current rate, wages would consume 92 per cent of the
projected operating revenues, compared with a 60 per cent average for the Class I railroads in 1920.

The reaction of the unions to a wage cut was as expected. They complained vociferously, proposed a cut in work force, and then stated that they would only accept a cut in wages if required by the Railroad Labor Board. The move by Phelan was based on two facts: the higher wages simply could not be paid since there were no funds available, and the cost of living along the M. & N. A. was (and still is) lower than in most parts of the country. Phelan also felt that he had some public sentiment behind him, for throughout the country railroad labor was becoming difficult to deal with and, as a result, was getting a very bad image, Actually, the government was generally blamed for creating wage scales that were too high during a period of declining cost of living and business recession.

Nevertheless, the two sides could not agree, and on February 1 the Harrison shopmen again walked off their jobs. It was the initial move in a strike that was to be one of the longest and most bitter ever to afflict a United States railroad, and one that would bring nationwide attention to the Arkansas Ozarks.* Operations continued after February 1, with supervisory personnel handling the bare essentials of shop work. The railroad and the unions met with the Railroad Labor Board on February 15, and that body gave a decision on February 21 which proposed that the wage reductions be accepted under protest; that the two sides negotiate further; and that another meeting with the Board be held on March 5. The unions could see nothing to be gained from further discussions with Phelan; he was adamant that the wages would be cut or the road would have to shut down. And the unions were not going to accept a wage cut without some kind of fight. This obvious impasse led to the expected. At 3:00 a.m. on February 26 there was a walkout of the engineers, firemen, hostlers, conductors, trainmen, yardmen, agents, telegraphers, train dispatchers, and maintenance of way men. The full strike was on!

General Manager Phelan was resolved to win the battle, and decided to operate on an "open shop" basis. With supervisors, quickly recruited experienced railroad men, and pure green hands

---

*A very thorough and readable account of this strike is given in the book by O. T. Gooden, which is listed in the section on References. The books by Bradley, Russell, and Farris also contain details on the strike.

recruited from the hills he managed to get operations under way March 5 with limited service between Harrison and Seligman. Shortly thereafter he was running a passenger train and a freight train throughout the length of the line. (The *Helena World* noted that on March 2 a special train arrived at Helena carrying 30 passengers, all of whom were aboard the return train when it left the next morning. It seemed clear that the men were strike breakers in the employ of the company. No troubles arose.)

The immediate animosity between the strikers and the non-union "scabs" can be imagined. Violence broke out all along the line but much of it was confined to the Harrison area where most of the workers lived; to assist civil authorities in preserving law and order in the area the Harrison Protective League was formed.

Business for January and February was bad, the deficit for the two months totalling $93,000 on income of only $234,977. Not all of this drop could be attributed to the national recession or to the brief cessation of operations in February. Bridge traffic from other roads appeared to have dropped, possibly due to the efforts of union employees on those roads. The word had gotten out that it was not safe to travel or ship on the M. & N. A. And to underscore the point, reports came on March 16 that two trestles had burned, one at Pindall and the other a sizable chunk of the Long Creek crossing at Alpena. At best, operations limped sadly and deficits grew.

Local sentiment against the strikers grew as rail service suffered and depredations continued. On March 19 Phelan stopped operations completely, his reason stated as follows in the March 25, 1921, issue of *Railway Age:*

> . . . The new employees are entirely satisfied with the reduced scale of wages and it has been clearly demonstrated that the new organization can operate the railroad efficiently and take care of public convenience and necessity; but since February 26 we have encountered lawlessness and interference in the way of intimidations and threats against new employees, the new employees and their families have been insulted by former employees, the new employees have been assaulted by former employees, and obstructions

have been placed on the railroad track and train bridges
have been burned . . .

The people and the authorities along this railroad are
familiar with conditions and while the railroad has used
every means at its command to protect trains and property,
that has been impossible. To attempt to continue train operation in the face of the depredations which have been
committed would endanger the lives of passengers and employees, and until federal and state authorities provide
adequate protection to trains and property of this railroad
between Neosho, Missouri, and Helena, Arkansas, we must
in the interest of safety discontinue the operation of this
railroad.

Mass meetings were held up and down the line, and citizens'
committees were formed to assist in policing the railroad property. On March 22 special trains, heavily guarded, brought many
of these citizens to a mass meeting at Harrison. On the basis of
this support, Phelan resumed train service on March 24, and on
April 6 hauled the citizens back to Harrison for another meeting.
At this time they demanded that the union officials staying in
Harrison would have to go. As described by Gooden, ". . . The
union officers were told that the people held them responsible for
the depredations and that they should leave the state at once. No
argument was permitted, and at the request of the union officials
they were given five minutes to confer. They agreed to obey the
request and immediately left the state by automobile. . ."

For the next two months, operations continued in the face of
many depredations: bridges were burned, spikes pulled, water
tanks drained or injected with sulfuric acid, abrasives thrown in
journal boxes, and so on. Intimidations continued, and there was
much physical violence. The road was desperately trying to hang
on to business; the motor car service between Joplin and Harrison
was resumed June 1 but because of low revenues was taken off
June 24. Special excursion rates to Eureka Springs went into effect
June 4, but visitors appeared to prefer to take the Frisco to Seligman and then use automobiles to go to Eureka. The first six
months of 1921 showed a colossal deficit of $396,900, and this did
not include interest payments for the period.

The Railroad Labor Board announced a national reduction in wages in June, and Phelan anticipated an equivalent further reduction in the M. & N. A. wages. But by July, Phelan had come to the end of his rope, and in rather abrupt fashion resigned from the railroad, the cause being noted as a complete nervous breakdown. His place was taken by J. C. Murray, Traffic Manager, who was officially appointed Receiver and General Manager by Judge Trieber on July 14.

Murray took stock of the situation quickly and saw that some $28,000 of the July payroll could not be paid because of insufficient funds in the treasury. He applied to Judge Trieber for permission to discontinue operations. Trieber had gone on vacation, but Judge F. A. Youmans at Fort Smith issued an order on July 23 that operations would be suspended on July 31 and appropriate embargoes on freight were being instituted. Such news was completely upsetting to many shippers, and it was estimated that more than 3,000 carloads of freight were ready to be shipped when operations stopped.

The last regularly scheduled train ran on Sunday, July 31, 1921. Cleanup operations moved foreign cars off the line and brought most of the locomotives and passenger train cars to Harrison. In an obviously biased report, the *Railroad Telegrapher* of August 1921 described a portion of the cleanup as follows:

> On August 4th, an extra backed into Harrison at 8:00 p.m., that had been sent north early in the morning, consisting of an equipment of nine empties, a coach and caboose, with a bunch of 'scabs' and their families. The engine was running on one side, having blown out a cylinder head before reaching Capps, the first siding north. Engine No. 9 came in from the south about 6:00 p.m. the previous day, with engines Nos. 3 and 5 dead, and a bunch of empties. They had been trying for over a week to get those dead engines moved from Outer Yard [Helena] to Harrison for repairs, but August 1st they were set out at Armstrong Springs on account of engine No. 9 running for water that day, being killed at Letona and having to be towed back to Searcy by another engine before it could fill its tank. Yardmaster and engineer Fitzgerald, switching in Harrison yards August

3rd, without a fireman or switchman, ran over the derail on
the north end of the rip track, and it took the official family,
lawyers, and all the entire day to get the rear trucks of the
engine tank back on the track again . . .

The same article noted that former General Manager Phelan
". . . is now enjoying the peaceful life of the banished in the
Ontario Woods near Ste. Marie, Canada."

As equipment was lined up in the Harrison yards there could
be little realization of similar actions to take place 25 years later.
The shutdown was definite, and was expected to last a long time.
The American Express Co. office at Harrison closed down, with
the horses being sent to St. Louis, the wagon to Joplin, and the
furnishings to Little Rock. The Harrison Electric Co. made arrangements to truck coal in from Bergman, ten miles away on the
Missouri Pacific. Eureka Springs citizens made an unsuccessful
attempt to operate privately the section of the line from Seligman
to Eureka.

This action seemed to mark the closing chord of a railroad
venture that was jinxed from its very inception. A *St. Louis Post-
Dispatch* headline stated that the "Missouri and North Arkansas
Quits Operation and Seems 'All In,' " and in the article it was remarked that the Receiver was expected to apply to the U. S. Court
for permission to sell all the property. Edwards Whitaker, president of Boatman's Bank in St. Louis and current chairman of the
North Arkansas noteholders' committee, stated that refinancing or
continuing operation of the property was "hopeless."

William Z. Ripley, Harvard professor and Interstate Commerce Commission consultant, remarked on the M. & N. A. as
follows:

> . . . it not only lies almost entirely in the inhospitable*
> Ozark region, but it is paralleled on either side by the lines
> of the Missouri Pacific. It is alleged that there is not a living
> for the property and that the only thing to do is to tear it
> up. It is evident from the map that the road neither begins
> nor ends anywhere, and it is difficult to see how it could

---

*Inhospitable to the development of railroads, in a physical and economic
sense.

perform any useful function except to serve the towns locally along the line. Whether they can afford sufficient business to keep it alive is open to question.

In view of Professor Ripley's remarks, it might be well at this juncture to recount the position into which the group of St. Louisans had gotten themselves with regard to this business venture. Back in 1906 they had bought the property for $2,000,000. Immediately afterward they invested almost $6,000,000 in extending the line to Helena and Joplin. Finally, in 1912-1913 they purchased some $2,000,000 in Receiver's Certificates. The total investment, then, came almost to $10,000,000. Some of the smaller investors had already bowed out by selling their interests at large discounts. The hardy group remaining, represented by Festus Wade, David Francis, Charles Gilbert, G. H. Walker, Edwards Whitaker, George L. Edwards, and R. McKittrick Jones, must well have thought at this point that discretion would be the better part of valor. The property might have a salvage value of as much as $3,000,000, or 30 cents on the dollar. But there was a stumbling block: would the government permit the people of this region, especially the 145,000 souls in the 5,400 square miles directly dependent on the railroad for service, to lose their railroad? The case could only be taken to the government; the *Post-Dispatch* remarked that "The only hope is Uncle Sam. The M. & N. A. may secure additional aid from the government as it is considered diametrically opposed to governmental policy to permit a railroad to be discontinued, but local (St. Louis) financiers are of the opinion that this is the only hope for a continuance of operation." And this philosophy of government aid was the one taken by Wade *et al* during the remainder of the year 1921.

Meanwhile, the lack of rail transportation began to be severely felt by Ozarks people. Eureka Springs and Harrison were more fortunate than most towns along the line, in that they were fairly close to alternate railroad connections, but even they were badly handicapped by the incredibly poor highways. There were no hard surface highways in the region, and "all-weather" roads of gravel were very rare. The usual case was for towns to be connected by dirt roads or trails with steep grades which were essentially impassable in wet or icy weather. In fact, only the larger

After the shutdown of operations July 31, 1921, rolling stock lined up in the Harrison yards was photographed from the top of the roundhouse. The two motor cars can be seen next to the employees' change house. A citizen guard protecting the rolling stock there during the strike is shown below. Left to right are engines No. 7, 20, 36, 30, coach No. 3 and two unidentified engines. Locomotive No. 17 is in the right foreground.

*(Two pictures: E. G. Baker)*

places such as Harrison and Eureka Springs had a few "all-weather" streets. The lack of rail transportation made it difficult and costly to bring in necessities from other parts of the country, and essentially eliminated the possibility of shipping out regional products of agriculture and manufacture.

Of the towns along the line, Leslie was perhaps the hardest hit. As mentioned previously, it was completely dependent on the timber products industry. The H. D. Williams Cooperage Co. had gone into bankruptcy in 1915 and had been reorganized as the Export Cooperage Co. In 1921, despite Prohibition, this company employed some 500 men, had an investment of over $1,000,000, and continued to operate the logging railroad described earlier in connection with the Williams Co. Along with other Leslie timber products companies, Export Cooperage was forced to shut down completely. Economic strife among the employees became so acute that the Red Cross was called in to help feed their children attending the local schools. The Leslie story in variation was repeated at other towns served by the M. & N. A.

Fortunately, Festus Wade and colleagues were not sitting idly by, waiting for an opportune time to apply for abandonment. Instead, they were developing an elaborate plan for putting the North Arkansas back on its feet. Their plan was complete by October 1921, and consisted of four parts: (1) a further reduction in the wage scale, (2) a greater share of the tariffs on freight transferred to and from the North Arkansas, (3) a loan from the U. S. Government, and (4) a complete reorganization into a new company. The plan was prosecuted during the period of October 1921 to April 1922.

Wade petitioned the Railroad Labor Board for a 25 per cent reduction from the wages being paid at the time of the shutdown. This would drop the annual payroll from $1,241,000 to $931,000, with the new figure still being 34 per cent over the payroll of 1917. His petition stated that if such a reduction were granted, the owners of the road would not receive any return on their investment until the wages were restored to the standard scale. Thus, if earnings were sufficient, the payroll would be higher than $931,000 and could be as high as $1,241,000 per year. This increment represented a kind of profit-sharing incentive for the workers and seemed reasonable to the Board. Wade made the petition on October 10 and it was granted February 18, 1922, in Decision No. 724. The unions refused to abide by the decision, and thereby surrendered their right to sympathy by trainmen on connecting roads; this would aid in the recovery of some lost interline traffic.

On December 9, 1921, Charles Gilbert and J. C. Murray applied to the Interstate Commerce Commission for a loan of $3,-500,000 under provisions of Section 210 of the Transportation Act. The loan was to be used as follows:

| | |
|---|---:|
| Retire receiver's certificates | $1,969,250 |
| Pay unpaid vouchers | 442,642 |
| Cover other current liabilities | 169,792 |
| Pay indebtedness to the U.S.R.A. | 292,000 |
| Cover miscellaneous debts and expenses | 126,316 |
| Provide additions and betterments | 500,000 |
| Total | $3,500,000 |

The loan was granted on April 4, 1922 under the following conditions:

1. The owners were to provide separately a sum of $560,-000, to be used for

| | |
|---|---:|
| Additions-betterments | $250,000 |
| Working capital | $250,000 |
| Competent supervision | 60,000 |

2. The loan was to be secured by $5,000,000 in M. & N. A. six per cent, 15-year gold bonds, as described below.
3. The loan was to be repaid in 15 years.
4. The company would elect an advisory board of 15 members, one from each county traversed, and there would be two additional members appointed by the Governors of Missouri and Arkansas. This board would have certain executive powers.

In January 1922 Festus Wade, representing the trustees for the noteholders, formally asked for foreclosure and sale of the railroad. On February 7 Judge Trieber ordered Receiver Murray to sell the properties, rights, and franchises of the M. & N. A. at public auction on April 10, for an upset price of $3,000,000. A new company, The Missouri & North Arkansas Rail*way* Co., would be organized to acquire the properties, rights, and franchises. This plan was pursued, with the new company being chartered on February 28, 1922 with Charles Gilbert as president, J. C. Murray as vice president and general manager, and J. M. McGaughey as secretary-treasurer.

The new company purchased the old company on April 10, 1922. It issued securities in the amount of $5,000,000 first mortgage bonds, deposited with the government as collateral for the loan, and in the amount of $3,000,000 in common stock at $100 par. The same investors were forced to remain with the new company because of the depth of their involvement. Actually, the only funds distributed to them were for the Receiver's Certificate payment less the $560,000 required under the terms of the government loan. Concurrently, the valuation of the property was dropped from $18,173,475 to $3,500,000.

The fourth part of the master plan dealt with freight tariff divisions. On December 8, 1921, Wade applied to the Interstate Commerce Commission for an increase of 25 per cent in the division of joint rates for freight traffic interchanged with the M. & N. A. As expected, the connecting roads raised loud objections. On the basis of 1917 operations, tonnage transferred to or from the M. & N. A. had this breakdown:

|  | Tons |
|---|---|
| St. Louis-San Francisco (Frisco) | 124,272 |
| Illinois Central | 60,885 |
| Kansas City Southern | 58,142 |
| Missouri Pacific | 58,027 |
| Missouri-Kansas-Texas | 39,264 |
| Chicago, Rock Island & Pacific | 33,718 |
| St. Louis Southwestern | 33,718 |
| Atchison, Topeka & Santa Fe | 33,335 |
| Total | 441,361 |

The I. C. C. calculated that the 25 per cent increase in divisions would, under normal traffic conditions, give the M. & N. A. an increased annual income of $265,000. The application was granted March 14, the railroad being successful in advancing a new application of the Transportation Act, as described by K. H. Koach in *Railway Age:*

It was pointed out that the Missouri & North Arkansas was included in a group of railroads whose total valuation was considered as the basis for the establishment of such rates as would yield an average return of six per cent on the combined investment. The petitioning carrier, it was stated, had earned nothing on its investment, while the connecting lines had thereby benefitted by this provision of the Transportation Act, and had received more than their share. This was held to be true even during the past year when the road has been out of service, since the M. & N. A.'s valuation was included in the group's total, upon which each road's earning capacity was based in so far as fixing rates is concerned. The [M. & N. A.] further contended that the Transportation Act contemplated that the small independent carrier was to receive the same return upon its investment as the larger railroads, and that this return should be equalized within this group, the same as would have been done if the Missouri & North Arkansas had been a branch of one of the larger trunk lines.

The sale on April 10 gave the green light for resumption of operations. Through the voluntary aid of citizens, the property had been well protected during the eight months of the shutdown. An inspection of the line showed it to be in better condition than anticipated, probably due in part to the large expenditures during government operation. Aside from tie replacements, occasioned by the eight-year life of untreated white oak ties, little maintenance was needed. The union forces elected to stay on strike, so Murray proceeded to rehire many of the people who were on the job in July 1921.

Mixed train service between Seligman and Kensett began on May 15. And Murray was taking no unnecessary chances; he had "protection" on the trains. Mrs. Loren Lack, of Leslie, Arkansas, remembers the first train south through Shirley. Her father, C. C. Halbrook, was depot agent at Shirley and during the strike had provided for his family by handling odd carpentry jobs; later he was forced to resign because he happened to have been an old-timer (though a non-striker). To quote Mrs. Lack:

Dad didn't resign before I had a chance to see and hear and worship 'Chilton' the strike-breaker. I don't know where he came from or where he went, but he brought the first train through, and he walked with glorious daring through the muttering mobs gathered at every station from Harrison to Kensett. His attire was impeccable; you could see yourself in his highly polished shoes. To a little girl who had been through the hunger and terrors of the strike he was 'beautiful' and he was Mr. God. . . . I guess he wasn't afraid of anything on earth and he probably loved the challenge of breaking a strike. He was really cold eyed and aloof, but he and Dad had a warm friendship that endured as long as they were associated. Dad left before Chilton did. He was probably just a Chicago gangster . . . but to this day I remember him as a savior.

And so operations resumed.

On May 24 Murray reported to St. Louis management on conditions as follows:

Work is continuing although we have been slightly delayed on account of rain and very greatly delayed on account of bridge material . . . and other supplies. Have arranged with the Kansas City Southern for temporary use of sufficient terminals at Neosho to operate to and from that point, and will open Neosho to Kensett June 4th. I will not be able to open south of Kensett until about June 15th. Berry movement is gradually increasing and the business on the district Seligman to Kensett is taking practically all available power. Am sending four engines Friday to the Pittsburg Boiler and Machine Co., Pittsburg, Kansas, for a general overhauling, and we are overhauling two in our shops, in addition to running repairs on power now in use. Work is progressing as well as can be expected, in connection with the repair of freight cars.

Have put in approximately 30,000 ties and have sufficient work trains on the line to take care of distribution. Am operating train between Neosho and Wayne handling both work service and the berries. Have 60,000 ties distributed. Have nothing further from organized labor and am not having any interference except at Seligman and Searcy. At these two points switches have been thrown causing derailments, but I am handling this in such manner as should eliminate further trouble.

The strikers here have been given to understand that we will stop operation about June 1st for about ten days and then commence operation employing men and paying standard wages. Even in view of this understanding, however, a considerable number of them are moving off the railroad.

Murray's view of the labor situation proved to be optimistic; no sooner had regular operations commenced in mid-June than a rash of depredations erupted. It seemed apparent to the citizens that the strikers were intent on closing down the road again. On June 18, bridge 35-2 burned. On June 20 it was bridge 344-8. On June 22 bridge 89-4 burned and, for good measure, acid was found in the water tank at Stark City, Missouri. The citizens offered rewards for the arrest and conviction of the bridge-burners. The unions, as would be expected, denied any connection with these depredations and proposed that the fires were caused by faulty ashpans on the locomotives and by the incompetent non-union enginemen. The renewed impediments to the operation of the railroad only served to further the resentment of the citizens toward the strikers. Reverend W. T. Bradley, a Presbyterian minister in Harrison, addressed the strikers this way during a July 2 sermon:

> There is but one way this trouble can be ended, and I appeal to you as the ones who have the power to end it. Harrison was happy and peaceful until you quit work, and its peace will not be restored until you go to work again. . . I appeal to you as red blooded men. I would be ashamed to sit around in the Court park and wear out my pants on those benches. I would blush to accept the dimes and quarters deducted from the pay checks of office boys and girls and clerks, and men who sweat and toil in other places and sent here to maintain you in idleness and help keep alive this unnecessary and dangerous strife. . .

The railroad operated with fair regularity during the remainder of 1922, but under oppressive difficulties. Depredations for the last six months of the year were summarized as follows:

| | |
|---|---:|
| Air hoses cut | 63 |
| Chemicals in tanks | 10 |
| Rails greased | 9 |
| Wrecking attempts | 7 |
| Bridges afire | 6 |
| Theft | 4 |
| Damage to property | 4 |
| Emery dust used | 3 |
| Total | 106 |

Such occurrences at regular intervals were bound to keep the citizenry aroused. The local leader of the strikers, an ex-conductor named J. T. "Pete" Venable, became a particular object of attack and in July he and two others were arrested on the rather vague charge of "conspiracy to murder the employees of the railroad." They were found guilty of collecting ammunition and dynamite for suspicious purposes. As more and more of the strikers became identified with questionable acts, the problem of ever reinstating them became more difficult; a settlement mutually acceptable to the people and the railroad might be well nigh impossible. On December 19, Thomas C. McRae, Governor of Arkansas (and whose name was later given to a company motorcar), issued a proclamation that the depredations were felonies and that a $300 reward would be paid for "The arrest and conviction of each and every person guilty of any of these or any future depredations. . ."

Despite the impediments, the railroad gave regular service during 1922, operating on 230 of the 253 days during the official April 12-December 31 period. A regular daily passenger train was operated between Neosho and Kensett (going into Joplin after November 15); a daily mixed train, carrying two coaches and a baggage car, between Kensett and Helena; and local freights servicing all stations at least three times a week. The operating ratio, operating expenses to revenues, for 1922 was a creditable 77.7 per cent and the final figures for the year showed a small net earnings of $4,222 on total operating revenues of $753,508. (The old corporation showed a deficit of $159,833 in 1922 prior to April 24.) Business was relatively light, only 189,440 tons hauled, but expenses were kept low. The railroad seemed to be getting back on its feet, despite the labor problems.

January 1923 proved to be the turning point of the strike. During the second week no less than eight bridges burned. One of these, bridge 78-8, a majestic 238-foot frame trestle in Livingston Hollow near Eureka Springs, made a spectacular fire and required a major rebuilding job. Bridge crews had to operate throughout the line and recovery operations would be slow. Such occurrences led J. C. Murray on January 13 to announce that the railroad simply could not afford to continue operations unless the occurrences ceased. The announcement concluded with these words:

> It is now entirely with the public as to whether or not they desire the continued operation of this railway, and their desire will be expressed entirely in the protective measures they may and will take.

Murray's announcement was made on Saturday morning. Over the weekend communications were rampant along the line from Seligman to Searcy. Telephone wires hummed and it is likely that company telegraph wires also were active. By Monday morning, January 15, armed men began to converge on Harrison from all locations, including inland towns such as Jasper and Clinton that were dependent on the M. & N. A. for service. About noon a special train from Leslie brought in many more men. The very atmosphere became explosive. Soon there were some 1000 men on the streets of Harrison, all armed with pistols, shotguns, or rifles. This apparently was the signal of a "showdown" to the strikers, and many of them left town immediately.

As if by special prearrangement, the crowd organized itself quickly for specific actions. Leadership was under a "Committee of Twelve" prominent citizens of the region, in effect a vigilance committee. Search squads were organized for the purpose of bringing in strikers and locating materials used in depredations such as emery dust, kerosene, and sulfuric acid. The strikers were to be interrogated by the Committee, and because of the number were scheduled over a period of several days. By and large, neither strikers nor law officers interfered with the methodical actions of the citizens. And Judge Shinn of the Circuit Court, currently in session, was apprised of all actions directly by the Committee.

As he was questioned, each striker or strike sympathizer was given an opportunity to renounce the union and its benefits and pledge loyalty to the railroad. If he refused, he was expected to leave town or "receive no protection." On late Monday some difficulty was experienced with a striking shopman named E. C. Gregor. He resisted being taken in for questioning, and only came after an exchange of gunshots. His answers to the Committee were unsatisfactory, and at its request he was detained under guard for the night. Sometime during the night the guards were overpowered and Gregor was taken away. Early the next morning his body was found hanging from the railroad's Crooked Creek bridge, just east of the shops.

The lynching of Gregor made national headlines. Reporters, possibly smelling blood, were sent in from major newspapers. In addition to the hanging, there had been some whippings and a bonfire had been made of the union hall furnishings. State militia were alerted. Some fifty deputies were sworn in by local law officers. But through it all, the Committee of Twelve went about its business carefully and methodically. During the rest of the week it completed its task, accumulating in the process copious notes and evidence which were turned over to the proper civil authorities. By Friday the committee broke up, confident that all bad apples had been eliminated from the barrel. From that point on, there were no further depredations of any consequence.

Much has been written on this uprising of the citizens along the North Arkansas Line. One cannot condone their taking the law into their own hands, but their actions were bred from months of hardship and antagonism which the civil authorities seemed completely incapable of handling. A special committee of the Arkansas State Legislature was appointed to investigate the actions, and for the next few weeks collected a great deal of information. This committee filed its report in May, and did not fix the responsibility for the depredations and acts of violence. It absolved the citizens, committees, and labor unions as organizations,

With its headlight moved to the center of the smokebox door, No. 14 demonstrates the "new look" of North Arkansas locomotives under President Stephenson's restyling program. In front of her are fireman Bradshaw and, right, engineer E. R. Tucker. Trestle 78-7, between Junction and the tunnel, was burned, it was thought by strikers, in January 1923. It is shown below as it appeared after being rebuilt.

*(Above: Fred Johnston; below: Orville T. Gooden)*

declaring that the evidence collected tended to show that "all the dastardly events sprang from seemingly innocent beginnings."

And thus peace returned to the Arkansas Ozarks in 1923. The road operated normally, and with the help of the citizens gradually recovered most of the business lost after 1920. Operations were routine: on-time trains, late trains, and (occasionally) wrecked trains. Typically, in late summer of 1923, northbound passenger No. 202 pulled into Shirley at noontime, about on schedule. At the throttle of American type locomotive No. 15 was one of the line's colorful engineers, "Windy" Mitchell. Taking care of things on the platform was C. C. Halbrook, the Shirley agent. Halbrook's daughter, Mrs. Loren Lack, tells of the events that immediately followed:

> My father had just rolled the mail float away from the train when he heard his telegraph call. He ran to answer as the train puffed out of the station. The message was urgent: 'Stop the train, a runaway engine is heading south!'
>
> Dad tore from the depot frantically waving his arms at the disappearing train. The conductor, who had just swung aboard the rear platform, gaily waved back as the train went out of sight around a curve. He thought dad was simply waving goodbye. Though Dad was on a handcar following the train almost instantly it was impossible to catch it. The trains crashed head-on about two miles northwest of Shirley. Dad was on the scene of the accident almost as soon as it happened, and the grinding impact of those two engines hitting remained with him all of his life. The fireman on the runaway engine was scalded to death. One passenger who was standing between two passenger cars was bruised when thrown to the floor. There were no other injuries. We never knew exactly what happened but were told that the engineer (on the runaway) was drunk. We also heard that he was unable to read, and had more-or-less guessed at his orders and had highballed through Leslie instead of stopping. . .

For the year 1923 there were $1,509,848 in revenues, but high maintenance costs plus the formidable $208,410 interest payment to the government caused a deficit of $87,307. As the year ended, so did the strike; on December 21 a settlement was announced that would (a) dismiss all cases against the strikers, thereby giving them clearance to work elsewhere, (b) release certain strikers who had been sent to prison, and (c) provide payment by the railroad of $500 to cover court costs of several of the strikers' cases. The union was glad to get out from under the unfavorable publicity and the continuing costs of benefits. The railroad was equally relieved, although it anticipated no change from the open shop arrangement. The strike had lasted for almost three years and was one of the longest ever to be called against a railroad.

The January 1, 1924, timetable showed a new daily manifest freight between Joplin and Kensett, stopping only at Neosho, Seligman, Harrison, and Searcy. At Kensett it connected with the regular daily mixed train to and from Helena. The Joplin-Kensett passenger run was a fixture by this time, its three or four cars pulled by one of the Americans (Nos. 15-17) or one of the ten-wheelers (Nos. 18-20).

The year 1924 came and went without unusual incident, the spring rains and washouts being almost routine. Whereas the neighboring White River Division of the Missouri Pacific had embarked on a project of filling all major trestles, the North Arkansas could ill afford to take such measures against the ravages of floods and fires. Particularly vulnerable to washouts were the trestles along Butler Creek and Leatherwood Creek, north of Eureka Springs, and along Clabber Creek between Freeman and Green Forest. For 1924 operating revenues were up slightly at $1,587,104, but the deficit rose significantly to $139,236.

The valuation of the property was announced by the Interstate Commerce Commission in June 1925. Based on June 30, 1919 values, the total came to $9,177,460 which, for rate-making purposes, was considered too low by M. & N. A. management. Hearings were held in late 1925 but the government valuation was not changed substantially. As things would turn out, the value of the work was principally for introspection by M. & N. A. management; whatever concessions might be made to the earnings potential of the railroad had already been made in the 1922 rate divisions case.

The public timetable for July 5, 1925 seemed to imply a "new look" on the line. The M. & N. A. was described as passing "through the heart of the Ozark Playgrounds, the Land of a Million Smiles" and serving "Eureka Springs and Heber Springs, famous Arkansas all-year health and tourist resorts." The one-sheet folder stated that the Red Ball Fast Freight made the Joplin-Helena run in 32½ hours southbound and 30 hours (because of lighter tonnage) northbound. The mixed train on the south end was replaced by a local freight, and a passenger train, often a motorcar with trailer, was added between Heber Springs and Helena. The second motorcar was put in regular shuttle service, four times daily, between Eureka Springs and Seligman. Spending for publicity and off-line traffic solicitation was up, and J. C. Murray seemed to be making a determined effort to make the road pay. But as the year went on, it was clear that the deficit would be even larger than that of the preceding year.

During the latter half of 1925, a separate event took place that would affect the North Arkansas. The Frisco Lines bought a controlling interest in a number of short lines, among them the 87-mile Jonesboro, Lake City, and Eastern in northeastern Arkansas. The acquisition of this line became official on November 1, 1925, and in the reorganization the vice president and general manager, a Mr. W. Stephenson, was shuffled out. He had been general manager of the J. L. C. & E. since 1919. Through his Frisco contacts in St. Louis he got together with Charles Gilbert, who was a somewhat reluctant M. & N. A. president because of his other obligations handed down from John Scullin. Stephenson had little difficulty in convincing Gilbert that he could take over the M. & N. A. and do something with it. Accordingly, Stephenson accepted an offer to become president and general manager, with headquarters at Harrison. His salary was set at $10,000 per year, a princely sum for the Ozark region, and the effective date was January 1, 1926. Appropriately, J. C. Murray resigned and Gilbert became chairman of the board.

The news caused a large stir at Harrison, where Murray was highly regarded, particularly in view of the comradeship built up during the long strike. But the 1925 closure of the books indicated that a change was needed; the deficit was $239,329.

*The Stephenson Era*

The new president and general manager of the North Arkansas, Mr. W. Stephenson, arrived in Harrison on Monday, January 3, 1926. His small welcoming group noted a slight, dapper gentleman of about fifty years of age. Expectantly, the *Harrison Daily Times* saw him as a ". . . genial-faced man, every ounce of whose probable 160 pounds avoirdupois radiates energy no less than reserve force." The Harrison townspeople soon learned that he was unmarried, that he had a male negro servant named "Jesse," and that for the Ozarks region he had some strange "city-type" mannerisms. And the railroad employees would find that he was a reserved and formal administrator who would not associate readily with the rank and file. Curiously, he chose not to reveal what the "W" stood for in the way of a first name (it stood for Wellington). In the future, his few close associates would call him "Steve."

Stephenson had spent some twenty years with the St. Louis Southwestern line, achieving a supervisory position in the transportation department before going to the Jonesboro, Lake City, & Eastern road in 1919 as general manager. As mentioned in Chapter V, he later became vice president of the J. L. C. & E. In several ways, his entrée to Harrison resembled that of Edward Wise back in 1911.

One of Stephenson's first actions was to have No. 100, the abbreviated (34-foot) business car acquired secondhand the year before, pulled to a spur track near the station and connected with electricity. This car was to be his Harrison home. Then he spent

Shortly after W. Stephenson took over the presidency of the North Arkansas,
he announced his intention to overhaul the property. He made the announce-
ments directly to business groups and also through the press, as may be
witnessed from this advertisement in the *Helena World* for January 21, 1926.
*(Helena Public Library)*

the remainder of the week with J. C. Murray, effecting the change of guard. During the following week he put No. 100 on the road and made a thorough inspection of the property. Assisting him was H. B. Agnew, former traffic manager of the J. L. C. & E., and one of several former associates that he would bring to Harrison.

In summary form, here is what Stephenson learned about the condition of the property in early 1926:

### Roadway

Embankments and ditches satisfactory. Weed growth heavy. Tie replacements lagging — with some 1,200,000 ties in service and 8-9 years' life for untreated white oak ties, about 150,000 replacements per year were needed; for the past 8 years only about 900,000 new ties had been inserted. Original 65-pound rails marginally-low in weight for present loadings. Very few tie plates in service.

Parts of the line never ballasted, mostly between Searcy and Helena. Less than half the line with good, weed-free ballast providing free drainage.

### Bridges

Several wooden trestles subject to washouts need replacing with steel girder spans. Many trestles need to be filled. Bridges between Seligman and Leslie marginally-light for present loadings.

### Structures

All buildings in good repair, but in need of painting. Several stations need cotton platforms and berry sheds. Some ore loading platforms are obsolete. Engine shed at Outer Yard (burned in 1921) needs to be replaced.

### Motive Power

Locomotives on hand, 24. Age range, 12 to 26 years. All serviceable, but many need repairs. Freight locomotives limited to 750 tons on 1.75% ruling grades. Facilities for light running repairs needed at Kensett, where both freight and passenger locomotives are turned. Shop facilities at Harrison adequate.

The much-photographed Narrows gateway between Seligman and Eureka Springs shows here the results of Stephenson's cleanup efforts. Weeds have been cleared, new ballast applied and right-of-way signs repainted. This picture appeared on the cover of the public timetable dated August 15, 1926. (*Louis Goodwin*)

*Rolling Stock*

Passenger cars dirty and antiquated; in need of complete refurbishing, including installation of electric lights. Of the 594 freight cars only 321 have steel underframes. Rolling stock for revenue service generally in poor repair.

*General*

Total employment of 900 probably too high. Cash position precarious, due to deficits in prior years. Volume of business too low ever to be profitable. Employee morale good, with M&NA Booster clubs established at several points. Image of line generally poor outside the region served.

By January 15 Stephenson was ready to make some rather bold statements. At a meeting of the Harrison M. & N. A. Booster Club he told some 150 members that much rehabilitation work on the road was necessary, and that over the next three years he would spend $500,000 to this end. Such an expenditure would be required, he said, before the road could be put on a paying basis. He would spend money to make money. And the North Arkansas would take on the appearance of a secondary main line of a large railroad system. His objectives were not unlike those of General Manager Wise 15 years earlier.

Stephenson soon had things humming. By January 22 his personal secretary from the J. L. C. & E., Miss Moselle Claire, was on the job at Harrison. By February 1 he had opened up an executive office in the Solomon Building at Helena, with the intention of spending a good portion of his time there (traveling and living, of course, in No. 100). New furnishings were ordered for his office there as well as for his office at the Kirby Building in Harrison. He made Agnew his general traffic manager and located him next to the presidential suite in Harrison. On February 11 he announced that the North Arkansas had "been fortunate enough" to secure the services of E. D. Lyons, recently of the J. L. C. & E., to supervise generally the physical rehabilitation of the line.

Still wheeling along, Stephenson announced on February 18 that henceforth the M. & N. A. would be known as the *Ozark Mountain Route* and that the slogan would be painted on all equipment. (Later, the slogan was changed to the *Ozarks North Arkansas Route,* with a specially designed shield-shaped insigne to go along with it. The change was made before the painters had gotten to the task.) He referred several times to the morale-boosting effect of coats of paint on equipment and other properties. And he spoke grandiloquently to the Harrisonites about a planned three-story brick (or stone) depot-office building for the headquarters city. He also let it be known that the company purchasing agents would buy only first-class materials, almost as if money was no object!

Thus, during early 1926 Stephenson embarked on a strongly motivated plan to improve image as well as service of the M. & N. A. He was going to banish such epithets as "The Clickety-Bang" road and "May Never Arrive" for M. & N. A.— in fact, he stated that the initials now stood for "Move — and no argument!" He boosted off-line traffic solicitations, put advertisements in newspapers, and published a large and pictorially descriptive public timetable — the first of its kind since the days of E. M. Wise. Although there is good evidence that Stephenson worried little about cost control, one must admire his will and confidence in tackling a difficult turnaround job. To underscore his own belief in a fruitful outcome, he spent personally almost $15,000 on 2,931 shares of M. & N. A. common stock, making him, after the Francis and Scullin estates, the largest stockholder of the company.

There was early evidence of the "new look" out on the line. Crews moved along to repair cattle guards, renew roadway and station signs, re-stencil mileage markers on telegraph poles, and even trim the trestle bulkheads with white paint. Weeds were cleared, and during the year a record 245,933 new crossties were inserted. The 56-pound rail on sidings was replaced with re-lay 65-pound rail, and a start toward adding heavier rail to the main line was made with the laying of three miles of new 70-pound rail near Grandview. To accommodate extra train movements, new passing sidings were added at Pender, Walden, Coin, Green Forest, Kensett, and other points. The *Harrison Daily News* of July 16 noted that "From an almost rundown, worn-out streak of rust, this road under the present management is fast coming into its own. . ."

At Harrison, the shops people were not sitting on their hands. A start was made on the construction of 75 cars to haul coal from a mine at Midway, Kansas, to the large coal chute at Junction and to the other coaling platforms at Harrison, Heber Springs, and Outer Yard. All locomotives were repaired, given a coat of black Duco, and, if in passenger service, equipped with larger turbogenerators. All locomotive headlights were re-positioned to the center of the smokebox. All coaches were redecorated, reupholstered and fitted with electric lighting systems. Selected passenger train cars were covered with steel sheathing to give them a more modern and substantial look. A very distinctive look was given to the passenger train cars by painting them "Pennsylvania red" (a dark red, Tuscan red, used by the Pennsylvania Railroad). These and other projects were not all completed in 1926, but moved at top speed during the year.

With all this rehabilitation work, movement of freight and passengers was not neglected. For the first time in years, a significant number of extra freights was operated. Tonnage for 1926 was 720,341, up from 552,829 the year before. Total revenues were up from $1,548,341 in 1925 to $1,759,084 in 1926, but because of heavy spending on maintenance of way and structures, the deficit was up from $239,329 to $367,902. This was according to plan, stated Stephenson. And he told the shareowners so in an attractive and informative Annual Report, the first published by the road in many years. But the report revealed one disturbing item: of the $210,000 government interest accrued during the year, only $56,270 was paid. Stephenson was propagating an interest-defaulting action begun two years earlier.

On January 9, 1927, a special train was run down to Helena by Stephenson. He took a group of businessmen to inspect a new $400,000 river terminal recently installed by the U. S. Government at Helena. This terminal promised to bode well for the M. & N. A.; freight rates to a large part of Arkansas would be made cheaper by combining barge and rail traffic and Helena had an advantage over Memphis because of the latter's expensive bridge toll and switching charges. The formal opening of the terminal was two weeks away, and this present trip was for an advance look. Charles Gilbert was along, and so was a businessman from Wichita Falls,

Texas, a Mr. Frank Kell. This latter gentleman did not join the group just to see the terminal properties; he was interested in the railroad as an investment. It is entirely likely that Stephenson and Gilbert kept him "cornered" most of the time during the trip. Much more will be said later about Mr. Kell.

The year 1927 started off in very good style for the North Arkansas. Some of the "new look" projects of Stephenson had been completed. They were exemplified by the appearance of locomotive No. 20, complete with full coat of black Duco, lowered headlight, white driving wheel tires, and red-painted cab panels. Attached to No. 20 were three Tuscan red passenger train cars. The train was photographed in Harrison and identified as the M. & N. A.'s "new electrically-lighted passenger train." This "new" equipment rolled in style to the Helena Terminal formal opening on January 24. As a special train it carried 150 people — employees, guests, and members of the 20-piece M. & N. A. Band from Harrison. The opening ceremonies were marred by rain and high water, but Stephenson lightened the employees' spirits by entertaining them with a reception at the Helena Y.W.C.A. Later in the evening the attending dignitaries had their banquet at Habib's Restaurant, with music provided by the M. & N. A. Band. The train and passengers returned to the various points along the line late that evening.

In support of the Stephenson image, business for the first quarter was profitable. The net after rents was $28,725 compared with a deficit of $48,132 for the same quarter a year earlier. This was a happy state of affairs for Stephenson, since he was playing his cash position very precariously.

For all the bright prospects, during early 1927 there were, literally, very somber clouds hovering over the line. The spring rains started early and were incessant. And in late 1926 there had been floods along the Ohio River and its tributaries. By March the Mississippi River was on the rise, and there was unprecedented rain in Kansas, Missouri, and Oklahoma. There was still no real cause for concern by the M. & N. A., since the Mississippi appeared well protected by levees, and the railroad was only vulnerable in a few places. By April 1 it was clear that there was

Eye-appealing handiwork of the Stephenson revitalization effort included the "newly electric-lighted passenger train" as it appeared in a company advertisement in 1926. Engine No. 20 has been repainted in black with Tuscan red panels on cab and tender, and has been equipped with a heavy-duty electric generator. The cars have been refurbished inside, sheathed with steel and painted Tuscan red with gold trim. At the rear of the train is business car No. 100 and behind the train is one of the gasoline-electric motor cars. During the great Mississippi flood in the spring of 1927 No. 17 is pushing an inspection flatcar along the inundated right of way just north of Georgetown, the water having overflowed from the White and Little Red rivers.

(*Above: E. G. Baker; below: Merritt McGaughey*)

going to be trouble: levees had broken near New Madrid, Missouri, on the Mississippi, and the White River had risen to flood stage. Water was lapping at the rails of that construction-troubled stretch of the M. & N. A. between Kensett and Cotton Plant. This was the section that traversed the bottom land of the White and Cache Rivers.

By mid-April, the Mississippi River had gone mad. Levees had broken from Cairo, Illinois, to the Gulf and thousands of square miles of land were under water. The White River was on its own rampage and had stopped all operations on the competing line to the north, the White River Division of the Missouri Pacific, from Cotter to Newport. The Missouri Pacific main line from Little Rock to St. Louis became impassable at several places. The only route open for trains between those cities suddenly became the M. & N. A. which was still high and dry north of Kensett. The management lost no time in attempting to exploit this fact. In the *Arkansas Gazette* on the morning of April 20 there was a prominent advertisement which read, in part:

> Missouri & North Arkansas Railway Co. maintains through service. No delay account high water. Between Central Arkansas and Kansas City — Kansas — Missouri — the North and Northwest.

And thus it was on Thursday, April 21, that dispatcher Merritt McGaughey drove out to the operations building near the Harrison shops to begin a hectic day of dispatching extra trains. As he was about to enter the building, he looked down toward the yards and was surprised to see one of the 30-class mikado freight engines with what appeared to be a long string of varnish behind it. Lo and behold! It turned out to be The Sunshine Special, crack Texas-St. Louis train of the Missouri Pacific, being detoured to St. Louis via Kensett, Joplin, and Pleasant Hill, Missouri. What an unusual sight it must have been, one Pullman after another, rolling through Harrison, Arkansas!

The *Arkansas Gazette* on that same morning described the situation under the headline, "Railroad Finds Way to St. Louis, Missouri Pacific Routes Trains Via Seligman and Joplin." The story read, in part:

The Missouri Pacific Railroad established train service yesterday between Little Rock and St. Louis by way of Kensett, thence to Joplin, Mo., over the M. & N. A. An express special carrying mail and perishable express left here [Little Rock] at 3:30 p.m. for St. Louis and Kansas City. An hour later the Sunshine Special left for the same points.

The Missouri Pacific plans to operate one passenger train daily, leaving here at 5:00 a.m. . . . The trip to St. Louis will require 26 hours and 23 minutes, according to the special schedule. A return train will leave St. Louis at 6:28 p.m., arriving here at 10:15 p.m. the following night.

Sleepers to Kansas City and St. Louis will be open at 10:00 p.m. This service will continue until flood conditions permit more complete service. . . A freight train loaded with freight for Little Rock left St. Louis last night to follow the same route as the passenger trains. . .

But this surge of traffic was short-lived. On April 22, some of the shops buildings became flooded when the White River back-up caused Crooked Creek to go out of bounds. And in a few more days the traffic flow was halted completely by a landslide which covered sixty feet of track near the tunnel. The Berryville people still talk about the through train that got stopped by the landslide and disgorged its passengers to look for alternate transportation at their city.

Chaos in rail transportation in Arkansas was nigh complete. Washouts and inundated track abounded. The Illinois Central incline and the new river terminal at Helena were both wrecked. There was no semblance of regular service anywhere. On the M. & N. A., 11 miles of track were underwater near Cotton Plant, and that city was completely isolated, with 1500 refugees living in boxcars.

The ravages of nature had turned on Stephenson. Revenues were down from $5,000 per day to $1,000 per day. On April 29 Stephenson advised Gilbert in St. Louis that there were insufficient funds in the treasury to meet the May 2 payroll. In response to this frantic statement, the directors of the M. & N. A. quickly agreed to apply for receivership. Jacob Trieber, still Judge of the U. S. District Court, Western Division of the Eastern District of

Arkansas, granted the receivership on May 3, 1927, and on the following day named Mr. W. Stephenson as Receiver. Authority was granted to issue $250,000 in certificates. As had happened two times previously, the North Arkansas was again bankrupt and at the mercy of the Court!

The flood crest passed Helena on April 26, and by May 6 service on the North Arkansas was partially restored through the troubled areas. There would still be floodwaters to encounter as late as June, but the worst was over in the Arkansas area. The M. & N. A., along with the thousands of affected people in the Mississippi Valley, took up the unsavory burden of cleaning up and rebuilding. This great flood of the Mississippi would, in the final analysis, have submerged the home of 750,000 people, inundated 28,000 square miles, and caused $355,000,000 damages. For the railroads, some 3,000 miles of line would have been submerged, and the final cost for rehabilitation would run over $10,000,000.

One effect of the flood on the North Arkansas did not become evident until September. At that time the large drawspan of bridge 293-0 over the White River at Georgetown developed a slight list to one side; train cars began to "lean" as they crossed, and the tracks at the span connection no longer matched well. Inspection showed that the piling under the drawspan pier had been scoured so heavily by the spring floodwaters that the pier no longer had an effective anchor. Correction might very well involve complete removal of the span and the rebuilding of the pier, a very expensive and time-consuming operation. List & Weatherly, a civil engineering firm of Kansas City, Missouri, was called in for help. That firm's opinion was that the span could be repaired in place by locating two new pier supports and bridging them with plate girders that would, in turn, support the span. But this would take time to design and install; in the meantime the old pier would be braced with temporary piling. While the piling went in, traffic was detoured via the Missouri Pacific-St. Louis Southwestern from September 15 to November 7.

It was necessary during 1927 for Stephenson to sell $61,000 worth of Receiver's Certificates, but he found a ready buyer in the Texan, Frank Kell. It had become apparent that Kell wanted

The North Arkansas always had its full share of wrecks. In the upper picture ten-wheeler No. 20 is in the ditch at Ozier Cut, just south of Harrison, in 1926. Below, several freight cars have been spilled when a trestle near Green Forest gave way, the date being about 1928. (*Above: E. G. Baker; below: Mrs. Alvin Simpkins*)

to buy into the M. & N. A., and it is appropriate here to give some background of the man. He was 68 years of age and had spent most of his business career in Wichita Falls, Texas. His main business was grain milling, and in this business he had prospered handsomely. But he was also interested in railroading, and had built two lines, the Wichita Falls & Northwestern, and the Wichita Falls & Southern, and still controlled them in 1927. In 1923 he and an associate acquired 52 per cent of the stock of the San Antonio, Uvalde & Gulf, and in 1926 they sold out profitably to the Missouri Pacific. His milling business had taken him to St. Louis where, in mid-1927, he purchased the George Plant Milling Co. and then placed his only son, Joe (his other six children were all girls), in charge of operations. One of his large mills, at Arkansas City, Kansas, moved many products over the Santa Fe and M. & N. A. en route to Southeastern U. S. markets; this undoubtedly accounted for his earlier interest in the North Arkansas. By late December 1927 he had decided to sell all but two of his mills (those at St. Louis and Arkansas City) to the General Mills Co. Thus unencumbered, he would be able to devote attention to that interesting Ozarks railroad that hauled his products from Joplin to Helena.

In late 1927 Stephenson purchased (for $6,000 in Receiver's Certificates) Kell's private railroad car which was officially Wichita Falls & Southern No. 99. Stephenson had coveted this car for some time, and it did indeed have an interesting history. Built in 1888 by Barney and Smith, it was the famous "Manitou" of the Colorado Midland railroad and was numbered No. 99. Kell had purchased the car in 1922 after the Colorado Midland was abandoned, and had preserved the magnificent interior and furnishings. At 65 feet in length, this new business car would permit Stephenson (and his man Jesse) much more freedom of movement than they had been having in No. 100.

Also in late 1927 Stephenson undertook to bolster the railroad's motive power situation. He purchased three locomotives from the Midland Valley Railroad: two consolidation type engines built by Baldwin in 1906, and one ten-wheeler built by Baldwin in 1913. The former had 30,000 pounds tractive effort and would be used in local freight service; they were given numbers 1 and 2. The ten-

In August 1928 one accident triggered another. Loads of steel bridge members shifted and derailed several flatcars, as shown above. Wrecker X-1 was called, and in its attempt to lift the cars it overturned, below. A Missouri Pacific wrecker had to clean up the mess. This happened between Georgetown depot and the White River bridge. *(Two pictures: Merritt McGaughey)*

wheeler had 29,500 pounds tractive effort and would be used in passenger service; it was given number 21. The three engines were in good condition and cost $35,872. In partial trade, Stephenson parted with the venerable General Electric motor cars, Nos. 102 and 103. The exchange was completed in December 1927.

Despite the flood problems, 1927 was reasonably kind to the M. & N. A. Total revenues were down only $76,472 to $1,682,612, and expenses were cut such that the deficit dropped to $257,984. If there had been no flood, operations for the year just might have been in the black. But in the 1927 Annual Report, Stephenson remained optimistic:

> The estimated cost of making . . . flood damage repairs to the property will be in excess of $200,000, and they will be completed during the year 1928. It has been our policy to make these repairs and renewals of a permanent nature, continuing the policy begun first of year 1926, of steadily improving the physical condition of the property and raising its general standard of maintenance.

In 1928 Stephenson continued with his rehabilitation program at full speed. Having caught up on crosstie renewals, he started reballasting the main line, and completed 25 miles during the years. A number of steel girder bridges were installed as replacements for washout-vulnerable trestles. A special gasoline-powered inspection car was constructed at the Harrison shops; this car would give the officials a real closeup view of the track. Perhaps the biggest job of the year was the renewal of the pivot pier at the Georgetown bridge. This was accomplished by installing five large cross girders under the pivot, with the ends of the girders supported by 48-pile clusters.

An interesting sidelight to this renewal job occurred just north of the bridge. The five heavy girders were being moved in on flatcars when they suddenly shifted and overturned the cars. Girders and cars were spilled along the embankment north of the rails. Wrecker X-1, a 75-ton Brownhoist job purchased new in 1913, happened to be at the bridge, waiting to unload the girders, so it moved quickly to the scene and prepared to retrieve cars and girders. But when it dug away at the load, it too overturned! So,

a Missouri Pacific wrecker was called in from North Little Rock
and finally, with much effort, got things back on the track. This
happened in August 1928.

The business car from Frank Kell was moved to Harrison for
"betterments." It received replacement trucks, steel sheathing, and
a row of heavy steel lockers under the floor that was the equivalent of a steel underframe. New interior furnishings were added.
And the exterior was given two coats of Tuscan red paint, with
the words "North Arkansas" placed on each side in 24-karat gold.
The cost was over $20,000, but this would now be a fitting home
for the chief executive officer of the M. & N. A.

Stephenson was prone to making costly decisions without adequate preliminary study and planning, and one of his most disastrous such decisions came in late 1928. To relieve his concern
over the relatively light freight motive power on the line, he
began shopping around for used locomotives that could better
handle the 1.75 per cent grades. Tonnage had been increasing,
and trains heavier than 720 tons required helper engines between
Seligman and Leslie. At the salvage firm of Hyman-Michaels he
was able to locate several secondhand consolidation type engines
that had been in service on the New York Central's subsidiary,
the Big Four, since 1907-1911.

These locomotives were attractive, big-boilered brutes that
were built by the American Locomotive Co. and which were rated
at 45,700 pounds tractive effort. They would permit 35 per cent
more tonnage behind a single engine; their mechanical condition
was good; and they were available at the East St. Louis plant of
Hyman-Michaels. But they did have a major shortcoming that
Stephenson did not appear to recognize fully: they had an axle
loading of 53,000 pounds. This was too heavy for the E-40 speci-
fication bridges between Seligman and Leslie, and according to
good operating practice called for rail weights of at least 90
pounds to the yard. To provide for this shortcoming would require
expenditures far outweighing the savings in increased hauling
capacity.

But the deal was made, Stephenson paying $7,750 each and
agreeing to take delivery on five engines in December 1928. They
arrived at Kensett just before Christmas, but the new year would

see them still there and immobile while the M. & N. A. engineering department deliberated over what to do about those light bridges.

For the year 1928 revenues dropped slightly to $1,654,466, but in keeping with the Roaring Twenties philosophy it seemed to matter little that there was a significant deficit of $245,069. During the year Stephenson cashed $188,000 in Receiver's Certificates, bringing the total to the maximum allowable $250,000. This total would be due for payment August 1, 1929, but an extension from the court was practically assured.

The year 1929 blossomed forth on a wave of prosperity that saturated the entire land. The M. & N. A., like so many corporations and individuals, was living heavy on the margin, as if the future could not possibly hold any reverses. As the fantastic bull market on Wall Street continued its upward climb, so did Stephenson continue his deficit spending. And why not? Weren't the trains rolling regularly and their tonnage increasing? Wouldn't it be just a short time before the urgent spending on upgraded facilities would no longer be necessary? On the basis of early reports, 1929 was going to be the biggest year ever!

Of course, there were minor setbacks, such as the one that took place on a cold February 19, 1929 night at Gilbert, Arkansas. As recalled by Jesse Moore, then a section man, southbound freight No. 211 eased to a halt to take on feedwater for the long climb up to the divide above Marshall. The time was about 11:00 p.m. and the depot was deserted. After the tank level had overflowed, the engineer whistled to the tail end, and eased the 30-class locomotive forward. Soon the train was rumbling across the three through-truss spans high above the dark waters of the Buffalo River. But as the train nearly cleared the bridge, a deck girder at the south approach gave way and sent nine cars hurtling to the gravel bar below. Miraculously, the caboose remained on the rails and no one was hurt.

A replacement span was ordered immediately, and a temporary span was built of timber. Back in service, this makeshift affair lasted just 129 hours and 45 minutes before a flash flood washed it out. Following this, operations were halted 129 hours and 15 minutes before service was resumed on a new steel span. The

After President Stephenson bought ten heavy consolidation engines from the Big Four, the locomotives were "dolled up" in the Harrison shops, and the first one out, No. 47, stood for an official photograph on the outskirts of Harrison. Stephenson's business car No. 99 is shown below at Neosho, completely refurbished and painted Tuscan red with gold trim. *(Two pictures: E. G. Baker)*

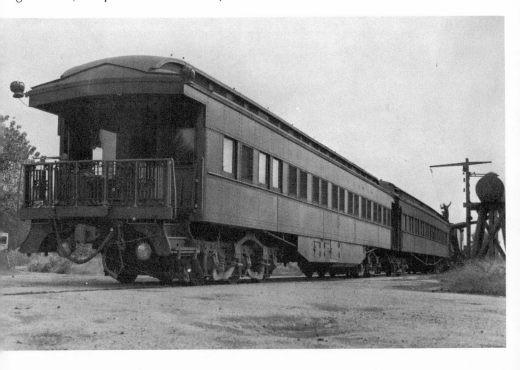

close agreement of these time intervals is a remarkable coincidence. The accident cost the M. & N. A. $8,568, a tidy sum in 1929.

The big consolidation locomotives caused quite a stir in 1929. In due course they were pulled to Harrison, numbered 40-44 (given a "40 Class" designation), and outfitted in North Arkansas livery. To accommodate them, bridge gangs got busy on the Seligman-Leslie section; they added a fourth stringer on each side of the trestles and strengthened all steel bridges. Bridge work for 1929 cost $95,338. In addition, 12.45 miles of 80- and 85-pound rail were installed at critical points such as the grades on either side of Alpena, the grade east of St. Joe, and the grade between Marshall and Baker. The big engines would be run as far south as Kensett, and at that point new shops facilities were completed which included a 70 x 120-foot, three-stall engine house. (Concurrently, the engine house at Heber Springs was retired.)

Stephenson elected to buy five more of the ex-Big Four consolidation freight locomotives in 1929, and what with the heavy spending on way improvement he was in a very bad cash position by mid-year. On June 21 he appealed to the court to authorize $500,000 in Receiver's Certificates, half of which would pay the $250,000 maturing on August 1. In his appeal he noted that he was $70,735 behind in wage payments and had almost $200,000 in other outstanding obligations. The court came through, speculators bought more certificates, and the deficit spending continued.

In mid-1929, Frank Kell made a move to take over control of the railroad. Working through St. Louis connections, he (and his business associates) offered to buy all shares of M. & N. A. common stock for four dollars a share. Although issued at $100 par, the shares had become essentially worthless, and Kell had no trouble in finding ready sellers. By October he had purchased 24,586 of the 30,000 outstanding shares, spending $107,000 according to later reports. Accordingly, the October 20, 1929 *St. Louis Post-Dispatch* ran the headline, "St. Louisans Sell M. & N. A. Railroad" and described the transfer of control to Kell:

> . . . Virtually all of the stock was owned in St. Louis, two of the large holders having been the John Scullin estate and

the estate of David R. Francis. The deal, which includes all
but scattered stockholdings, transfers control of the railroad
to Kell and his associates . . .

It was interesting to note that 1,791 shares remaining of those
purchased by Richard Kerens were *not* offered for sale to Frank
Kell.

The announcement of the sale of the road came just days
before the stock market crash. October 24 was the first bad day
and harked back to October 24, 1907, when J. P. Morgan and
others came to the aid of the sagging economy. Black Tuesday
came on October 29, and, although not known at the time, the
Great Depression was under way. Unquestionably, Frank Kell and
his associates must have had many misgivings about their rash
investment in the Ozarks North Arkansas Line.

Nevertheless, Kell called a special meeting of the Board of Directors on November 9 at which he was elected a member as well
as president of the company. His 34-year-old son, Joe, was also
elected to the board and was made vice president. Stephenson,
retained the titles of receiver and general manager. The St.
Louisans, including Charles Gilbert, J. D. P. Francis, Isaac H.
Orr, and James H. Grover, took their official exit from affairs of
the North Arkansas. The new board of directors was largely
Arkansans.

Revenue freight tonnage for 1929 soared to a record high of
851,912, a 49 per cent increase over 1928. Much of the increase
was due to petroleum shipments from the newly opened Seminole
Field in Oklahoma along the Rock Island Line; these shipments
were routed Wheatley-Helena to avoid the expensive Memphis
gateway. Total revenues were up 17 per cent, to $1,933,824 and
the annual deficit was shaved slightly to $214,304. A big factor
in the deficit was the $141,000 increase in maintenance of way
and equipment. By the end of the year, outstanding Receiver's
Certificates totalled $385,000.

The year 1930 was characterized by the general slide into the
depression. But there was no sudden impact. Petroleum shipments
held up well, though their haul was relatively short. Regular
through and local freights were maintained throughout the year,

and helper service was quite common despite the presence of the 40-class engines. In June, Receiver's Certificates were increased to $600,000, and at the end of the year $533,000 were outstanding. Total revenues for 1930 dropped 15 per cent to $1,632,444, but the deficit was up to $254,475. Significantly, passenger revenue dropped almost 50 per cent, and the daily passenger train run was shortened to Neosho-Kensett. The drop was due in good part to the development of improved highways in the Ozarks, and to win back some of the passengers the M. & N. A. received permission in December to lower the passenger fare from 3 cents per mile to 2 cents per mile. A particular problem was the opening of a bus line from Little Rock to Springfield, Missouri, that paralleled a portion of the North Arkansas route.

In 1931 the economic bite really began to hurt. Revenues were down to $1,185,951, with passenger revenue falling from $67,259 to $25,351. Local freights were cut off, the "through" freight making local calls and, at times, doubling as the mixed train from Kensett to Helena. The passenger train was shortened to two cars, baggage-mail and coach. Additions and betterments dropped precipitously, but did include the laying of 6.6 miles of new 90-pound rail between mileposts 115 and 122. Total employees dropped from 604 to 488 during the year, the cuts coming primarily in maintenance of way and equipment. As traffic fell off it was painfully apparent that those ten big consolidation locomotives, "Stephenson's Folly," were really not needed!

In 1931 Stephenson had arranged to get the Receiver's Certificate limit raised to $700,000 and, strangely enough, had been able to sell all but $25,000 of them. But as 1932 dawned, a source of funds appeared; in January the Reconstruction Finance Corporation was created by the Hoover administration to lend money to needy railroads, banks, agricultural agencies, industry, and commerce. And the M. & N. A. management lost no time in attempting to take advantage of it. On February 6, Federal Judge John Martineau authorized Receiver Stephenson to apply to the RFC for a loan of $1,000,000. The amount was later increased, and on March 1 Stephenson submitted an application to the RFC for a loan of $1,250,000. This amount seemed to fall on deaf ears,

The third No. 2 stands before the Kensett enginehouse, above, about 1930. It appears to be providing steam for some extraneous purpose. The Harrison shops are pictured below, looking east, in 1929 or 1930. The main line is farthest to the left. The building next to the track scales housed an inspection car. Other prominent buildings, left to right, are the operations headquarters, the stores building, the backshop and the six-stall roundhouse. The passenger depot is out of the picture by about 1400 feet.

*(Above: Earl Saunders; below: E. G. Baker)*

for on June 23 the loan application amount was amended to $575,000, to be used as follows:

| | |
|---|---:|
| Taxes for 1930 and 1931 | $ 50,235 |
| Unpaid wages | 85,416 |
| Open accounts | 80,000 |
| Interest on Receiver's certs. due 2/1/32 | 13,860 |
| Bills due on crossties and coal | 149,489 |
| Interest on Receiver's Certs. due 8/1/32 | 21,000 |
| Redemption of 25% of $700,000 rec. certs. | 175,000 |
| Total | $575,000 |

The Interstate Commerce Commission ruled that:

> The need for the loan is clearly evident. At the time of filing the application it was estimated that there would be available on April 1, 1932, the sum of $2,000 to meet the above obligations, and the cash forecast by months for the remainder of the current year, without allowance for their payment, showed an estimated balance at the close of the year in the amount of $6,675. . . Effective in part on June 1, and fully on July 1, 1932, the applicant made a 23% reduction of salaries of all employees on a monthly basis, and a reduction in forces, resulting together in an annual payroll saving of $72,000. The price of track ties has been reduced from 5 to 8 cents per tie,* indicating a saving of $7,000 per annum, and the cost of coal used by the applicant has been reduced 20 cents per ton,* which will result in a further saving of $8,000, making a total saving in operating expenses of $87,000.

The Commission finally approved a loan for $400,000, with the redemption of 25 per cent of the Receiver's Certificates being eliminated. For this, the railroad would be required to deposit with the RFC $400,000 additional Receiver's Certificates having an absolute first lien on the property.

---

*The average cost of an untreated white oak tie in 1931 was 52 cents and in 1932 43 cents. The peak price had been 75 cents in 1929. The average cost of a ton of coal in 1931 was $2.93 and in 1932 $2.82. In 1933 the cost would drop to $2.62. The peak price had been $3.94 in 1924.

Whether Frank Kell objected to the higher priority certificates (he and his associates owned most of the outstanding issue of $700,000) or whether the RFC thought the railroad to be a poor risk is not clear. The public announcement was that the loan was denied by the RFC. With the very precarious cash position of the railroad considered, there was a distinct likelihood that operations would have to cease.

But the line managed to eke out its existence in 1932 when the Great Depression led voters to the polls to usher in the New Deal. Expenses were cut to the bone; for example, out on the line there were only 72 section hands under 44 foremen and tie replacements dropped to 65,254 — half of the needed amount. Since there was so little cash, employees found that paydays were being missed, the railroad informing them that the amounts would be made up just as soon as "foreseeable" business improvements came along. Wellington Stephenson became more and more of a recluse, spending his time in Business Car No. 99 pondering over the situation. The petroleum business dropped off greatly as more and more of the material was transported by pipeline. Forest products, such as logs, ties, lumber, staves, and so on, shipped out on the line dropped to 33,350 tons for the year, compared with annual tonnages of 300,000 to 400,000 back in 1913 to 1917. Passenger revenues were down to $15,749, although mail revenues held up nicely at $49,478. To cap things off, the Citizens Bank in Harrison failed, taking with it $24,663 in M. & N. A. deposits.

When the books were closed for 1932, they showed a $382,846 deficit on total operating revenues of $838,829. As usual, the deficit included $210,000 due on the 1923 government loan, but no interest had actually been paid in years. The remaining portion of the deficit, instead of coming out of Receiver's Certificates as it had in the past, came from "accounts and wages payable" and this liability item stood at $436,743 at the end of 1932. The employees and the creditors were supporting the railroad!

Early 1933 brought with it the Roosevelt administration and its many depression-curbing policies. If there was optimism about, Frank Kell did not partake of it. He owned most of the Receiver's Certificates and attempted to unload them for as low as 85 cents on the dollar. Of course, there were no takers, but several parties

As far as local residents were concerned, the North Arkansas could move pretty well. The passenger train was called by some "The Jackrabbit." Above, the train is moving right along, behind No. 19, near Bellefonte. Below, heavy consolidation No. 44 is bringing a solid train of tank cars southbound, pulling into the siding at Arlberg to pass the northbound passenger train, sometime in 1931. *(Two pictures: E. G. Baker)*

did consider such a purchase seriously. Strangely, Frank and Joe Kell did not appear to take an active part in managing the railroad; they seemed to have confidence in the competence of W. Stephenson. And that gentleman seemed at a complete loss as to how to deal with the poor business conditions.

In April the Interstate Commerce Commission gave the railroad permission to operate trucks over a route from Little Rock to Seligman, to help it "control freight business that is now being lost to truck lines. . ." as the April 6 issue of the *Boone County Headlight* stated. But this venture was given up in July because, contrary to the understanding of the M. & N. A., franchises had been granted to other companies to operate trucks over the same route. Meanwhile, business on the railroad was poor, maintenance was almost nil, and more paydays of the employees were passed. Lon Holder, then foreman of a bridge gang, tells of a visit with Mr. Stephenson in Car 99 at which Jesse, the colored servant, served a very delicious meal. Stephenson told Holder that he and his crew would have to be patient about their back pay; he had a plan for reorganization that would make it possible to handle all amounts in arrears. But such talk did not do much for hungry families, and resentment toward Stephenson mounted.

Sometimes the resentment broke into open defiance. One day Stephenson ventured out into the shops area on inspection. As he threaded his way through the equipment he brushed by the large steam hammer. Suddenly — wham! — the hammer fell on two carefully placed track torpedoes. Stephenson jumped to the terrifying noise, but he said not a word and continued on his way. It was almost as if he had expected such an act. He knew the feelings of the people, and he knew that his time was about up.

The climax of the Stephenson era came on June 21, 1933. On that day three spokesmen for the employees made an appointment with Stephenson at his office in the Kirby Building in downtown Harrison. Just how the spokesmen were chosen is not known for the railroad still operated on a non-union basis. However, they carried out their assignment well.

Just how the conversation went in Stephenson's office is subject to some speculation. The spokesmen demanded the resignation of Stephenson as well as two of his close associates, H. B.

Agnew, general traffic manager, and J. B. Silaz, general superintendent. What means of coercion was used can only be imagined; but it is significant that by the very next day all three men had left town!

The general auditor, Lewie A. Watkins, was appointed receiver; L. N. Bassett, a veteran operating man from Kell's Wichita Falls and Southern line, was appointed general manager and J. E. Halter was appointed general superintendent. Stephenson moved to Kansas City, but in general little further was ever heard from the three officials who left the North Arkansas so suddenly.

Lewie Watkins, 37 years of age at the time, had joined the M. & N. A. accounting department back in April 1922, and in addition to his duties as general auditor had, since October 1932, been functioning as assistant general manager. He had the strong support of Frank Kell as well as of C. F. Spouse, of Pittsburg, Kansas, one of the principal creditors (coal for locomotives). As will be seen in later paragraphs, Watkins was a capable and level-headed administrator, and probably the best possible choice for promotion to chief operating officer.*

Watkins was presented with a situation that would be relished by few. Employee morale was at rock bottom, with wages and salaries 4½ months in arrears. Taxes were very delinquent. Relations with the shipping public were poor. The Federal Court showed a general attitude of disgust over the situation. Watkins was under the gun.

Watkins' first move was to ensure loyalty from the employees. He met with them and assured them that the back pay would be made up. Then he went about the obvious needs of increasing business and decreasing costs. On September 23 he revised schedules to extend passenger service back into Joplin from Neosho, and he consolidated the manifest freight and mixed train south of Kensett. In November he opened up a small but adequate depot at Neosho and discontinued paying the Kansas

---

*In a personal communication to the author, Mr. Watkins recalled that "the [Federal] judge said to me, the newly appointed receiver, that the court would give me 90 days in which to show some definite signs of pointing the affairs of the property in the direction of becoming self-sustaining. He also commented caustically on the delinquencies in wages and taxes."

The two men above picked up the North Arkansas from the throes of depression and receivership and made a money-maker out of it for several years. Frank Kell from Wichita Falls, Texas, left, bought most of the receiver's certificates in 1927-1933, and then purchased the road at public auction in 1935. Lewie Watkins, right, was receiver and later president. American type No. 17, an example of an attractive passenger engine, was photographed at Harrison in 1935. As can be seen here and elsewhere in these pages, North Arkansas shopmen took great pride in the appearance of the road's locomotives. *(Below: E. G. Baker)*

City Southern for use of facilities at that location. In a like manner he moved the M. & N. A. out of the Missouri Pacific depot at
Kensett into a small M. & N. A. depot. He retired a number of
obsolete locomotives, including the early consolidations, Nos.
10-14, preparatory to obtaining scrap metal value for them. And
on the side of new business, he encouraged the activation of mills
for producing white oak staves, since the 21st Amendment was
rapidly being ratified by the states, and there was a distinct
demand for whiskey barrels.

Thus, 1933 ended on an upturn. Tonnage was up slightly to
437,327; revenues were up slightly to $894,780; and the deficit,
including the $210,000 owed to the government, dropped to $199,-
323. The very important criterion of operating ratio (ratio of
operating expenses to operating revenues) was down from 100.34%
in 1932 to a very respectable 79.26% in 1933. Accounts and wages
payable were still high at $485,477, but Watkins had been making
good on his promise to cover regular payroll payments and, in
fact, do some catching-up on back pay. A significant event of the
year was the re-establishment of labor unions on the railroad; this
came about after Watkins was required by the new National
Industrial Recovery Act to post notices reminding workers of their
right to organize, effectively inviting union organizers to move in.

The year 1934 was generally uneventful on the North Arkansas. Watkins continued to run a tight ship, and he chased down
all possibilities for saving money. After much effort and some
agony he was able to effect a compromise settlement of delinquent taxes, as well as to obtain a substantial reduction in tax
assessments from Arkansas and Missouri. In August he was permitted to discontinue the new passenger service between Neosho
and Joplin; records for eight months' operation showed only four
passengers per day on the average, with total revenues of $5.12
per day being far offset by $27.40 per day expenses. An item in
the *St. Louis Post-Dispatch* on August 13 stated that the M. &
N. A. now owed two months' back pay to the employees; Watkins
was working down the backlog. By the end of 1934 the accounts
and wages payable were down to $331,913, which exhibited re-
markable progress. For 1934 the operating ratio was 79.86%; total
revenues were $922,581: and the deficit, again including the

$210,000 government interest item, was down to $187,755. It is significant to note, also, that expenditures for maintenance of way were up; 103 section hands under 40 foremen installed 118,581 crossties and otherwise began to trim up the property.

The performance of Watkins plus signs of an upturn in the economy brought Frank Kell back into the act. Had it not been for the government debt, the railroad would have operated slightly in the black for both 1933 and 1934. So far, he had invested about $800,000 in the railroad and in return had recovered only a modest amount of interest. Accordingly, he petitioned John E. Martineau, Federal Judge for the western division of the eastern district of Arkansas, for foreclosure and sale of the property. On January 22 Martineau instructed the appropriate attorneys to prepare an order of sale. In February notices were posted that the entire railroad would be sold between 10:00 a.m. and 4 p.m. on Tuesday, March 12, 1935, at the south door of the Boone County courthouse at Harrison. The minimum bid was fixed at $350,000, and a deposit of $10,000 was required of all bidders.

Proceeds from the sale (after deducting expenses of sale) were to be used to pay off claims in the following order of priority:

1. Taxes due to states and counties          $     16,153.00
2. Wages due employees                          70,738.95
3. Receiver's Certificates                       700,000.00
4. Interest on Receiver's Certificates       119,460.00
5. Various accounts and judgments payable    142,409.49
5. Principal and interest of the bonds of the
   railroad held by the U. S. Government     5,655,628.18
7. Unsecured notes of the railroad           75,000.00
8. Materials and supplies furnished the
   railroad prior to receivership          130,745.13

On April 10, 1935, a new railroad company filed articles of incorporation with the Secretary of the State of Arkansas. The company was the Missouri & Arkansas Railway Co., and capital stock was set at $918,000. For the 9,180 shares of $100 par stock, subscribers were listed as follows: Frank Kell, 8,992; Joe A. Kell, 180; L. A. Watkins, L. N. Bassett, J. M. Wagley, Roy W. Milum, C. M. Crowell, T. N. Flinn, W. P. Watkins, and G. M. Toney (all directors), one each. The Missouri & Arkansas was organized to take over the rights, franchises, and properties of the Missouri & North Arkansas.

According to Joe H. Schneider, master of sale, on March 12 the $350,000 bid of Frank Kell for the M. & N. A. was the "highest, best, and only" bid. Accordingly, the deed for the property was conveyed to Frank Kell who, in turn, conveyed it to the Missouri & Arkansas Railway Co. in exchange for all of its capital stock. This last act was effective at 12:01 a.m. on April 16, 1935, after which time the Missouri & North Arkansas was no more! The slate was clean at last!

**MISSOURI AND NORTH ARKANSAS RAILWAY COMPANY**
W. STEPHENSON, RECEIVER

**1930**                    No. A **533**

**Pass** ---Mr. C. S. Kirkpatrick---
          Chief Engineer,
ACCOUNT    Missouri Pacific Lines.

**BETWEEN ALL STATIONS**
UNTIL DECEMBER 31, 1930 UNLESS OTHERWISE ORDERED AND SUBJECT TO CONDITIONS ON BACK
VALID WHEN COUNTERSIGNED BY MYSELF OR J. F. STITT.

COUNTERSIGNED                              *W. Stephenson*,
                                                      RECEIVER

# The Missouri & Arkansas

When the Missouri & Arkansas came into being at 12:01 a.m. on April 16, 1935, there was certainly no celebration along the line. In fact, things were reasonably quiet. The two-car passenger trains, Nos. 201 and 202, were tied up at the Kensett yard and at the Neosho depot. The regular freights, Nos. 211 and 212 were handling the routine along the way; if on schedule they were both threading their way along the bluffs of the Little Red after making a meet at Arlberg. The only telegraph stations open were at Seligman, Heber Springs, and the dispatcher's office at Harrison. The night crew at the Harrison shops was minimal, its only pressing concern being that a 40-class engine be ready for the northbound freight when it pulled in at about 4.00 a.m. For sure, however, there was now a debt-free air pervading the property, and after so many years of insolvency, that could be real cause for celebration!

There was cause for general optimism, too. The Great Depression was loosening its grip on the economy. Railroad carloadings were on the increase, and on the M. & A. the employees were getting their back pay and were convinced that with their new management the railroad would go places.

Of course, there were big losers in the reorganization of the line, the biggest by far being Uncle Sam; he lost his $5,665,628 in loan principal and interest. The $132,409 owed to various suppliers and clients also went by the wayside. After deducting the amounts for taxes and back wages, $263,108 of the $350,000 sale price was returned to Frank Kell as holder of the Receiver's Certificates. His other $436,892 in certificates plus $119,460 in unpaid interest resulted in naught. Nonetheless, Kell had himself a railroad at a cost of about one million dollars, including common stock, Receiver's Certificates, and unrecovered interest.

Officers announced on April 16th appeared to be well chosen. Frank Kell would be chairman of the board and his son Joe would be president. L. N. Bassett became vice president and general manager. Transportation superintendent was J. E. "Jack" Halter, who had started with the M. & N. A. at Searcy in 1910, and who had been singularly successful in dealing with the operating crews. Lewie Watkins became general attorney and auditor while continuing his residual duties as receiver of the Missouri & North Arkansas.

In August the Interstate Commerce Commission ruled against the planned issuance of $918,000 capital stock and limited the issue to the purchase price of $350,000. Of the 3500 shares at $100 par, one share each was issued to directors L. N. Bassett, L. A. Watkins, Morris Wilkins (general manager of Kell's Arkansas City, Kansas, flour mill), and R. W. Milum. The other shares were issued in the name of Frank Kell (2725), Joe Kell (170), and Frank Kell's six daughters (100 each).

For several months the attention of the top management was devoted to developing an economy minded organization. For example, it was painfully clear that there could be no long range plan for the heavy 40-class locomotives. Certainly the nine existing units (one was forcibly retired in 1934 when it was fired up with no water in the boiler) were not all needed; because of their damage to the track an attempt had been made to confine them to service north of Harrison where track and embankment were in comparatively good shape. Why not scrap them and get some cash for operating funds? Almost immediately, Nos. 46, 47, and 48 were marked for the scrapper.

The year 1935 ended with a modest net of $29,200, some 4.3% of total revenues. And this sum could go into surplus, something unheard of since 1917. By the time 1936 was well under way, a vigorous and forceful "new look" was apparent all along the line. Townspeople noticed that a new coat of paint was being applied to their depots. A new, circular insigne of the M. & A. replaced the old shield shaped equivalent of the M. & N. A. And, best of all, Lewie Watkins became executive vice president in March.

With the strong backing of the Kells, Watkins went to work on the problem of developing more on-line customers. He initiated a survey of important raw materials in the territory; of interest were lead, zinc, manganese, silica, limestone and other minerals; a vast amount of merchantable timber; and labor-agricultural potential for the business of canning fruits and vegetables. Detailed information and inventories were obtained, and efforts were then made to attract exploitation capital. For example, the search went beyond the hardwood timber (now mostly cut) near the right of way to stands of first and second growth pine that could be brought in by truck; then creosote treating plants were located on the line as shippers.

Even though the promise of mineral wealth in the Ozarks had never materialized for the railroad, geologists and mineralogists were hired to take a new look at the deposits and their data were conveyed to outsiders by new publicity campaigns. To enable the small mining operators to get started, the Manda Corporation was formed to lend them money and pay them in cash for their less-than-carload shipments of ore.

A particularly important mineral development was the discovery of a high grade silica (glass sand) deposit at Everton, the small station 15 miles south of Harrison. Mining operations of the Everton Silica Sand Co. got under way in the spring of 1936 with two types of support from the M. & A., investment capital, and the boiler of engine No. 16 for stationary steam generation. This mine continued to be an important silica producer until the railroad stopped operating in 1946; in 1939 it was sold to Silica Products Co., prominent producer at Guion, Arkansas, on the White River near Batesville. Other Manda developments included a large lead and zinc mine at Stark City, Missouri, a rock crusher near Heber Springs, Arkansas, and a wood products operation near Harrison.

These and other efforts helped the company to show a profit of $47,981 on total 1936 operating revenues of $1,043,008, the first million dollar year since 1931. In a seemingly premature action, the directors voted a cash dividend of $35,000, essentially all of which went to the Kells. Although there was the hint that the Kells were starting on a process of bleeding the property, the dividend action was actually at the urging of Watkins. The publicity of a large cash dividend, something essentially unheard of on the North Arkansas, would convince outsiders that this railroad was really on the move forward.

No person anywhere was happier about the railroad's turn for the better than an 18-year-old Harrison youth named E. G. Baker. Born into a family of "North Arkansans," he had developed an early infatuation for the trains that puffed in and out of Harrison. At almost any time of day or night, when not in school, he could be found roaming the yards, chatting with the trainmen and shopmen, or riding along on the family pass. He was one of few who recognized the value of recording the North Arkansas trains photographically (as the pictures in this book attest). Baker was known as "Harrison's No. 1 Rail Nut."

One winter afternoon in Neosho, Baker decided to "bum" his way back to Harrison on an oil tank car of southbound Red Ball No. 211. So, while the freight was easing off the Kansas City Southern iron, he jumped aboard and settled himself for a real fling at hoboing. The train had about 30 cars behind consolidation engine No. 49, and rolled out of Neosho about six hours late. No sooner had the train crested the 0.8% grade at Stark City when a cold north wind began to bring in a mixture of rain and sleet and E. G. Baker began to wonder about this lark; but he decided to stay put until the train stopped at Wheaton. This time, however, No. 211 really was a manifest and it clanked right on through Wheaton in sleet that had the young man near frozen on that skimpy tank car footboard. So Baker started toward the caboose, crawling because of icy catwalks that were far from steady. Right on through Wayne the train rolled, the agent handling the switch onto the Frisco.

At last, Baker found the warmth and hospitality that is characteristic of freight train cabooses. Once inside, he could enjoy a cupola view of the night landscape that now was being touched by flurries of snow. And before long he was treated to a plate of hot biscuits, eggs, ham and red-eye gravy.

The Brill gasoline-powered motor car, purchased by the M. & A. in 1937 for service between Kensett and Helena, made six round trips weekly with rarely a breakdown until cessation of operations in 1946. The 30-class mikados were steady work horses on the North Arkansas, and were especially useful on the south end where bridge ratings were low but grades very slight. No. 33 is pictured below, possibly in the yards at Joplin, about 1937. (*Above: National Museum of Transport; below: Earl Saunders*)

Passenger operations are here depicted at Harrison on two days in May 1938, before the advent of the streamliners. Above, No. 21 pulls the north-bound train past the operations office. The lower view, taken four days later, shows the same train, this time behind No. 20, meeting No. 18 in the yards.

*(Two pictures: E. G. Baker)*

No. 211 rolled on through Seligman, meeting the northbound passenger No. 202 while it was at the depot, and finally made its first stop for coal and water at Junction. The trip on in to Harrison might have been perfect for the young railfan, but when the train started down Capps Hill, with the lights of Harrison visible in the valley below, the conductor yanked the emergency cord, bringing things to a jolting halt. The trucks of a freight car were on the crossties. Rerailing the trucks was not easy on a snowy night, and No. 211 made Harrison by about 3:00 a.m. Though E. G. Baker had not, by any means, lost his love for the M. & A., he did decide to wait until spring before playing hobo again.

Returning to the economic development of the M. & A., there is one peripheral event that must be recorded. The Crescent Hotel at Eureka Springs, for years almost a symbol for the North Arkansas, was forced to close its doors. In 1933 the off-season operation of Crescent College, using hotel facilities, had come to an end. Now, in 1936, the hotel ceased operation and the property was sold to Norman Baker, a pseudo-physician who would operate it as a hospital for about two years. This development was a far cry from the days when the passengers detrained by the hundreds and took the various public conveyances up the hill to the magnificent Crescent. By 1936, Eureka Springs had lapsed into a quiet hill town in a picturesque setting, with much of the tourist business passing it by. Very few passengers got on or off the dusty dark-red coaches after they had been backed up the grade from Junction.

Some significant developments were under way in passenger train service on the M. & A. In 1937 a new gasoline-powered motor car was purchased from the J. G. Brill Co. and was placed in service between Kensett and Helena. The car was given No. 605; it seated 28, had a compartment for baggage and pouch mail, and cost the princely sum of $7,805. This car represented a definite improvement over the mixed service which consisted of adding one or two passenger train cars to the regular freights for the run between Kensett and Helena. Until the end of operations, this streetcar-looking affair would be a familiar sight, bouncing along the rough track through the cotton and rice fields of alluvial Arkansas.

Spurred on by a 1937 net income of $21,135, despite heavy expenses for washout repairs, management turned to the need for improving passenger service north of Kensett. At its February 6, 1938 meeting, the board voted to purchase two more gasoline-powered motor cars. And these cars would not be of the plain Jane variety such as the Brill car. They would be honest-to-goodness *streamliners,* in keeping with the trend started a few years earlier by the Union Pacific and Burlington railroads. The two cars would cost $94,942 and would be purchased from American Car and Foundry. By executing equipment trusts, it would be necessary to make an initial cash payment of only $18,584. When the news got out, employees and railroad friends up and down the line could hardly wait until the cars made their appearance.

As luck would have it, this decision to spend money was followed shortly by a real need for money. Heavy rains in the spring of 1938 resulted in extensive washouts in May. In the vicinity of Beaver, some 15 trestles and 2.67 miles of track had to be completely rebuilt. And the tab for this work came to about $46,000. More of the luck of the North Arkansas!

Nevertheless, planning for the streamliners went forward. By June 19 they were ready to leave the builder's plant at Berwick, Pennsylvania. They were real beauties! Spectacular enough to warrant separate exhibition tours before reaching M. & A. rails at Helena, and newsworthy enough to merit a special article in the June 11 issue of *Railway Age.* By June 26 they had been checked out and were ready to start their runs in replacement of (and on the same schedule as) the venerable steam-powered passenger trains. In fact, this date bore the death-knell for Engine No. 17, which pulled its train into Harrison on June 25 and then went almost directly to the scrap track.

The streamliners were christened; No. 705 took the name of THOMAS C. McRAE, after the man who was Governor of Arkansas during the critical stages of the Great Strike in the early 1920s. No. 726 took the name of the ex-Governor and Federal Judge JOHN L. MARTINEAU. Each car was 75 feet long, carried 33 persons in air-conditioned comfort, and had baggage plus railway post office compartments. The cars weighed 33 tons light and were powered by a 200 HP Hall-Scott horizontal engine with special

Streamliner No. 705, the THOMAS C. McRAE, and its twin, the JOHN L. MARTINEAU, began regular service between Neosho and Kensett on June 26, 1938. The 705 is shown above, rather battered, at Harrison depot about 1940. Sometimes the gasoline-powered "Blue Goose" streamliners needed assistance. Below, No. 21 has just helped one of them into Harrison. *(Above: Garland Case, courtesy* RAILROAD MAGAZINE; *below: E. G. Baker)*

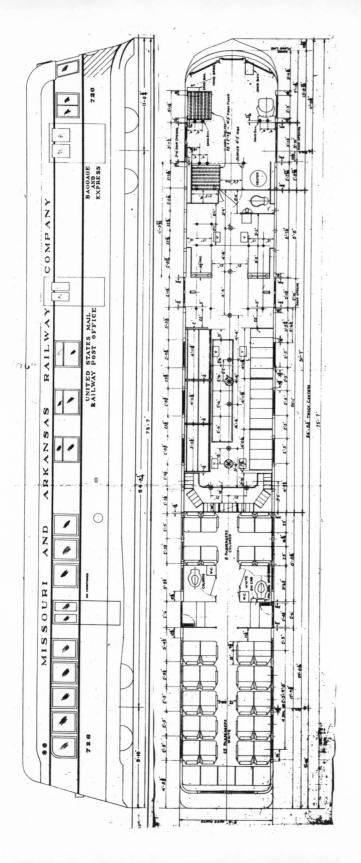

Plan and elevation drawings of streamliner No. 726, the JOHN L. MARTINEAU show a car about 4½ feet longer than the 1912 gas-electric cars (page 102), but with less than half as many seats, and with more space for baggage and railway post office than for passengers. (*American Car & Foundry Co.*)

heavy-duty transmission to cope with the M. & A. grades. The exterior was blue and white, leading inevitably to the sobriquet "blue goose." As the cars took their regular turn each day of the week, crowds gathered at every station between Kensett and Neosho to see them come and go.

The December 10 issue of *Railway Age* noted that the "Missouri & Arkansas (motor car) units prove economical and attract business on light traffic line" and included the following cost comparisons for one car vs. one steam train (based on July 1938):

|  | Rail car | Steam train |
|---|---|---|
| Fuel | $ 811.65 | $1,158.35 |
| Material-maintenance | 69.60 | 373.34 |
| Cleaning & supplying | 270.06 | 142.23 |
| Lubricants | 27.18 | 39.05 |
| Engine house expense | – | 244.70 |
| Shop & store expense | 98.49 | 246.80 |
| Coal chute man – Junction | – | 26.97 |
| Fire insurance | 23.33 | 4.35 |
| Turn at Neosho | 46.50 | 46.50 |
| Seligman-Wayne trackage | 80.91 | 161.82 |
| Livestock killed | 11.00 | 246.00 |
| Depreciation | 387.16 | 328.43 |
| Payroll taxes | 117.51 | 177.83 |
| Total for month | $1,943.39 | $3,196.37 |

For two cars, the saving was $2,506 and because of the improved service, passenger revenue was up $500. Thus, a $5,000 per month loss was cut to $2,000 and there was hope of eliminating it entirely. The savings did not, however, come up to the $4,240 monthly payment to American Car and Foundry that was to run for 18 months.

Although the improved economy of passenger operations was indeed encouraging, freight made up the major part of the business — and this part declined in 1938 along with a minor recession in the general economy. Bridge traffic held up reasonably well, but freight originating on the line dropped from 348,878 tons in 1937 to only 207,997 tons in 1938. Total revenue dropped slightly below the million dollar mark, but by deferring some maintenance

Three of the six mikado freight engines purchased from the Atlanta, Birmingham and Coast line appear below, in May 1929, at the Harrison engine yards. At the left is A. B. & C. No. 201 after being converted to M. & A. No. 51; the next is A. B. & C. No. 206 before conversion to M. & A. No. 53; beyond M. & A. No. 21, at the far right, is A. B. & C. No. 202 before it was converted to M. & A. No. 52. This latter engine appears above with its new number, and the headlight moved to the center of the smokebox cover. *(Two pictures: E. G. Baker)*

and cutting other expenses, Watkins managed to show $6,400 net income for the year.

Hitler's 1938-1939 endeavors in taking over Austria and Czechoslovakia caused wartime preparations in the United States to pick up sharply. A boom in railroad traffic seemed on the way, and the M. & A. management suddenly realized that their freight motive power might not be adequate for the upcoming job. The fiasco of the 40-class consolidations has been noted several times earlier; by early 1939 only four of them remained in serviceable condition. The 30-class mikados were needed south of Leslie where the grades were modest. To meet the need, four used locomotives were located at Southern Iron & Equipment Co. in Atlanta, Georgia, and on March 28, 1939, the M. & A. board approved their purchase.

These were mikado freight locomotives that had seen over 25 years of service on the Atlanta, Birmingham and Coast line. Careful inspection showed their mechanical condition to be almost perfect. Their axle loading of 47,000 pounds was much more favorable than the 54,000 pounds of the 40-class engines. Further, their tractive effort was slightly greater and they could be rated at 1,000 tons on the 1.75% grades north of Leslie. The purchase price of $5,800 each, with $1,800 down and the remainder over eight months, was attractive. By May they were at the Harrison shops being repainted and modified in appearance by having their headlights positioned at the center of the smokebox cover. They were numbered 50 through 53 and classified simply as "50-class." On test and afterward, they were regarded highly by the M. & A. enginemen.

With these motive power expenses in 1938 and 1939 plus a gnawing concern that maintenance was not adequate, the M. & A. management decided to follow an old North Arkansas tradition and really go into debt in order to raise needed cash. On March 29 application was made to the Interstate Commerce Commission to borrow $175,000 from the Reconstruction Finance Corporation. (It will be recalled that in 1932 a $575,000 application for a M. & N. A. loan was turned down by the R. F. C.) The money was to be used for the following purposes:

| | |
|---|---:|
| Retire debt on ACF motor cars | $ 60,000 |
| Purchase four more freight engines | 26,500 |
| Flood damages in 1938 | 33,000 |
| Treated piling and bridge materials | 25,000 |
| Six miles of 70- and 80-pound rail | 17,000 |
| New ditching machine | 6,000 |
| Retire bank note | 7,500 |
| Total | $175,000 |

As security for the loan, certificates of trust on all serviceable equipment would be issued.

This loan application resulted in a visit by two examiners from the Railroad Division of the R. F. C., Messrs. W. W. Sullivan and T. A. Hamilton. These men made a motor car inspection of the property on May 23-26, 1939, and their report constitutes a detailed and historically valuable appraisal of the railroad facilities and operations at the time. Their evaluation of the M. & A. was reasonably favorable. They complimented the operating management on its efficiency in moving tonnage, and agreed with the move to stay in the passenger business with the new rail motor cars. They felt that motive power was adequate for existing levels of business. And they agreed with the policy, which some might call "parasitic," of not owning freight cars for interline service.* But they did take management to task on lack of upkeep of fixed facilities — the dire need for ballast, improved drainage, and new rail on the south end, for example.

Thus, despite the seemingly favorable comments, the inspectors recommended against the loan. There was insufficient collateral for a $175,000 loan. And a $400,000 loan would do more justice to the railroad's needs. The loan application was turned down by the R. F. C. So much for that!

Operations continued well in 1939. The "Blue Geese" made their regular daily trips on schedule, laying over at night in new sheds constructed for them at Neosho and Kensett. The "new" 50-class locomotives showed such good performance that in Octo-

---

*This policy had forcibly gone into effect in the early 1930s when obsolete wooden equipment was being retired and no funds were available for purchasing replacements.

ber management elected to purchase two more of the ex-A. B. & C. mikados. Numbered 54 and 55, they were out on the road in December. The year-end financial results were not bad: $1,107,939 operating revenues with $38,736 net income.

However, 1939 was marred by tragedy. Late in the year there took place in far-off Texas an event that proved to be the most important turning point in the railroad's career. Joe Kell was killed. His instant death resulted from an automobile accident five miles south of Wichita Falls. The date was November 21, just before the Thanksgiving festivities at Frank Kell's house. Joe Kell, aged 44, was Frank Kell's only son and his hope to see the M. & A. through to success. Joe had become quite interested in the business, and did a lot of off-line selling of its services. But now he was dead, and the father was understandably grieved. Little did the people in Harrison, Arkansas, know that this tragic event would lead to the demise of the railroad.

At a special meeting of the M. & A. board on January 2, Lewie Watkins was elected president. Frank Kell, of course, remained chairman of the board, but at age 79 and with the grief of his lost son, his interest in the railroad waned; in fact, he asked Watkins to look around for a buyer of the property.

One early action of 1940 was the incorporation, on January 5th, of the Missouri & Arkansas Transportation Co. This subsidiary of the railroad would provide an integrated truck-rail activity on the north end of the line. Less-than-carload shipments would be picked up and consolidated at central points for transshipment by rail, if needed. Furthermore, business was extended into Little Rock; common carrier routes were Gateway, Arkansas (just south of Seligman, Missouri) to Kensett, Shirley to Little Rock, and Heber Springs to Little Rock. Trucks were purchased, and operations were under way by April 1.

The specter of right of way rehabilitation needs continued to haunt Watkins, and he decided to attempt to raise $540,000 by selling 4%, 25-year bonds. After all, the image of the line was good (for one thing, Watkins had been spending about $3,000 each year on advertising), not only in the region but with connecting roads that had come to recognize the reliability of the M. & A. Permission to carry out this financing was requested of the I. C. C.

in June. Alas, permission was not granted! It appeared that Watkins would have to generate needed cash the long and hard way.

As the European War continued to heat up in 1940, business moved well along the line. Freight was up to 645,000 annual tons. The single through train was maintained, with frequent double-heading between Seligman and Leslie. Total revenues rose to $1,201,742, and the net was $40,276. The surplus now stood at $163,257. Fortunately, the shareholders didn't arrange a cash dividend for themselves.

Buyers of the property had been sought by Watkins, and one of them evinced a serious interest: Eagle-Picher Mining Co., which had been moving considerable freight on the line out of Joplin. Details for purchase were worked out, and just as the company was ready to make a firm offer, more misfortune befell the North Arkansas. Frank Kell died.

Kell died on September 17, 1941, at the age of 81. Although he had not taken a strong interest in the M. & A. since his son's death two years earlier, he had supported Watkins in the management of the road. But he was gone now, and after settlement of his estate, the 3500 shares of stock would be distributed as follows:

| | |
|---|---|
| Mrs. Frank Kell | 1354 |
| Mrs. Joe Kell | 170 |
| Six Kell daughters at 328 each | 1968 |
| Total | 3492 |

with the other eight shares being owned by officers of the company.

Lewie Watkins had been president for nearly two years by this time. He had never been one for ostentation and the handsome ex-Colorado Midland business car No. 99 was of little value to him. If he wanted to inspect the right of way, he went by motorized hand car. And if he wanted to "visit" along the line, he used a company automobile. But in October 1941 he put the No. 99 to good use. He organized a special train to move up and down the line as an advertising and public relations activity. Dubbed the "President's Special," the train comprised coach No. 5 plus the No. 99. Businessmen from the various communities were treated to the elegance of No. 99 and were doubtless well impressed.

Train 211, the southbound manifest, above, tackles the 1.75% grade just south of Harrison on December 29, 1940; No. 49 heads toward the camera with No. 52 back in the train. Below, both engines have passed the camera but continue to fight the grade. According to E. G. Baker who took both pictures, "The stack music was terrific on this curve."

Engine No. 40 with freight train 212 makes a run for the Capps Hill grade about two miles north of Harrison. The date is early 1941. In August of that year, doubleheaded southbound freight No. 211 works the grade between Alpena and Batavia. The lead engine is mikado No. 53; the second engine, well-spaced because of bridge loading problems, is unidentified. The rail here is 90-pound and, for the North Arkansas, the ballast condition is excellent. *(Two pictures: E. G. Baker)*

Shortly after this it became clear that the Kell heirs were not interested in such public relations. The No. 99 was parked in the Harrison coach shop and used very little before being sold in 1946 to M. & A. engineer Dick Ligget at Kensett. The car stands today, sans trucks, across the street from Ligget's home.

But back to 1941, the year when Frank Kell died: there were other important events late that year. One was, of course, the bombing of Pearl Harbor on December 7. The impact of this event on the United States and the world is well known; the impact of it on the Missouri & Arkansas will be told in due course. And on the same day — December 7 — another calamitous event befell the railroad. The Kirby Building, housing the executive offices of the M. & A., burned. All was lost, save vital records stored in a fireproof vault. More of the usual tough luck of the North Arkansas!

The year 1942 brought with it the rigors of full-scale war on both sides of the globe. Needs for conserving gasoline and rubber caused people and freight to begin returning to the railroads. Plants for manufacturing explosives sprang up, some of them situated to ship their products via the M. & A. The surge was felt on the railroad, and while dealing with it, Lewie Watkins had little time to worry about the Kell heirs. But they had time to worry about him. They wanted some connecting link between their 3,492 shares of stock and the operation of the railroad.

The link was provided in the form of a Mr. Malcolm Putty, 39-year-old husband of Mary Josephine Kell Putty, one of the six daughters of Frank Kell. Putty had been in the retail automobile business, but with no new cars being produced he was available for work more related to the war effort. Accordingly, in May 1942 he and his family moved to Harrison and he became executive vice president. It would be hard to imagine anyone less qualified for the job, but there he was! The Texas end of the link was held very firmly by another son-in-law, Orville Bullington, who had married Sadie Kell back in 1911 and who had been general counsel for the M. & A. since its organization. To further enforce the link, Willie May Kell, only unmarried daughter of Frank Kell, was elected chairman of the board. Watkins was surrounded!

Despite their general antipathy for the railroad* the Kells might well have been pleased about its pickup of business. No longer could the single freight train handle the load; extra trains were assigned to both local and through traffic. Workers in the office of the Joplin Union Depot often were impressed by the number of cars set out for the southbound M. & A. "Red Ball" freight and they would notice that a yard switch engine would have to give the freight an uphill push when it left town. Track gangs worked tirelessly to inspect and replace worn-out rails in the Ozark hills and replacement rail weight was as high as 100 pounds to the yard! The years 1941 and 1942 were busy ones, as the following figures show:

|                | 1942        | 1941        | (1936)      |
|----------------|-------------|-------------|-------------|
| Total tonnage  | 899,086     | 719,652     | 576,915     |
| Total revenue  | $1,729,768  | $1,359,196  | $1,043,008  |
| Expenses       | $1,426,726  | $1,130,332  | $ 857,479   |
| Net income     | $   42,008  | $   24,025  | $  47,981   |

The Kells could see that expenses were going up as fast as revenues so they voted themselves a $17,500 dividend in 1942.

The war year 1943 was more of the same. Double-headed freights getting in each other's way and too long for many of the sidings. Local freights plying all three districts. Rail motor cars having frequent breakdowns and needing assistance from the steamers. For the year about 25 per cent of the passenger train miles were pulled by ten-wheelers 18, 19, 20, or 21. Of real concern, however, was the accident situation.

During 1943 there were no serious accidents such as collisions, but the regularity of minor derailments indicated unsafe operation over parts of the line, especially south of Harrison. In 1942 there had been 71 mainline accidents costing $32,863. In 1943 there were 94 mainline accidents costing $53,875 and there were many more accidents on sidings. Of the 1943 mainline accidents, 65 were attributed directly to track conditions:

---

*At the same time they appeared to condone the Frank Kell railroad near at hand, The Wichita Falls & Southern.

North Arkansas historian and photographer, E. G. Baker, was perched on a hillside just east of the Harrison yards when he caught the lower view of southbound manifest 211 on February 8, 1942. Doubleheaded by mikes 54 and 55, in that order, the train was rumbling across Crooked Creek bridge and gaining momentum for the climb up to Ozier summit. At the Highway 62 crossing near Green Forest, above, engines are laboring as they head the westbound manifest into another of those 1.75% grades.

Engine No. 54 is headed north on the S-curve that included the deck lattice girder bridge just east of Alpena. World War II put a heavy bind on the motive power situation and several engines were leased from other roads. Below, No. 1915 is one of two locomotives leased from the Rock Island. It was later purchased and, retaining its Rock Island number, gave good service to the railroad.

The sad-looking mogul No. 14, above, was one of two leased from the Wichita Falls & Southern. In this instance the lease rate was too high and the engine's mechanical condition very poor. Below, mike No. 51 leads the freight easily around the curve that leads to Alpena station. The head brakeman has climbed down from his "doghouse" to get in the picture. (*Above: John B. Allen; three pictures: E. G. Baker*)

| | |
|---|---:|
| Rough track | 36 |
| Broken rail | 10 |
| Alignment | 7 |
| Worn rail | 3 |
| Soft track | 2 |
| Track frog | 2 |
| Miscellaneous | 2 |
| | 65 |

Although freight train miles were up 22% over 1942, it was pain-fully clear that the track was inadequate and that tie-ups due to accidents were excessive. The only immediate solution seemed to be to slow down the trains even more, until they almost literally crept along through the hills and across the flatlands on the south end. The average over-all freight train speed dropped to 9.9 miles per hour, with an actual running time of 16 hours from Joplin to Heber Springs.

Still, the tonnage was hauled. The total of 1,021,071 tons for 1943 was 14% above the previous year. Movements over the line showed the following breakdown:

### Average Daily Tonnage, 1943

| | Manifest South | Local South | Manifest North | Local North |
|---|---:|---:|---:|---:|
| Joplin-Harrison | 1,865 | 928 | 1,509 | 645 |
| Harrison-Heber Springs | 2,265 | 1,133 | 1,760 | 784 |
| Heber Springs-Helena | 1,891 | 1,379 | 1,465 | 1,080 |

The locals were run as extras, but were out on the line all week-days. This permitted the manifests to move steadily if *very* slowly.

Another problem which worsened during 1943 was motive power. In February arrangements were made to lease two small mogul-type locomotives from the Wichita Falls & Southern through the good graces of Mr. Bullington and his connections with the Kell ownership of that road. Unfortunately, the locomo-tives turned out to be sad looking and badly worn castoffs that would have to be converted from oil-burning to coal-burning. And the lease was at the exorbitantly high rate of $35 per day for each engine! Could this indicate overt action on the part of the Kells? It would seem so.

These moguls retained their W. F. & S. numbers of 14 and 15. They were assigned to local service on the south end but, according to later testimony, they were mechanically inadequate and were seldom used. This made it necessary to continue to keep all five of the 30-class mikados busy south of Kensett, with the north end load carried by the six 50-class mikados and the 4 remaining 40-class heavy consolidations. The remaining locomotives on the roster, ten-wheelers 18, 20 and 21, were kept busy with rescuing the motor cars, switching in the Harrison yard, and movement of light local freights. The situation was aggravated by the usual need to doublehead the manifest between Junction and Leslie* with the helper engine often having to go one way "light" (no train) because of unreliable schedules.

The year 1943 ended with financial figures showing a high turnover of money but a low net income. Revenues soared to $2,178,125 but because of such extra operating expenses as high overtime due to accidents and slow train movements, the net income came down to $27,256. The entire *modus operandi* had portents of trouble and during the latter part of 1943 there were evidences of labor problems that could even portend disaster. . .

Since the strike of 1921-1923, labor problems on the road had not been severe. Working conditions were reasonably good. Wages had remained lower than the national average, but there was a corresponding living cost advantage in the territory served by the line. Open shop conditions had prevailed until 1933, and after that time management-labor relations had been amicable. General wage increases had been negotiated for January 1, 1939, and February 15, 1942, and in the frenzy of moving wartime traffic the overtime pay received by the operating unions had kept them satisfied. Further, "there was a war to be won." But, inevitably, the M. & A. workers, both operating and non-operating, were to be stirred up by national railroad labor unrest in the latter part of 1943.

During the summer the Brotherhoods started national demands for the substantial increase of $3 minimum per basic day. This was unrealistic, of course, and certainly not allowable under

---

*The double-headers were characterized by having several freight cars between the two engines. This was to prevent overloading of bridge sections.

Things are quiet around the Harrison depot as the northbound streamliner THOMAS C.

the "Little Steel Formula" which permitted a 15% maximum increase over wage rates of January 1941. The unions (including the M. & A. workers) had received a 10.5% average increase in 1942 and now they wanted another 40%! The Emergency War Board had, in May 1943, recommended increases averaging 64 cents per basic day or 8 cents per hour; this was unacceptable to the unions. On September 25, the National Railway Emergency Board recommended that the workers receive only 4 cents per hour, in order to comply with the 15% allowable increase over 1941. Understandably, this second action made the railroad workers quite unhappy!

Even though the unions had a "no-strike clause" in their contracts, they made strike threats. On December 18 the operating unions voted to walk out on December 30. They were thwarted in this move by President Roosevelt, who took over the nation's railroads on December 27 and granted interim increases of 9 cents per hour. Eventually, on January 22, the railroads were returned to their owners. The 9 cents per hour increase held, with retroactive payment to April 1, 1943. Non-operating unions got 9-11 cents per hour increases.

But the M. & A. management elected not to go along with the national decision. The stated reason was that there was not enough money in the treasury for the required $115,000 retroactive pay. Yet the local unions insisted that any increases had to be on the retroactive basis. Ultimately, on March 20, 1944, the trainmen voted 119 to 1 to strike at 6:00 a.m. on March 28. The walkout was averted by calling in the National Mediation Board. Also, the Office of Defense Transportation (ODT) was asked to investigate the railroad's ability to pay; to this end Mr. Samuel W. Fordyce III, a Kansas City Southern executive* on loan to the ODT, made an inspection of the property.

The Fordyce report was issued on May 21, 1944. It included a great deal of factual data on the railroad, and its conclusion that the railroad could not afford the back payment of wages was well documented. Fordyce included some specific suggestions for making the line more able to increase wages:

---

*And grandson of Colonel S. W. Fordyce, distinguished St. Louis capitalist and builder of the Cotton Belt railroad through Arkansas and Texas.

1. Modify the Joplin terminal agreement to permit the M. & A. to pay a more equitable (and lower) portion of the cost of operation.
2. Obtain lower and much more realistic lease terms from the Wichita Falls & Southern, covering the two locomotives plus freight cars.
3. Eliminate $16,000 annual cost of "unnecessary executives."
4. Revise the Kensett terminal situation which required that locomotives be returned to Harrison even for light repairs.
5. Eliminate passenger service.
6. Operate only one freight train each way daily.
7. Avoid high overtime charges by hiring additional trainmen.
8. Get rid of the M. & A. Transportation subsidiary.

While not all of these recommendations were practicable, several did give Watkins food for thought and were later followed up. More importantly, the Fordyce report gave the unions food for thought . . . that perhaps the railroad really couldn't come up with all of the back pay. But how much could be recovered? That was their question, and negotiations continued.

In June, the unions voted in favor of a strike on July 13. At the last minute, the National Mediation Board requested a deferment, which was granted. A new mediator arrived July 18, so Lewie Watkins cancelled his plans to be an Arkansas delegate at the Democratic National Convention in Chicago and negotiations resumed at Harrison. There was pressure on Watkins by the Kells who didn't want any wage increases, and felt that the unions would not go through with a strike during wartime. But, lo and behold! On Friday, July 28, all operating employees were out "on vacation." A strike had been called for 9:00 p.m. Thursday evening, with provisions that all trains be taken to terminal points.

With such drastic action, July 28 became the day for settlement. Both operating and non-operating employees agreed to wage increases of from 9 to 11 cents per hour, retroactive to July 1, 1944. The settlement seemed to be a reasonable one from the viewpoints of both sides. Even the Kell family had to agree that

The end of operations was not too far away when the day shift at the Harrison shops gathered for the picture on the opposite page.

(*Garland Case, courtesy* RAILROAD MAGAZINE)

The depths to which track maintenance descended are shown in this view at Junction
looking toward Seligman, in 1946. In the distance is a coaling station. In earlier year
there was a trestle-type coal chute located to the left and just behind the camera.

(C. E. Hull

the railroad could not have been shut down with the continuing heavy load of wartime tonnage to be moved.

Thus, the labor situation was taken care of, and attention could now be given to other pressing matters. The M. & A. Transportation Co., plagued by a shortage of tires and parts, was dissolved on August 1. To alleviate the motive power squeeze, arrangements were made to lease five consolidation type freight locomotives for a combined cost of about $200 per day. Three of these came from the Cotton Belt and were 40-year-old ex-Erie coalburners; they were assigned numbers 60-62. The other two came from the Rock Island and were somewhat less venerable. They too were coal-burners,* and they were not renumbered from their Rock Island designations 1915 and 1972. This added motive power carried the M. & A. into 1945 with few troubles in pulling the freight.

As proposed by Fordyce, an attempt was made to eliminate passenger service. By this time enough synthetic rubber and rationed gasoline was available to take passengers away from the road. Applications were filed on October 17, 1944, hearings were duly held and protests were extensive. Before the Arkansas and Missouri commissions could act, the railroad decided to go along with promises for more business and withdraw the abandonment applications.

Misfortune, that long-time bedfellow of the North Arkansas, struck again on December 4, 1944. On that date the large backshop building at Harrison was destroyed by fire. Insurance coverage was only $23,000 — much less than the cost of replacement. One would think that this unexpected expense, together with the increased cost of labor, would put the M. & A. directors in a cautionary mood; instead, on December 7 they declared a $35,000 dividend! Perhaps the justification was in the record $89,999 net income on $2,575,273 gross for the year. After deducting the dividend, the surplus stood at $278,912. Certainly a decent sum, but how obvious it was that the physical facilities of the road were barely holding together, and that the ultimate rehabilitation

---

*Unlike other railroads of the region, the M. & A. had never converted to oil for locomotive fuel. Perhaps the answer was in a long-standing and favorable business arrangement with the Pittsburg & Midway Coal Co.

would be very costly. Unfortunately, it was equally obvious that the Kells had no long-range plans that covered the rehabilitation problem.

In fact, the idea was to sell the property as soon as possible. Back in October some sale negotiations had been carried out with undisclosed principals through the Chase National Bank in New York. These and other negotiations were short-lived. However, in early 1945 another prospect was located. On January 7, President Watkins announced to the press that "an agreement has been reached for sale of the line to Samuel N. Summer and associates of Columbus, Ohio." The actual sale price had not yet been agreed upon, but transfer of the property was scheduled for June 15. This was good news for all, since it was common gossip by this time that the disinterested Kell heirs were out to get rid of the road, one way or the other.

Possibly spurred on by these negotiations, Watkins agreed to having the American Locomotive Co. study dieselization of the M. & A. Their recommendations were given in a report dated January, 1945. A total of ten 1000-HP Alco-GE diesel locomotives would handle all manifest and local freight needs. Passengers would be handled by motor cars or not at all! The diesels would cost about $1,000,000 less scrap value of the steam locomotives. As many as three units would be used on each manifest and would run through from Joplin to Helena. On the basis of 1943 tonnage (unrealistically high for postwar operation), the purchase of such units would show a 25% annual return, based on savings in maintenance, fuel, and employee time. If the local freights were eliminated, fewer diesel units would be required. If the proposed sale would go through, it might be possible to place orders for postwar delivery.

The idea of getting the road out of the Kell clutches was an attractive one to employees, customers, and friends. Hopefully it would also be attractive to the prospective purchasers. Timetable No. 7, issued February 25, 1945, showed optimism in a full complement of passenger motor cars, manifest "Red Ball" freights, and tri-weekly locals. As usual, the timetable was detailed and informative, even giving locomotive and passenger car rosters. Reconstruction of the backshop building got under way January 10, and the plans called for a modern structure that would be much more attractive than the one it replaced. Things were going well until misfortune called again, this time in the form of heavy spring rains.

March was a wet month in Arkansas, with the result that the White River and its tributaries began to overflow along the south end of the M. & A. On March 20 about 3½ miles of track at Enright (mileposts 285-288, just north of Georgetown) went underwater. This particular section went under in 1927 and on other occasions, so this inundation was nothing new or unexpected. In fact, a substantial amount of stone riprap had been installed to hold the embankment in place.

Somehow, strong currents developed in the overflowing backwaters, and on April 4 a sizable section of the embankment washed away completely. In fact, later observations showed that a large hole some 70 feet deep had been dug precisely in line with the track!

The wartime traffic had to move, and arrangements were made to detour the through freights between Kensett and Fargo. Routing was via main lines: Missouri Pacific between Kensett and Fair Oaks; Cotton Belt between Fair Oaks and Fargo. The connecting spurs at Kensett and Fargo were not well designed for these movements, and at each interchange it was necessary for the train to back up for a considerable distance. The detour was 62.4 miles versus 28.5 miles direct, but it was over smooth, heavy rail on good rock ballast, and the higher speeds this permitted might keep time losses to a minimum. Of course, it would be necessary for the M. & A. to pay the cost of "pilots" over the foreign route.

The waters stood over the Enright section for several weeks, and preparations for repairing the washout were delayed. With the coming of V-E Day on May 7, ending World War II hostilities in Europe, there was still no repair action on the south end. The diverted freights continued to move, though much slower than expected. Traffic was heavy on the routes and the delays to the M. & A. freights were such that on occasion the crews reached their 16-hour work limit and had to be replaced out on the detour. The Brill motor car made its regular run between Cotton Plant and Helena, swinging around at the north end of the run on an improvised turntable at McClelland.

While the washout situation dragged out over the summer, bad news was received about the sale of the property to the Ohio interests. According to Interstate Commerce Commission records, the deal fell through over a difference of $50,000 in the purchase price. Another misfortune for the M. & A. Meanwhile, the expensive re-routing of trains continued to be a drain on the treasury.

Clearly, the washout should be repaired in some way. The task was far from insurmountable, and Lewie Watkins knew it. But it seemed that his Texas bosses would not give him independence of action and at the July 14 meeting of the M. & A. board of directors, he submitted his resignation with the effective date of August 1. The resignation was accepted, but Watkins did agree to remain as vice president and treasurer, primarily in a consultative capacity. Malcolm Putty was elected president as his replacement.* An operating man from the Rock Island, C. C. Fertig, was brought in as general manager.

And still the gap in the line existed. The war with Japan ended September 2, concurrent with the start of repair work. A 1,600-foot "shoo fly" detour was built around the gaping "blue hole," and on October 26, almost seven months since the washout, traffic between Kensett and Fargo once again moved over M. & A. rails. For the rest of the year operations were smooth enough, but the move into peacetime started cutting into the tonnage. For example, shipments of high-rated explosives reached 2,617 carloads in 1944; in 1945 the total was 1,539, and the shipments had been eliminated completely by the end of the year.

The financial results for 1945 were terrible: operating revenues were down 16% from the previous year, and stood at $2,158,641; and for the first time the M. & A. net was in the red — to the tune of $319,196! The question might well be asked: "How could such a drastic change in net income happen?" The answer is in the following figures:

---

*Putty had been elected president of the Wichita Falls & Southern on January 1, 1944, Orville Bullington moving up to chairman of the board.

The crew gets in the picture with big No. 40 before the last freight run north out of Harrison on September 6, 1946. One of the last passenger runs on the M. & A. is depicted below, as cream cans are unloaded at Eureka Springs. The JOHN E. MARTINEAU had been battered by a collision four days earlier and generally seems ready for the grave. Open windows indicate that the air-conditioning is not in service. By this time the other streamliner had been so badly damaged that it had to be replaced by a steam train. (Above: E. G. Baker; below: C. E. Hull)

War and weeds appear to be taking their toll as No. 50, above, pulls the northbound freight out of Harrison yards in 1944 or 1945. No. 20 and its two-car consist have just concluded the last passenger run on the North Arkansas. The date is September 7, 1946, and the train has arrived at Harrison from Kensett. Before being tucked away, train and crew stand for a final photograph. *(Two pictures: E. G. Baker)*

| | 1944 | 1945 |
|---|---|---|
| Total operating revenue | $2,575,273 | $2,158,641 |
| Railway operating expense | | |
| Transportation | 858,041 | 1,017,357 |
| Other | 1,176,456 | 1,185,449 |
| | 2,034,497 | 2,202,806 |
| Railway tax accruals | 187,008 | 35,613(cr.) |
| Rents payable | | |
| Hire of freight cars | 158,995 | 220,713 |
| Rent for locomotives | 44,142 | 72,691 |
| Other | 19,551 | 19,653 |
| | 222,688 | 313,057 |
| Other income | −41,081 | 2,413 |
| Net income | $89,999 | −$319,196 |

It can be seen that the "transportation ratio" (transportation expense to operating revenue) soared clear out of proportion, because of the detoured freight and general slow movements. Train accidents were the highest ever — 152 accidents per million engine miles, compared with an average of 8.3 for the western Class I railroads. It can also be seen that the slow train movements accounted for much higher per diem charges on freight cars, since the total cars handled was about the same for the two years. The net effect of all this was that the surplus, which had built up to more than $300,000 in early 1945, was completely wiped out.

The new year of 1946 saw the Missouri & Arkansas Railway Co. as a completely lost cause. Clearly, the owners were pulling out. Station buildings were being sold, and even replacement rail was being sold instead of installed. The high accident rate continued for maintenance of way work was desultory and generally uninspired. The road was losing money every month. The specter of death was hanging over the entire property.

To add to this grievous picture, new labor problems arose. On a national scale the unions began agitation for increases in wages — following the patterns set in 1943. There was the continuum of negotiation, strike vote, strike deferment, mediation . . . finally ending in President Truman taking over the railroads and forcing a compromise settlement on May 26 of 18½ cents per hour, with 15 cents per hour retroactive to January 1. The unions were still not happy; this represented less than 12% increase for many of the workers, not as much as they claimed the cost of living to have increased.

Naturally, the M. & A. was not going along with such a settlement. Putty stated flatly that there would be no wage increases; if the workers chose to strike, he would simply close down the business. Funds were just not available. Nevertheless, the Brotherhood of Railroad Trainmen took a strike vote, and then scheduled a walkout at 6 p.m. on Friday, July 19. Knowing this, the M. & A. board called a special meeting on July 17 and resolved to apply for abandonment if the walkout took place.

The walkout didn't come off. The men weren't that eager to quit, and they knew that Putty was serious in his intentions not to pay an increase. The delay was attributed to pending mediation in Washington. But the future of the road was clear. Mayor E. T. Parker of Harrison sent out an urgent plea for purchasers of the road to come forth; he stated that the owners were known to be negotiating with a scrap dealer to take over the property. The July 25, 1946 issue of the *Harrison Daily Times* had this comment:

> Demise of railroad predicted. The last hours [of the railroad] are passing quietly despite the [labor] dispute. After years of serious and strenuous fighting between management of the M. & N. A. railway and its employees, it comes as an anticlimax that the final death struggle is unmarked by the customary controversy.

Jesse Lewis Russell, prominent North Arkansas newspaperman, remarked that the "Swan song of the M. & A. railroad is now in the making . . . it may be said that as an enterprise it was conceived in speculation and born in desperation. . . " And now it was dying in silent despair.

The month of August dragged by, with wage talks continuing through the National Mediation Board. Through the heat of the summer, things seemed pretty lifeless along the line, but news did develop late in the month. On the morning of August 23, motor car No. 705, the THOMAS C. McRAE, left Neosho on schedule and proceeded to make its routine stops along the line. At the controls was Joe Cowan, a veteran of steam days on the railroad; the rest of the crew included A. J. Heath, conductor, and a brakeman. Also aboard was a mail clerk, an expressman, and about 10 or 12 passengers.

Cowan pulled out of the Alpena station at 11:41 a.m., 37 minutes late, chugged along the steady grade up to Batavia, and then began to coast down the grade to Harrison. As he neared the grade crossing for highways 62-65 just north of Harrison, he was clicking along at the maximum allowable speed of 35 miles per hour. Also nearing the crossing was a milk truck driven by Floyd Hair. As the reader has surmised, motor car and truck met at the crossing, the impact derailing the motor car, demolishing the truck, and killing both Cowan and Hair.

Fortunately, there were no other serious injuries. The motor car was judged to be lost to continued service, and was set aside to be cannibalized for parts to keep the other motor car running. Engine No. 20 and two of the ancient passenger cars were called into service, and engine No. 21 was brought up from the south end for standby. On September 2, the other motor car, the JOHN L. MARTINEAU, collided with a truck and car at the highway 62 crossing just west of Green Forest; there were no serious injuries, but motorman Claude Gibson was unable to complete the run to Neosho. (His car had killed a Bellefonte farmer three months earlier, and that plus the present and August 23 incidents completely unnerved him.)

And so the clouds of death continued to envelop the M. & A. On Thursday, September 5, at 2:30 p.m. notice was served to management that the freight trainmen would go off the job at 6:00 p.m. Friday, and the passenger trainmen would do the same at 6:00 p.m. on the following day. Compliance of the passenger and freight enginemen with this edict was expected. The unions had previously promised that the railroad would have at least 48 hours' notice of a walkout, but with this short notice, about all management could do was place an embargo on incoming shipments and do a bit of last minute clearing of cars containing perishables.

The freight trains (manifest only, the locals had long since been taken off) were duly tied up at terminals: No. 11 at Harrison and Helena, and No. 12 at Heber Springs and Joplin. On the following day, September 7, the passenger trains made their last runs in peace and quiet. If railfans had been interested, they would not have had much notice to arrange to ride the last runs. The Brill "doodlebug" made an uneventful round trip out of Kensett and was then backed into the motor car shed at the Kensett yards. The JOHN L. MARTINEAU left Neosho on schedule, dropped its final cargo at the Harrison depot around noontime, and wound up parked beside the Harrison roundhouse. Engine No. 20 pulled its two dusty, red cars up from Kensett to Harrison without fanfare. After pausing at the Harrison depot it backed the train over to the yards and bowed to a "last amenity" a pose for the camera of Harrisonite E. G. Baker. Thus ended all scheduled movements on the M. & A.

During the week of September 8 regular engineers and firemen, aided by officials as crew members, were used for mopping-up operations. On September 11, the enginemen joined the striking trainmen. By September 13 only about 150 foreign cars remained on the line. By September 20 these cars were removed, and shutdown arrangements were complete. The last wheels had turned. The North Arkansas Line was well along in its final death struggle. . .

**Missouri and Arkansas Railway Company**

**1936**

~ Mr. H. R. Thompson - No. 231

**Pass** Traveling Freight Agent
Federal Barge Lines

GOOD BETWEEN ALL STATIONS UNTIL JANUARY 31, 1937, UNLESS OTHERWISE
SPECIFIED HEREON, AND SUBJECT TO CONDITIONS ON BACK

VALID WHEN COUNTERSIGNED BY MYSELF OR D. C. KUDER

COUNTERSIGNED BY

VICE-PRES. & GEN'L. MGR.

The last steam run came into Eureka Springs September 6, 1946. The locomotive is unidentified, but likely No. 21. The southbound train appears to be relaxing the rule requiring trains to back into Eureka Springs from Junction. The last locomotives to move on the North Arkansas finally came to rest just west of the roundhouse at Harrison, below. Freight engine No. 40 was used for mopping-up operations while No. 20 and No. 62 were used for general switching. The time is September, 1946, and the engines will not move until salvage operations begin in April 1949.

*(Above: C. E. Hull; below: E. G. Baker)*

Winter of 1946-1947 finds the Eureka Springs depot deserted, above, with no markings on the train bulletin and piles of crossties that will have to be shipped out by truck. By 1948 weeds had overgrown much of the right of way. The picture below was taken from tracks at Beaver (Narrows in the early years), looking east toward the White River bridge.

*(Two pictures: C. E. Hull)*

# Chapter Eight

# Demise and Reincarnation

The Missouri & Arkansas Railway operations did halt in September 1946, and there could be no mistake about that. Almost as if an "operation mothball" had been planned and activated, supervisory crews put things in an orderly condition and then they disappeared from the open scene. Mikado locomotives 34 and 36 were stored in the Kensett engine house, along with the Brill motor car No. 605. Mikados 32 and 33 plus several cabooses and service cars were left in the open at Heber Springs. Various pieces of company rolling stock were grouped at Neosho, Eureka Springs, Leslie, and Kensett. All the rest of the locomotives and rolling stock were lined up in and around the Harrison roundhouse. Clearly, there was no thought of early resumption of operations. In some ways, history of 1921 seemed to be repeating itself; but there was one important difference, the closing down of the road was accompanied by no violence over labor-management differences.

The Kells lost no time in unburdening themselves of their albatross. By approval of the board of directors at a special meeting on September 16, Malcolm Putty prepared an abandonment petition and mailed it to the Interstate Commerce Commission on September 21. The reasons for asking for abandonment were the expected ones: insufficient traffic, high costs of operation, and a history of consistent losses. When the petition became public knowledge, a number of petitions to intervene were submitted to the ICC, one of them in the name of the State of Arkansas by

Attorney General Guy E. Williams. On October 30 the ICC Questionnaire, asking for detailed background on the abandonment petition, was returned to the ICC by Putty.

The filled-out Questionnaire was a sad commentary on the attention, or lack of it, given to the property by the Kells during the last years of operation. Of the 23 locomotives owned* only 13 were listed as "serviceable," and of those only four were considered in 75% or better condition. The rail was stated to be generally curve-worn, surface-bent, and in need of tie plates. Ballast was adequate only north of Harrison. Tie condition was "poor, particularly between Kensett and Helena"; about 20% of the ties were creosoted** and in good shape while most of the rest were in poor shape and 25% of them required immediate replacement. Steel bridges were thought to be in good condition, save one: the large swing span across the White River at Georgetown would have to have a new and very expensive center pier. Service equipment, shop machinery, and so on were all given an inferior rating. Importantly, the net salvage value of the property was listed as $828,361.

Rumors flew fast and thick about the sale of the property to salvage dealers. As would later be revealed, a purchase contract was actually signed on November 15, 1946. The purchasers were noted only as "Meyer P. Gross, of South Orange, N. J., and Associates." Also as later disclosed, the contract amount was $645,000, with the purchasers to assume about $155,000 in outstanding debts.

During operation of the M. & A., the Kell family had received $87,500 in dividends and $258,831 in salaries, rents, and other payments. It was generally concluded that the Kells profited excessively from the sale, since the "purchase price" in 1935 had been $350,000. Actually, as stated in Chapters 6 and 7, Frank Kell had invested about a million dollars in the road. Thus, the Kells

---

*Including Nos. 60, 61, 62, 1915 and 1972, purchased from the Cotton Belt and Rock Island in early 1946. Nos. 14 and 15 were still around, but were still on lease from the Wichita Falls and Southern.

**Creosoted crossties and bridge members had been used only since 1940. Of the 1,371,000 ties in the main line, 203,791 were creosoted. Of the 295 open deck pile and frame trestles, 105 had creosoted piling.

got their money back, and the Gross interests picked up the property at its salvage value. It would be difficult to question these business dealings.

The new ownership of the road moved rapidly. At a board meeting on November 18, new officers and directors were named:

| | |
|---|---|
| E. R. Vallance | President and Director |
| M. D. Putty | Vice President |
| S. A. Joffe | Secretary-Treasurer and Director |
| L. A. Watkins | Director |
| W. P. Watkins | Director |
| D. D. Mundree | Director |

Vallance, Joffe, and Mundree were newcomers, and represented the new owners. Elmer Vallance moved to Harrison from Wichita, Kansas, where he had worked for the Arkansas Valley Railway (earlier Arkansas Valley Interurban) for over 35 years, being General Manager when the road was abandoned. Putty's appointment was obviously transitional and he moved back to Wichita Falls. Joffe and Mundree remained in the East with the owners' management activity.

The identity of the purchasers was revealed in the transfer of the 3,500 shares of M. & A. stock:

| | |
|---|---|
| Saul S. Frankel, Rochester, N. Y. | 1,747 shares |
| Murray M. Salzberg, New York, N. Y. | 1,048 " |
| Harry E. Salzberg, New York, N. Y. | 350 " |
| Meyer P. Gross, South Orange, N. J. | 262 " |
| Morris H. Snerson, White Plains, N. Y. | 88 " |
| | 3,495 shares |

The other five shares were, for legal purposes, issued to the five directors.

This group was well known in railroad circles as the "Salzberg interests." It was not entirely a salvage group and had the reputation of picking up short lines and operating them so long as they were profitable. In 1946 they were operating four lines, and had recently scrapped another, the Arkansas Valley Railway. Which, of course, explains why E. R. Vallance made the move to Harrison.

A minimum staff maintained headquarters in the operations building at the Harrison

As 1946 closed, the dusk of inactivity had settled over the North Arkansas. Motorists entering Harrison from the south on Highway 65 could not help but notice and wonder at the mute locomotives and rolling stock lined up in the yards below. There was a strange silence pervading the shops where, for so many years there had been a familiar clang. Crossing frogs at Kensett, Fargo, Wheatley, and North Lexa had been pulled up. Debris was beginning to accumulate and clutter the mainline tracks, with only the chill of winter preventing weeds from obscuring the rusting rails. No longer could the residents of Marshall hear the southbound manifest "stack talk" as it fought its way up the hill to Baker or the "Blue Goose" streamliner sound its horn for the crossing east of town. Along the line the reaction was the same: "We sure miss those trains!"

There was life, however, in efforts of the citizenry to save the railroad from the Salzbergs. In early 1947 Arkansas State Senator Ernest Nicholson of Harrison introduced a bill that would permit the state to appoint a receiver of the M. & A. The bill passed, but before Governor Ben Laney could sign it into law, the owners moved quickly to petition for federal receivership. This was to be an equity, not bankruptcy receivership. The petition alleged that the property was not insolvent but that a receivership was necessary in order to prevent waste and avoid a multiplicity of suits. On February 14, 1947, Federal Judge John E. Miller acted favorably on the petition and appointed as co-receivers W. S. Walker and C. C. Alexander. Both men were residents of Harrison and had prior experience with the M. & N. A. Walker had been an M. & N. A. attorney and Alexander, executive vice president of the Security Bank, had been a director of the M. & N. A. for about six years. Thus, the North Arkansas was back in receivership for the *third* time in its turbulent career!

Abandonment hearings began on February 24 in Little Rock, with ICC examiner Jerome K. Lyle presiding. Considerable testimony was taken, most of it to the point that abandonment of the M. & A. would work a severe economic hardship on the region served. One interesting and important point developed was that after removal of Office of Price Administration price ceilings on steel scrap in late 1946 the salvage value of the M. & A. had risen with scrap prices and was now figured at $2,032,396. According to ICC policy, this was the price that the owners could now ask for the property, and there were no purchasers around that could pay the price.

After the second day of hearings, Arkansas Attorney General Williams asked for an adjournment of the hearings until the state could make an economic survey of the future profitability of the line as well as the economic potential of the region. The increased price of the property did appear to introduce new concerns, and the examiner granted a 60-day adjournment.

The state and the citizens joined forces in obtaining an appraisal of the property, each contributing $15,000. The prestigious consulting engineering firm of Coverdale and Colpitts was engaged to make a fast study of the rehabilitation needs and profit potential of the M. & A. To head the study was a Partner of the firm, Miles C. Kennedy, a man of considerable reputation in railroad engineering* and a director of several lines. Mr. Kennedy and his party started their survey at Neosho on March 11 and worked their way down the line in a motor inspection car. For most of their work, however, they headquartered at the Seville Hotel in Harrison.

The Kennedy study turned out to be interesting, if somewhat academic. It sought to establish the potential profitability of the road *if* it were placed in first-class condition and operated efficiently on a "secondary mainline" basis. The rehabilitation called for was extensive: all new 90-pound rail, 447,000 new creosoted crossties and switch ties, new ballast throughout, overhaul of the Georgetown bridge, and so on. And the total cost would be $7,-597,000! Further, $1,000,000 would be needed for diesel power. Including purchase from the Salzbergs, less credit for scrap, the total required investment would be around $9,000,000.

Kennedy figured that with such first-rate facilities the road could net some $532,000 annually from a $2,058,000 gross. This would represent a six per cent return on the total investment, marginal at best. And what sort of angel could be found with nine

---

*And co-author (with G. H. Burgess) of *Centennial History of the Pennsylvania Railroad Company, 1846-1946*, published in 1949.

million dollars of venture capital at his disposal? Yes, the study did seem to be a bit on the academic side.

When abandonment hearings were resumed in Little Rock on April 22, Mr. Kennedy presented his report and gave his interpretation of the handling of the road by the Kells:

> When Frank Kell died there was a distinct showing in the operating statistics . . . that when or with the death of Mr. Kell a lot of indifference suddenly developed in the whole operation and nobody could have devoted much attention to it without getting better results . . .

Attorney General Williams called many other witnesses to the stand, and all of them testified to such Kell directives as high rents on the locomotives from Wichita Falls, deferment of essential maintenance, and so on. But all this seemed after the fact and not pertinent. When Meyer P. Gross appeared on the witness stand, he simply concurred with the Kennedy report; some nine million dollars would be required to put the property back in first-class operating condition, and in his opinion this would not be a judicious investment. The hearings ended on April 24 with testimony on the public need for reactiving the rail service, not necessarily on a first-class basis.

On May 14 the State of Arkansas asked for the appointment of new (and presumably more favorable) receivers. Judge Miller chose not to do this, but did appoint a third co-receiver, Jordan B. Lambert of Helena. Lambert was known to be a strong advocate of reactivating the road. Miller charged co-receivers Walker, Alexander, and Lambert to seek a stay of abandonment for at least 90 days, during which time they were to formulate a plan for resuming operations.

This charge was not an easy one to deal with. The receivers strove diligently to locate bona fide purchasing interest. Several potential investors were brought in to inspect the property, including the Kansas City Southern and Rock Island railroads, the former secretary of war Harry Woodring, Kelly Gibson, a Tulsa businessman, and others. A "Citizens Rehabilitation Committee," headed by Lambert, was formed to develop local interest in purchase.

But no purchasers could put up the two million dollar minimum to take the road off the hands of the Salzbergs. So the receivers tried another approach: why not get the court's permission to issue receiver's certificates and force the owners to operate the road? The receivers thought they could sell $100,000 in certificates locally, with which amount they could put the Harrison-Seligman section back in operation. After all, this section produced about 36 per cent of the on-line revenue in recent years. For the first 12 months, they estimated $367,000 gross and $56,000 net before taxes and interest. A Kansas City civil engineer, H. C. Lamberton, in a later report corroborated their finding that the Seligman-Harrison stretch was in pretty good condition and could be placed in operation in 30 days with an outlay of $55,000.

The receivers presented this plan to Judge Miller in a report dated August 6, 1947. But there were too many "ifs" and Miller turned it down. From this point on, there were many more "plans" for resuming operations, but no real venture capital. Understandably, the owners were getting impatient. They would gladly sell the property for the net salvage value of $2,000,000, but if there were no buyers, then they wanted to get on with the business of tearing up the rails and reclaiming their $800,000 investment. Because of continuing plans, and at the instigation of the State of Arkansas, the Interstate Commerce Commission seemed in no hurry to come to the aid of the Salzbergs. Finally, on August 9, 1948, the I.C.C. handed down the decision for abandonment, with a final date of October 9 allowing 60 days for a possible purchaser. The Commission had concluded that highways would serve the area adequately and that the high cost of rehabilitation had discouraged all prudent investors.

This decision opened the way for a group of businessmen from Helena and Cotton Plant to deal directly with the Salzbergs on the purchase of the line between those two cities. A mutually satisfactory agreement was reached, and this encouraged the same business group to consider purchasing the Harrison shops and yards and then constructing a new nine-mile line north of Harrison to connect with the Missouri Pacific near Bergman. Such a line had been discussed for years as an alternate rail outlet for

The author snapped these views of the Kensett yards in April 1949, just before abandonment became official. The left view is to the south and shows some of the crude equipment used there. The right view shows the engine-house with extension built for the motor cars. Resting quietly in the stalls are locomotives 36 and 34 and Brill motor car 706.

Harrison, and the Missouri Pacific had considered it favorably from time to time.

As the October 9 final abandonment date approached, the citizens began to get frantic. They prevailed on Governor Ben Laney to appeal to the I. C. C. for a 120-day extension, in order to permit the State Legislature (which would re-convene in January) to consider purchase of the road by the State of Arkansas. Both the Salzbergs and the new Helena-Cotton Plant group opposed the extension. On October 8, the latter group filed articles of association for the Helena & Northwestern Railway Co., an organization to purchase and operate the 53.5 miles of line from the Cotton Plant depot to the Illinois Central connection at Helena.

The I. C. C. denied Governor Laney's appeal, but in a last minute pressure play acquiesced and extended the deadline to December 7. A new argument was to be heard by the full eleven-man commission on November 12. The pressure, incidentally, was applied on I. C. C. Chairman William Lee by the eminent Arkansas Senators John McClellan and J. William Fulbright.

At the Washington hearing on November 12, Attorney General Guy Williams sought a further extension of time in order to make further efforts for sale. He said, "We believe that the next legislature will do something about it. Governor-elect Sidney McMath has promised the people he will do everything in his power to get the railroad running again." He went on to say that the legislature might be asked to appropriate several million dollars to finance purchase and rehabilitation. He asked for 120 days and got them. The abandonment date would now be April 9, 1949.

In early 1949 it became clear that the State of Arkansas was not going to put up any money for the M. & A. The down-state legislators particularly opposed the idea. But the Salzbergs were not certain that some new delaying tactics might not be developed. For example, the state was considering a special tax on scrap iron that could be directed toward the Salzbergs but not to others selling scrap. To bring things to a head, the Salzbergs decided to make a positive move toward settlement. Their intentions were announced in the February 21, 1949, Harrison Times under the large headline "Owners Plan to Resume Operation of M & A Railroad."

Remains of streamliner 705, the THOMAS C. MCRAE were still at Harrison when they were photographed in the summer of 1948, two years after its encounter with a milk train. Steam action returned to the North Arkansas for a time. In April 1949, below, No. 20 is fired up to assist in salvage work south of Harrison and in rehabilitation work north of there. The locomotive was transferred to the books of the Arkansas & Ozarks and operated as late as December 1949. (*Two pictures: C. W. Witbeck; below: courtesy National Museum of Transport*)

One problem in rehabilitating the Seligman-Harrison segment by the Arkansas & Ozarks was the tunnel. This 1948 view of the east portal shows that some clearing will be required. *(E. G. Baker)*

The Salzberg plan had these key elements:

1. Operation of the Seligman-Harrison section by the owners.
2. Sale of the Cotton Plant-Helena section to the Helena and Northwestern, as previously planned.
3. Sale of the Heber Springs-Kensett section to a Heber Springs group headed by businessman A. C. Kennedy.
4. Operation of the Harrison-Leslie section by the owners, but with a guarantee by the citizens that there would be no losses.
5. Abandonment of Neosho-Wayne, Leslie-Heber Springs, and Kensett-Cotton Plant sections.

This plan had some appeal to the citizens. The line south of Leslie had been heavily damaged by Little Red River floods a few weeks earlier; thus it represented a problem of rehabilitation and would be best left alone. The Kensett-Cotton Plant segment had a long history of washouts and problems with the large bridge at Georgetown; furthermore, it could be by-passed by use of the Rock Island between Searcy and Wheatley. The Neosho-Wayne segment was not a large producer of revenue, and was in effect paralleled by the Frisco. The real question was whether the Harrison-Leslie segment had enough business potential to warrant a guarantee by the citizens.

The Salzbergs demonstrated the seriousness of their intentions by applying to the Arkansas Public Service Commission for a charter to operate the Seligman-Harrison segment. The charter was approved on March 4, 1949, in the name of the Arkansas & Ozarks Railway Co. Authorized capitalization was $400,000. Several residents of Harrison and Berryville were listed as subscribers to initial stock, but the major owners would be, of course, the Salzberg group. Final approval of the Arkansas & Ozarks by the I. C. C. would have to wait for formal abandonment of the M. & A.

Various last-ditch efforts to save the entire line continued, but when the final abandonment date of April 6 arrived, there was no appeal for an extension of time. Thus came the end of the Missouri & Arkansas Railway as an operating entity; some months later, on

July 14, it would be finally dissolved as a business. The demise of the M. & A. represented the longest railroad abandonment to have taken place in the United States.*

After the April 6 abandonment decision, activity mounted in three separate efforts: salvaging of track, bridges, equipment, and other properties that would not be used in the residue operating schemes; rehabilitation of the Arkansas & Ozarks line from Harrison to Seligman; and rehabilitation of the Helena & Northwestern line from Helena to Cotton Plant. Unfortunately, there was little activity connected with the plans to reactivate the Harrison-Leslie and Heber Springs-Kensett segments, and these plans fell by the wayside.

Salvage operations were headed by James Ashley, a veteran operating man whose background included assignments with the Salzberg interests. After arriving in Harrison and sizing up the situation, Ashley elected to put ten-wheeler locomotive No. 20 back in operation to handle movements of salvaged materials as well as to serve the A. & O. in its rehabilitation needs. No. 20 had weathered for almost three years but appeared to be in sound condition. To the surprise of everyone, the "old girl" fired up nicely and moved easily!

Crews wielding acetylene torches attacked the faithful and defenseless locomotives parked in and around the shops. No. 20 was used to pull the monsters into scrapping positions. Only No. 21, another ten-wheeler was spared; Ashley fired her up for use as a standby for No. 20. Separate crews moved in on the locomotives stored at Heber Springs and Kensett. Track gangs started in at Leslie and worked their way north, taking up all rails, reusable crossties, and miscellaneous scrap metal. Many station buildings and some bridges were left in place, their cost of removal exceeding their salvage value.

By the end of the summer of 1949 most of the salvage operations on the north end were completed. Between Leslie and Cotton Plant, track removal went more slowly and was not completed by the end of the year. In this section, the only through-truss

_____

*In terms of route miles owned, the next longest at the time being the Colorado Midland (261 miles).

bridge to be dismantled was the one at Georgetown; some of the others survive to this day.

Efforts to place the Arkansas & Ozarks and Helena & Northwestern lines in operation proceeded concurrently with the aforementioned salvage work. For convenience in this narrative, the stories of these two lines will be told separately and will cover their entire corporate lives.

### Helena & Northwestern Railway

Organizers of the H. & N. W. were J. H. Crain, a wealthy lawyer and landowner of Wilson, Arkansas; E. T. Hornor, banker and automobile dealer of Helena; J. B. Lambert, Helena realtor and one of the receivers of the M. & A.; Ben C. White, traffic manager of the Southwest Veneer Co. at Cotton Plant; and Helena businessmen W. J. Denton and Otis Howe. These people enlisted the aid of an experienced railroad man, C. W. Ferguson, of Star City, Arkansas, for planning of operations and to serve as secretary to the board of directors (which board comprised the gentlemen listed above). The first board meeting was held September 30, 1948; articles of association were filed with the Arkansas Secretary of State on October 8, 1948; and on the following day application to the I. C. C. was made for a certificate of public convenience and public necessity authorizing acquisition and operation of the 53.5-mile section of the M. & A. between Cotton Plant and Helena.

Authorized capital stock was $100,000 preferred (5% cumulative) at $100 par and $100,000 common at $100 par. By the time of final M. & A. abandonment on April 6, 1949, over $100,000 had been raised and the Helena-Cotton Plant trackage had been purchased from the Salzsbergs for $300,000. For the latter $100,000 was paid in cash and a first mortgage note was signed for the remaining $200,000. The purchase price included some 30,000 creosoted crossties from Kensett-Cotton Plant segment, about a third of the total and a high fraction for the M. & A. (But it was necessary for the H. & N. W. to remove these ties.)

The purchased line was not in dreadful condition. The rail was all original 65-pound variety, but because of light loadings

As backup for No. 20, locomotive No. 21 was fired up at Harrison. The June 1949 picture, above, shows her at work in the Harrison yards. Down on the south end, the Helena & Northwestern started operations in September 1949 with ex-Apalachicola Northern steam locomotives 200 and 201. Oil-burner 201 is shown below in the Helena yards.

*(Above: E. G. Baker; below: H. K. Vollrath collection)*

and absence of curves, it was in good condition. Of the 12 pile trestles, 10 had creosoted piling, but none of the 26 frame trestles had creosoted members. With the ties purchased from the M. &. A., about half of the total on the main line would be creosoted. With weeds removed, some drainage ditches opened, and crossing frogs at Fargo, Wheatley, and North Lexa replaced, the line could be deemed operational.

By mid-summer of 1949 three crews were out reworking the line, and two steam locomotives had been purchased. The latter were located at the Apalachicola Northern engine house in Port St. Joe, Florida. Built by the Cooke Locomotive Works in 1922, both engines were originally equipped with cabbage stacks for wood burning. On the A. N. they had been obsoleted by diesel power, but for the H. & N. W. they were a real answer to an urgent need. Their light axle loading of 27,000 pounds would be kind to the old track, their mechanical condition was sound, and they cost very little more than their value as scrap metal. The longer range thinking of the H. & N. W. was, of course, to use diesel power.

The Missouri Pacific Lines went out on strike on September 9, 1949, and this deprived Helena industry of sorely-needed rail service. Pressure mounted for the H. & N. W. to go into operation and at least handle switching chores on cars routed to and from the Illinois Central connection. On September 14 the Illinois Central transfer ferry "Pelican" made a special trip across the Mississippi to pick up the "new" locomotives of the H. & N. W. On the next day one of the engines, coal-burner No. 200 (the other engine, No. 201, was an oil-burner), started switching service.

Preparations for line-haul service were expedited, and the announcement was soon made that the first train to Cotton Plant would depart from Helena on October 11. Thereafter, there would be a round trip daily except Sunday with departure from Helena at 6:00 a.m. and arrival at Cotton Plant at 11:00 a.m.; for the return trip departure from Cotton Plant would be at 1:00 p.m. with arrival at Helena at 4:00 p.m. While one engine was on the road, the other would handle switching at Helena. No provision was made initially to turn the engines at Cotton Plant, although the turntable and other facilities at Helena would be used. Carload only freight would be handled.

The big opening day of October 11 arrived, but it was destined to have its difficult moments. No. 201 with 12 cars and a caboose was lined up at the Illinois Central water tank, but because the crew was called late, it didn't get moving until 8:00 a.m. At Cotton Plant, schools, banks, and stores were scheduled to close for the grand arrival celebration at 11:30 so the event was rescheduled for 1:30 p.m. But there were unexpected delays at the business office (ex-depot) at West Helena; problems of switching cars at Wheatley and Fargo; and things got further and further behind schedule. Frustration set in on the crew: Ray Thomas, engineer (formerly M. & A.); T. C. Edwards, fireman; C. C. Adkinson, conductor; and Fred McEntire and Fred Bell, brakemen. General Manager Ferguson rode along impatiently.

Meanwhile, the Cotton Plant greeters dwindled in number, only a few hardy souls sticking it out. At 4:00 p.m. there was the shrill blast of a steam whistle, and townspeople began to run for the depot. Alas! It was only the whistle of a veneer plant signalling a shift change. Finally, at 5:07 p.m., the real locomotive whistle was heard, and No. 201 rolled up to the old M. & N. A. station. Several hundred loyal citizens gathered about the first train into town in over three years. Despite the delays, everyone seemed happy.

Troubles continued on the next day. On the return trip, with eight cars out of Wheatley, the train was halted at Moro because of a suspicious-looking trestle. The *Helena World* headlined it "Helena's New Choo Choo Bogged Down Near Moro Because of Weak Bridge; Officials are Undaunted." Soon afterward train movements settled into routine activity.

At the end of 1949, there was a net loss of $1,030 on $42,638 gross business, not bad for a start. About 60 carloads a week were averaged. Stock subscriptions at the time had reached $127,900, but these had barely covered the down payment to the M. & A. plus the costs of locomotives, rolling stock, and right of way rehabilitation. Cash stood at only $2,191. Still hopes were high for an improvement in general economic conditions (1949 and 1950 before the Korean War were recession periods) and a gradual buildup of H. & N. W. business. The hopes included the securing of bridge traffic from the Cotton Belt and the Rock Island.

During 1950 it became clear that the H. & N. W. was in for trouble. Business continued to lag. The right of way needed additional attention, bridges needed rebuilding and the roadbed needed the advantages of ballast. Interest to the Salzbergs went past due and interline settlements lagged. The steam locomotives clearly did not represent the motive power efficiency that was needed. And, to top it off, there was a mutual dissatisfaction between General Manager Ferguson and the Board of Directors.

Positive action was taken to correct these problems. A 70-ton diesel locomotive was purchased from General Electric. Ferguson was replaced by Walter Shannon, M. & N. A.-M. & A. agent at West Helena for many years. An application was made for a $400,-000 loan from the R. F. C., proceeds of which would be used to pay off the Salzbergs and improve the physical facilities. The final financial data for 1950 showed $170,637 operating revenues, $156,430 operating expenses and a net loss of $26,883 after taking into account taxes and equipment rents. At the time $55,758 was still owed on the $68,150 purchase of the diesel locomotive, and the 1950 payment of $40,000 on the $200,000 mortgage held by the Salzbergs had been passed. Clearly, the only thing that could bale out the company was a significant increase in business.

All of the H. & N. W. news in 1951 was of the bad variety. In February, J. H. Crain resigned as president and Fred W. Schatz was elected to take his place. Messrs. Hornor and Shannon went to Chicago to attempt to get the Rock Island to route freight via H. & N. W. and the Wheatley connection. On April 27 the Salzbergs filed suit to foreclose the $200,000 mortgage. On May 21, the stockholders resolved to place the railroad in bankruptcy. Shortly afterward, the I. C. C. refused permission for the railroad to apply for the R. F. C. loan. Finally, on July 11, the stockholders voted to abandon the property. The abandonment application to the I. C. C. listed these reasons:

1. For the 17 months ending May 31, net losses totalled approximately $43,000.

2. Current indebtedness covering unpaid open accounts, interline settlements, and unpaid installments on the funded debt totalled approximately $182,000.

3. The Rock Island and Cotton Belt lines had refused to open through routes to enable the H. & N. W. to handle overhead traffic through the Helena gateway.

4. The I. C. C. had turned down the R. F. C. loan.

5. The officers and directors of the company had exhausted all possible means to continue the operation of the company, and further operation on a sound financial basis would not be possible.

The local business of the H. & N. W. had consisted of rice, cotton, wood products, logs, and general merchandise. Most of the shipments ran through between Cotton Plant and Helena. Without bridge traffic, and with minimal business generated at intermediate points, a 53.5-mile line could not be supported.

Interstate Commerce Commission hearings were duly held, and operations of the H. & N. W. continued on a bare-bones basis. On November 2, 1951, abandonment was authorized and the trains stopped rolling. The two years of operation had been a trying and expensive experience for a small group of Arkansas businessmen. After liquidating all assets it turned out that the $78,800 in common stock was completely worthless.

One asset liquidated was the right of way, trackage, and related facilities between Cotton Plant and Fargo. This property was sold for $50,725 to the Cotton Plant-Fargo Railway in January 1952. More will be said about this six-mile short line that today represents the last operating segment of the old North Arkansas Line.

## Arkansas & Ozarks Railway

It has been noted that on March 4, 1949, the Salzberg interests obtained an Arkansas charter to operate the Arkansas & Ozarks Railway Co. On March 14, this newly chartered company applied to the I. C. C. for authority to acquire and operate the 65.93 miles of M. & A. from Seligman to Harrison, plus the 3.16 miles from Freeman to Berryville. On April 11, the application was amended to include the 2.01 miles from Junction to Eureka Springs. The April 6 abandonment order for the M. & A. cleared away the obvious hurdle, and although the I. C. C. would not finally approve acquisition and grant a certificate of public convenience and necessity until January 19, 1950, preparations for operation went forward.

The main line from Seligman to Harrison had been better maintained than the rest of the line south of Harrison. Some 35.5 miles had replacement rail of 70 pounds or heavier. Occasional attempts had been made to ballast the line with creek gravel and chat. There were 66 wooden trestles, mostly of the frame bent type because of problems in driving piles into the rock bottoms of creek beds. For certain, it was 65.93 miles of up-and-down railroad, and it included that 2.6% killer grade just south of Seligman.

Capital stock in the amount of $200,000 was issued, in exchange for the property acquired, to the following:

|  | per cent |
|---|---|
| Saul S. Frankel | 25.0 |
| Murray M. Salzberg | 40.0 |
| Meyer P. Gross | 7.5 |
| Morris H. Snerson | 2.5 |
| Maurice Schwartz | 12.5 |
| Herman Schwartz | 12.5 |
|  | 100.0 |

who were owners, in the same proportion, of the M. & A. at the time of abandonment. Salzberg, Gross, and Snerson were given control by the I. C. C., and Gross functioned as the front man in all A. & O. dealings of the owners. The group advanced the A. & O. $40,000 in first mortgage 4% notes. An additional $200,000 stock was authorized, and there were minor subscriptions from citizens of the area. The books were kept open for one year, until March 4, 1950, for additional subscriptions, but such were few.

President of the A. & O. was S. A. Joffe, who had been affiliated with the owners at Rochester, New York; he moved to Harrison in April. In charge of rehabilitation was Joseph C. Bussey, general manager of the Salzbergs' Des Moines and Central Iowa line, and former chief engineer of the Monon line in Indiana. J. E. "Jack" Halter, mentioned earlier in these pages and formerly assistant chief operating officer of the M. & A., was named general superintendent of the A. & O. The public announcement was made that the A. & O. would employ about 40 people.

Rehabilitation work started in April, concurrently with salvage work at Harrison and points south. Newspaper reports in May stated that a large crew was busy overhauling the Harrison-Berryville section and that another crew was at work north of Berryville. A slide at the tunnel kept the crews separated. Ten-wheeler No. 20 was officially transferred to A. & O. No. 20 and pulled work cars out of Harrison; the *Kansas City Star* of May 4, 1949, ran the headline "Old No. 20 is Rolling Along the M. & A. Tracks" and said further that "The engine now toots its way along a two-mile stretch of track through the picturesque Ozarks hill country and rapidly will expand its run as the line is reconditioned." In time, the slide at the tunnel was cleared and weeds were burned away. Faulty ties were replaced by ties taken up from the south end and inadequate rail was also replaced by south end material. Many sidings were removed for scrap. No attention was given to station buildings other than attempts to sell or lease them.

Operating plans for the A. & O. were developed by mid-1949. Initially, there would be three round trips weekly between Harrison and Seligman. A traveling agent would service the communities of Alpena, Green Forest, Berryville, and Eureka Springs. No less-than-carload freight would be handled. A crew of three (engineer, brakeman, conductor) non-union people would be used on each freight run with an added brakeman in Arkansas if the train length exceeded 23 cars, in compliance with the state full crew law. Diesel motive power would be used, and to this end two 70-ton diesel-electric road-switchers were ordered from General Electric. These units were rated at 660 horsepower and 41,300 pounds tractive effort; each one could pull about 20 empties or about eight loads up Seligman Hill. If indeed a significant amount of outbound freight from Harrison could be generated, then there would be a continuation of the usual "doubling" of the hill.

Preparations for startup lagged during the latter part of 1949, ostensibly because the diesels were not ready and old No. 20 was not up to the regular chores of freight hauling. It was not until November 30 that the first diesel, No. 800, arrived on the scene. On the morning of that date Jess Watkins, veteran M. & A. engineer, and his fireman Ross McCullough steamed up No. 20 and ran it "light" over to Seligman to pick up the diesel. Mr. Joffe and Lon Holder, maintenance supervisor, went along for the ride. By late afternoon they had returned with No. 800 in tow.

Formal opening of operations was finally set for February 1, 1950, even though the second diesel unit, No. 900, had not yet arrived. Plans were made for suitable opening ceremonies at Harrison, with the Harrison High School Band to provide suitable music. Inclement weather forced a postponement of the ceremonies, although operations did begin. In fact, on Friday, February 3, the first return train from Seligman arrived at Harrison at 7:00 p.m. with two carload shipments. And on February 5, the second diesel was brought in. Opening ceremonies were rescheduled for Wednesday, February 8, at 10:30 a.m.

This time, things went off on schedule. As related by Bob Foresman in the *Tulsa Tribune,*

> Harrison is as proud as a new papa with twins. The old Missouri & Arkansas railroad resumed operations Wednesday under a new name, the Arkansas & Ozarks railroad . . . There was a big ceremony when the first train rolled up to the old passenger depot. It was a freight train, since passenger service has been abandoned.
>
> Two new General Electric diesel engines powered the train, and when it came round the bend the Harrison High School band struck up a tune. Then came speeches by rail officials, mayors and shippers from stations up and down the line.

S. A. Joffe pointed out that the A. & O. had spent $150,000 for the diesel locomotives and $100,000 on track rehabilitation. Now it was up to the citizens to make it all worthwhile. Charles C. Wine, chairman of the Arkansas Public Service Commission, made the principal address and admonished the people that "The future of this new road is in your hands. It must have your financial sup-

Arkansas & Ozarks opening ceremonies were held at Harrison. Above, the ritual begins as the train pulls out of the yards past the operations office. New diesels 800 and 900 are connected for multiple-unit operation. Below, the train approaches the crowd at the old passenger depot. Opposite above, the Harrison High School Band looks on, after speeches have concluded, when the train pulls on past the station. One of the new diesels is shown, opposite below, crossing high trestle 78-7 near Junction, en route to Harrison. (*Three pictures: Clyde Newman; opposite below: J. M. Gray*)

port." Included in the crowd were some oldtimers who witnessed the arrival of the first train into Harrison back in 1901, among them Dr. Troy Coffman, a dentist, J. L. Russell, newspaperman, G. F. Rea, father of Ralph Rea, the local postmaster and others. The event was covered by a special broadcast over Tulsa radio station KVOO. Yes, Harrison seemed proud of her new railroad — for the moment, at least.

Operations on the A. & O. soon settled into a routine. All trains were run as extras. Northbound runs to Seligman were on Monday, Wednesday, and Friday, the crew laying over in Seligman and bringing the train back on the following day. Two ex-M. & A. cabooses, Nos. 300 and 301, were used together with a dozen M. & A. holdover ballast and flatcars for work equipment. Freight to the A. & O. from the Frisco was the usual — building materials, petroleum products, feed, general merchandise. Outbound freight included drinking water from Eureka Springs, forest products, and farm products. The sound of the diesel horn of outbound freights as they moved up Dry Jordan valley in Harrison became a familiar message to the townspeople; not like the melody of the North Arkansas steamers, to be sure, but infinitely better than the silence of 1946-1949!

During 1950 the old shops buildings at Harrison were gradually vacated and disposed of. A new two-stall engine house of cinder block construction was installed to accommodate the diesel locomotives. The A. & O. headquarters were set up in the old dispatcher's office of the M. & A. The local operating reins were turned over to Jack Halter, General Manager, with S. A. Joffe departing to other Salzberg interest locations. The normal payroll list of the A. & O. broke down as follows:

| | |
|---|---|
| Executive | 1 |
| Clerical — general | 5 |
| Maintenance of way and structures | 24 |
| Maintenance of equipment | 3 |
| Transportation | 1 |
| Trainmen and engineers | 4 |
| | 38 |

The end of 1950 showed operating results (for 11 months) of 2,285 carloads, 80,713 tons, and $144,997 revenues. Because of normal startup problems, there was recorded a net loss of $38,626.

The years 1951, 1952 and 1953 proved to be reasonably good ones for the A. & O. Statistics were:

|  | 1951 | 1952 | 1953 |
|---|---|---|---|
| Carloads | 3,425 | 3,125 | 3,639 |
| Tons | 113,387 | 104,487 | 116,033 |
| Operating revenues | $210,896 | $246,933 | $232,606 |
| Operating expenses | $193,646 | $177,564 | $192,240 |
| Net income | $ −8,578 | $ 40,810 | $ 7,637 |

By the end of 1953 the $40,000 first mortgage had been retired, about 80,000 crossties laid and dependable service for customers had been established. The Class II short line seemed to have found a place for itself. If an energetic yet "tight" operation could be maintained, a respectable profit could be anticipated.

For some reason, things began to change in 1954. Service to customers began to deteriorate. There was no solicitation for new business, and no new industries "happened" to locate along the line. Maintenance of way began to be deferred. Indications were that the Salzberg owners had lost interest in the A. & O. Operating deficits became the rule:

|  | Deficit |
|---|---|
| 1954 | $ 5,349 |
| 1955 | 14,694 |
| 1956 | 32,361 |
| 1957 | 41,703 |
| 1958 | 59,626 |

During these years, operations were as routine as clockwork: three freights up and three freights down each week. However, there was one interesting break in the routine in 1956. On Monday, May 14, the regular freight got away from Harrison at 11:15 a.m. Between engine No. 800 and caboose No. 300 there were four empties and one load of strawberries. The train made it into Seligman, after stopping to switch two cars into Berryville and to pick up a car of water at Junction, when it was discovered that a carload of strawberries, in refrigerated car REX 6240, had been left behind in Harrison.

A crew was called, and at about 11:00 p.m. engine No. 900 left Harrison with the one car. After crossing the truss bridge at Beaver and moving along Poker Bluff, the train started to cross bridge 73.2 across Butler Creek when the structure began to crumple. Engine No. 900 fell, cab-end first, 36 feet into the six-foot-deep waters of Butler Creek. The three crew members, all in the cab, crawled to safety. The refrigerator car remained delicately balanced at the end of the bridge. On May 17 No. 800, which had been marooned in Seligman, pushed a Frisco work train with wrecker down to the scene of the accident. By May 21 repairs had been completed and No. 800 left Seligman with 21 loads and 1161 tons. The A. & O. was back in business.

Going back to the financial problems of the railroad, it was clear by 1959 that the Salzbergs were no longer interested in making the railroad profitable. And on January 19, 1959, they found their way to get out. On that date the Federal Government filed a condemnation suit to acquire title to 27.7 acres of land in and around the town of Beaver. This land was in the Table Rock Dam reservoir and it included 2.7 miles of A. & O. main line. The dam had been built recently, and it was felt that under certain high water flow conditions the trackage would be submerged. On January 22 a court order was entered which directed the A. & O. to surrender possession of the 2.7 miles of line within five days, with the railroad being permitted to use the line at its own risk.

The owners were, of course, entitled to compensation. It is entirely likely that they could have gotten the government to elevate the line the 3 to 5 feet required to maintain the rails above the 931-foot elevation of the Table Rock Dam flood level. This had been done in many similar situations. However, the owners chose to claim that the condemnation action had severed the line and, in effect, made it useless. They proposed that the government take over the road and operate it or instead build a connection from Harrison to the Missouri Pacific at Bergman so that the line from Seligman to Junction could then be abandoned.

Diesels 800 and 900 and caboose 300 are shown above at the north end of the Seligman yard. Diesel No. 900 took a dip into Butler Creek early on May 15, 1956, when the timbers of bridge 73-2 gave way. Resting precariously on the east end of the trestle is a refrigerated carload of strawberries. (*Above: C. E. Hull; below: H. C. Lamberton*)

After the mishap shown on page 259, the Frisco work train came, left, with the wrecker SF 99028 at the front. At the right the diesel is being pulled up to the east approach by a block and tackle driven by the wrecker.

*(Two pictures: Lon Holder)*

By 1959 the A. & O. had become a real "bare bones" operation. There were now only 19 employees, 10 of them in maintenance of way and structures. Managing the operation under tight orders from the Salzbergs was Lon Holder, who had become general manager upon the death of Jack Halter on May 15, 1958.

The end of the A. & O. operations came unexpectedly on May 5, 1960, when torrential rains in the Leatherwood Creek drainage area caused a washout of trestle 75-7 plus weakened trestles and damaged track for several miles in the vicinity. Besides No. 75-7, the trestle of most concern was No. 73-2, the one that had collapsed under engine No. 900 in 1956; inspections showed that it had been seriously weakened. The railroad placed an embargo on incoming shipments and proceeded to make a leisurely "study" of the cost and proper methods for repairing the damage.

The days went by and there was no apparent action by the owners of the A. & O. Shippers were left completely in the dark over plans for resuming service. There were 51 freight cars of other lines stranded on A. & O. tracks and there was no apparent concern about them. Finally, Attorney General Bruce Bennett appealed to the I. C. C. to force the road to do something about the public's need for service. Governor Orval Faubus asked Congressman J. W. Trimble to look into the matter. On May 31, 75 businessmen from Eureka Springs, Green Forest, Berryville, Alpena, and Harrison met at Green Forest and drew up a petition for filing with Judge John E. Miller of the Federal District Court. The petition pointed out that the A. & O. had no authority to "abandon operations." Little did they realize that on May 27 the A. & O. board of directors had met to authorize an application for abandonment of the entire operation. The application was filed with the I. C. C. on June 9, the reasons given being the expected ones: several years' losses, and severing of the line by the U. S. Government.

The return to the I. C. C. questionnaire was filed by the A. & O. on June 28. It disclosed that the estimated salvage value of the property was:

| | |
|---|---:|
| Rails, bars, spikes and appurtenances | $332,500 |
| Ties | 150,000 |
| Rolling stock and equipment | 115,000 |
| Real estate | 50,000 |
| | $647,500 |

It also pointed out that the cost of repairing the May 5 flood damage was estimated to be about $12,000. The questionnaire also went into some detail on how well the local industries could be served by common motor carriers.

The 51 stranded cars were moved off the line on July 7. A bulldozer was used to make a "shoofly" embankment around

This is the bridge that did in the Arkansas & Ozarks. Trestle 75-7, between Beaver and Junction, was washed out on May 5, 1960. Rather than repair the washout, the owners elected to apply for abandonment. Two months later 51 stranded freight cars from other railroads were taken around this bridge on an improvised "shoofly." *(Lane Baird, courtesy Lucius Beebe)*

bridge 75-7, and a temporary track was laid. The 51-car train was moved with one diesel in front and the other at the rear with no occupants in the diesel easing its way across the shoofly. At Beaver the front diesel was cut into the spur; then the cars were pushed gently across bridge 73-2 at Butler Creek. A Frisco engine was then brought down from Seligman to complete the job of getting the cars off the A. & O. tracks. Thus, the diesel locomotive weight was not put on bridge 73-2. The job done, the two engines ran on back to Harrison to await the outcome of the abandonment petition.

Abandonment hearings were held on August 25 and 26. There were a number of witnesses who testified to the utter necessity of the railroad, but their arguments were weakened by the amount of business that had been transferred to trucks. It would seem that the area could indeed be served by highways. It was disclosed that a group of capitalists was considering opening a glass sand operation near Green Forest, and the 25 cars per week of sand would make the difference between profit and loss for the A. & O. However, nothing came of this or other business possibilities subsequent to the hearings, and in due course, on April 7, 1961, the I. C. C. ordered abandonment.

The last-ditch efforts came forth, one of them being an attempt to pass a law that would place a prohibitive tax on the scrap materials from the road (very much as had been attempted at the time of the M. & A. abandonment). But all was to no avail. The two diesel engines were taken from Harrison to Bergman on lowboy trailers in mid-November.* Residue rolling stock was reduced to scrap metal. Removal of rails began on the last day of 1961. By spring all rails were gone, except for those on the Berryville stub; these stayed on the scene until August 14. By the end of 1962, all odds and ends of the A. & O. business were closed out.

Thus, the A. & O. might well have stood for the Alpha and Omega of the North Arkansas Line. Where the first trains had run in 1883-1901, the last trains ran in 1960. The luck of the North Arkansas had run out.

---

*The engines were sent to another Salzberg line, the Fort Dodge, Des Moines & Southern Railroad. So far as the author knows, they are still in operation on that Iowa short line.

In June of 1961 water backed up behind Table Rock Dam to the level of the railroad in the vicinity of Beaver, as the view west from the top of the Narrows bluff will attest. The Interstate Commerce Commission had by then already ordered abandonment.

(*H. C. Lamberton*)

## Cotton Plant-Fargo

The last vestige of the North Arkansas Line is the six-mile Arkansas short line from Cotton Plant to the Cotton Belt connection at Fargo. As mentioned earlier in this chapter, this section was purchased from the Helena & Northwestern, the deed being transferred in January 1952 and the purchase price being $50,725. The Southwest Veneer Co., needing a direct rail outlet, was the primary motivating influence but there was strong support from all Cotton Plant businessmen.

The C. P.-F. was incorporated December 11, 1951 and was financed by the sale of $17,600 capital stock plus a long-term loan of $43,700. This permitted purchase of the property, purchase of a small Plymouth industrial-type diesel locomotive, minor rehabilitation work and a reasonable amount of working capital. The president and general manager was (and still is) David Bush of the Southwest Veneer Co.

Operations commenced April 1, 1952 and continue today. The C. P.-F. operates on a low-budget basis, much like an industrial switching road. There were six employees initially, but this number has been reduced to three. The company does about $30,000-$35,000 annual business and shows a tidy profit. Trains operate irregularly and an operating employee may "wear several hats" during the course of a week's work. The track and right of way are in reasonably good condition. Headquarters are maintained in a small building opposite the old Cotton Plant depot, which now sports a coat of fresh paint and serves as a meeting hall for a workers' union local.

✓   ✓   ✓

This chapter spans the years during which the Salzberg interests had control of the North Arkansas property. It is easy to estimate how well those interests did from a financial point of view. Based on published information, the financial results are about as follows:

*Return*

| | |
|---|---:|
| Sale of property to Helena & Northwestern | $300,000 |
| Salvage value of Arkansas & Ozarks | 647,000 |
| Other salvage values: | |
| Neosho-Wayne trackage | 170,000 |
| Harrison-Cotton Plant trackage | 900,000 |
| Locomotives, rolling stock, miscellaneous | 270,000 |
| | $2,287,000 |

*Investment*

| | |
|---|---:|
| Original purchase from Kell family | $800,000 |
| Rehabilitation of Arkansas & Ozarks | 250,000 |
| Net loss on Arkansas & Ozarks | 264,000 |
| Interest on original purchase, 1946-1949 | 126,000 |
| | $1,440,000 |
| *Profit* | $ 847,000 |

If the Salzsbergs had been permitted to go right ahead with abandonment of all of the property back in 1947-1948, their profit would have been close to $1,200,000. The "experiment" with the A. & O. was costly to them, and these figures show why they were anxious to close up shop once it was established that the A. & O. could not become a big moneymaker. It is unfortunate that the Seligman-Harrison section could not have been purchased at net salvage value (about $370,000) by local interests that would have made every effort to make the road pay. But it didn't happen. . .

As these photos taken January 26, 1962 suggest, the A. & O. was fast disappearing from the scene. Above, the track has been removed, stranding the diesel house, left, and the operations building, right, as well as the caboose in the background and other facilities. Caboose No. 300, below, which made most of the runs to Seligman, is left high and dry and will soon be burned. (*Two pictures: W. J. Husa*)

The "President's Special" operated in mid-October 1941 as a public relations move. Above, the passengers and crew are photographed on the station platform at Neosho. Left to right: J. D. King, conductor; Bill King, brakeman; Ray Skelton, fireman; Lewie Watkins, president of the M. & A.; (road foreman of engines, unidentified); Jess Watkins, engineer; Vacara Gazzola, businessman of Forest City, Arkansas; J. R. Tucker, general manager of the M. & A.; Burke Mann, Forest City businessman; and W. A. Little, traffic manager of the M. & A. Below, the special is ready to roll south from Harrison, with white "extra" flags on No. 21. The consist is coach 5 and business car 99.

*(Two pictures: E. G. Baker)*

# CHAPTER NINE

*Epilogue*

The foregoing chapters have traced the history of the North Arkansas Line and have recounted its many ups and downs. The line had a relatively brief span of life; after full completion it lasted less than forty years. The reasons for the line's demise have been given, but it is of value here to summarize them so that the reader may take on some final perspective in the matter.

Major contributors to the fall of the North Arkansas were:

1. Territory not productive of revenue
2. Speculative-type construction
3. Difficult topography
4. Absentee ownership and management
5. Plain hard luck

The first of these, non-productive territory, was not foreseen by the original builders. They were advised of many income-producing potentials in Arkansas: excursion travel to Eureka Springs and other points of interest in the Ozarks, unlimited supplies of hardwood timber, untapped sources of mineral wealth, and developing agriculture that would produce many products for rail shipment. But the responses to these advices are now painfully clear: excursion travel, and passenger travel generally, dried up to nothing; the timber was cut and not replaced through reforestation; the mineral deposits were found not to be rich enough to warrant extensive mining and the agricultural potential north of Searcy turned out to be about as thin as the layer of topsoil on

These 1967 scenes suggest the scope of operations on the Cotton Plant-Fargo, last vestige of the North Arkansas. Motive power is provided by a Plymouth diesel, above. At Cotton Plant, below, the diesel points toward Fargo, six tangent miles away, where there is a connection with the Cotton Belt line.

the strata of Ozark limestone. Very little manufacturing industry developed in the region, partly because of a lack of interest by the State of Arkansas in industrial development. These territorial factors also mitigated against the parallel competitor, the White River Division of the Missouri Pacific; except for glass sand and stone, there are few local products being shipped in quantity on that line.

The speculative-type construction shows up in the comparison of the North Arkansas with the White River line given earlier. The North Arkansas suffered from light rail, sharp curves, and heavy grades. On much of the line the only ballast ever used was dirt. However, the justification for the high cost of construction of the White River line might well have been questioned at the time. Still a more substantial North Arkansas would have been better prepared to resist washouts, floods, and the wear and tear of heavy locomotives.

The topography of the chosen route was such that there was a ridge-jumping succession of grades north of Leslie. This required expensive helper service, and in many cases, doubling of the steeper hills. Much of the maintenance of way and equipment expense could be related to the effect of the grades and sharp curves. Whether a better route through the territory could have been found is doubtful. As William Z. Ripley put it, the region was "inhospitable" to railroads.

Ownership of the line was for many years located in St. Louis. When the Kells took over, ownership location shifted to Wichita Falls, Texas. In many instances, absentee ownership was the cause of near-disaster; there were the excesses of Wise and Stephenson, the parsimony of Phelan, and the lack of support for Watkins. Of course, local ownership could not be expected in a region of low economic level; still, a closer concern from a faraway ownership would have been helpful.

Plain hard luck seemed to haunt the North Arkansas through-out its life. The Tipton Ford collision, the floods in the Lower White River valley, the fires in the shops and general offices were examples of bad luck. The labor problems were partly hard luck and partly a result of the region being unable to support adequate wages. Perhaps the most unfortunate event was the untimely death of Joe Kell, noted earlier as the single incident that led to the decline and abandonment of the property. One final item of hard luck to mention, although in retrospect it might be termed bad judgment, was the decision to build the road from Leslie to Helena instead of from Leslie to Little Rock.

From this summary it might be concluded that the North Arkansas was doomed almost as soon as it was completed. In a sense, this was true. However, such a specter did not prevent the employees from giving their greatest possible efforts at all times. In railroad circles, the North Arkansas was known to have a cadre of devoted and hard-working railroaders. In their everyday work there were as many colorful events as could be found on any other line. They may have worked for second-class wages, but they certainly were not second-class railroad men, and some of the flavor of their work has been indicated in this book.

And so the M. & N. A., with its well-known epithet "May Never Arrive," never quite arrived as a corporation. But as a part of the life of the citizens of the Ozarks country of Arkansas, it was always on time.

✓     ✓     ✓

Aside from the short stretch of rail line from Cotton Plant to Fargo, there are very few traces today of the North Arkansas Line. Some trackage exists at Neosho, Searcy, and West Helena. Truss bridges at Beaver and on both sides of Shirley are still standing. Station buildings can still be seen at Beaver, Eureka Springs, St. Joe, Berryville, Marshall, Pangburn, Kensett, Cotton Plant, and West Helena. Embankments can be identified at many points north of Searcy, and it is possible to drive the old right of way between Shirley and Rumley, Leslie and Baker, and Beaver and Seligman. Remaining at Harrison are the backshop building and the Arkansas and Ozarks diesel house. As times goes by, the signs of the line are fading — leaving only the memories of those who knew the line so well. Before very many years, they too will be gone.

On this and the following three pages is a sampling of North Arkansas depots. The one at Cotton Plant, photographed about 1930, was the only M. & N. A.-built station with an integral pavilion. The building was still standing in 1969. Olvey, below, was viewed in the fall of 1915. Agent B. G. Lewallen, right, has things ready for No. 202, northbound. Perhaps the LCL of crated turkeys is destined for Thanksgiving tables. At the right is student telegrapher Merritt McGaughey, who later became a dispatcher for the road. (*Above: Mrs. W. H. McCain; below:Merritt McGaughey*)

A shelter and mail crane served Elk Ranch, above. A number of these structures were used along the line. The shelter at Gilbert, below, had a locked compartment for baggage and express. The Gilbert depot building was sold in 1945 and the shelter was fabricated of materials from the fire-damaged backshop building at Harrison. Both pictures were taken in 1946. *(Above: C. E. Hull; below: J. M. Gray)*

The small stucco building at Neosho, photographed in 1948, was built in 1933 to obviate the expense of sharing the Kansas City Southern depot. Fargo is shown below, as it appeared about 1935. The view is north along the Cotton Belt right of way, with the gate shown in its normal position, against the North Arkansas.

*(Above: A. B. Johnson; below: John W. Barriger)*

The station at Heber Springs, 1949 photo above, was one of the larger frame buildings erected by the North Arkansas. The handsome stone structure at Leslie, 1948 photo below, looking north, was built in 1914 as a consolation when the shops were removed from that community. The building still stood in 1969.

*(Above: E. G. Baker; below: C. W. Witbeck)*

The prefabricated structure above replaced the large depot at Seligman in 1966. The view is toward the southwest, and the North Arkansas house track is still in place this side of the depot. At Joplin Union Depot, the expanse to the right of the platform once contained a roundhouse and other terminal facilities used by the North Arkansas. The view above is to the north, and the Kansas City Southern main line is to the far right. When the picture was taken in the summer of 1968, only one passenger train each way on the K. C. S. was using the depot.

At Searcy the North Arkansas tracks, with their original 65-pound rails are used for occasional switching by the Doniphan, Kensett & Searcy line. The above photo was taken in 1965. In the lower view the old right of way shows the steady grade at the Missouri-Arkansas state line, looking toward Seligman.

The view above shows the remains of trestle 73-2 with White River in the background. The town of Beaver is about a half-mile to the left. Bridge 73-7 at Beaver, below, not only still stands but is central to a proposed scheme to reconstruct a few miles of the North Arkansas from Beaver to Elk Ranch, as a tourist attraction. These pictures were taken in 1967.

The Crooked Creek bridge at Harrison still stood in part, when the picture above was taken in 1965. From this bridge E. C. Gregor was hanged during the 1921-1923 strike. In 1969 business car 99 was in retirement at Kensett. If it could dream and reminisce, no doubt its thoughts would go back through a long career that started in 1888 on the Colorado Midland, shifted in 1922 to the Wichita Falls & Southern, and finally moved in 1928 to the North Arkansas where it became the living headquarters for president W. Stephenson. Now its coat of cheap white paint is peeling to expose the many layers of Tuscan red that identified North Arkansas passenger equipment. Would that it could be saved by an aficionado who would put it back on the high iron!

# *Chapter References*

CHAPTER 1

Branner, John C., *Annual Report of the Geological Survey of Arkansas*. V. *The Zinc and Lead Region of North Arkansas*, Little Rock (1900).

Chance, H. M., *Rush Creek, Arkansas, Zinc District*, Trans. Am. Inst. Min. Engrs. *18*, 505 (1890).

Donovan, Frances R., *I Have Found It*, unpublished manuscript, Eureka Springs, Arkansas (no date). In Carnegie Library, Eureka Springs.

Eureka Springs Railway Co., *First Annual Report – 1883*, by R. C. Kerens. In New York Public Library.

Harper's Weekly, *An Arkansas Watering Place*, December 18, 1886.

Kalklosch, L. J., *The Healing Fountain*, Eureka Springs, Arkansas (1881).

Mills, Nellie A., *Early Days at Eureka Springs, Arkansas (1880-1892)*, Free Will Baptist Gem, Monett, Missouri (1949).

Mills, Nellie A., *Other Days at Eureka Springs*, Free Will Baptist Gem, Monett, Missouri (1950).

Missouri Railroad Commissioners, *Annual Reports*, 1879-1887.

Muir, R. L., and White, C. J., *Over the Long Term* . . ., J. & W Seligman and Co., New York (1964).

Overton, Richard C., *Gulf to Rockies*, The University of Texas Press, Austin (1953).

Pinkley- Call, Cora, *Eureka Springs – Stairstep Town*, Times- Echo Press, Eureka Springs, Arkansas (1952).

Rayburn, Otto E., *The Eureka Springs Story*, Times-Echo Press, Eureka Springs, Arkansas (1954).

St. Louis & San Francisco Railroad, *Annual Reports*, 1879-1888.

West, George, *Railway Penetration into Northwest Arkansas*, Daily Times-Echo, Eureka Springs, Arkansas, April 24, 1905.

CHAPTER 2

Allhands, J. L., *The Colts* (J. B. Colt and Son Co.), America's Builders, *2*, No. 3 (1954). George Pepperdine College, Los Angeles, California.

Bain, H. F. *Preliminary Report on the Lead and Zinc Deposits of the Ozark Region*, U. S. Geological Survey, Dept. of Interior, Washington (1901).

Dodson, Lucille R., *The Missouri & North Arkansas Railroad Comes to Berryville, Arkansas*, Carroll County Historical Quarterly 5, No. 1, 17 (March 1960).

Irland, F. W., *The Missouri Pacific Railway Co. – Handbook*, Buxton and Skinner, St. Louis (1910).

Kearney, John W., *The Summit of the Ozarks*, Matthews and Northrup, Buffalo, New York (1903).

McInturff, O. J., *Searcy County, My Dear*, a history of Searcy County, Arkansas. Marshall *Mountain Wave*, Marshall, Arkansas (1963).

Rayburn, Otto E., *The Eureka Springs Story*, Times-Echo Press, Eureka Springs, Arkansas (1954).

Rea, R. R., *Boone County and its People*, Press-Argus, Van Buren, Arkansas (1955).

St. Louis & San Francisco Railroad, *The Top of the Ozarks*, Wallace and Tiernan, St. Louis (1900).

Shiras, Frances H., *History of Baxter County*, Mountain Home, Arkansas (1939).

Smith, Kenneth L., *The Buffalo River Country*, The Ozark Society, Fayetteville, Arkansas (1967).

Spalding, W. A., *How the St. Louis and North Arkansas Railroad Was Built from Eureka Springs to Harrison*, Berryville (Arkansas) *Star-Progress*, November 30, 1950.

CHAPTER 3

Burton, W. J., *History of the Missouri Pacific Railroad*, unpublished manuscript, July 1, 1956. In company files, St. Louis.

Crump, Bonnie L., *Unique Eureka*, Eureka Springs, Arkansas (1965).

Hackett, Glen, *Early History of Shirley, Arkansas*, Graduate paper, Arkansas State Teachers College, Conway (1957).

Missouri Pacific – Iron Mountain System, *The White River Country in Missouri and Arkansas*, 3rd edition, St. Louis (1906).

Parmelee, L. R., *Helena and West Helena – A Civil Engineer's Reminiscences*, Phillips County Historical Quarterly *1*, No. 2, 1-28 (December 1962).

Railway and Locomotive Engineering *21*, 97-98 (March 1908), *Missouri & North Arkansas 2-8-0*.

*Railway Age 41*, 890-891 (June 1, 1906), *The White River Division of the St. Louis, Iron Mountain & Southern Railway*.

Yarnell, Mrs. Ray, *History of Searcy's Railroads from 1870-1937*, Searcy Centennial, Searcy, Arkansas (November 23, 1937).

CHAPTER 4

Allonby, Charles, *Death Passed Them By*, Tulsa *World* Sunday Magazine, July 5, 1964.

American Engineer and Railroad *Journal*, 353 (September 1911), *Seventy-Foot Gas-Electric Motor Cars.*

Campbell, Don G., *50th Anniversary of Disastrous Missouri Train Wreck on August 5th*, the Local (Kansas City Chapter, National Railway Historical Society), 2-4 (August 1964).

Clayton, Powell, *Aftermath of the Civil War, in Arkansas*, Neale Publishing Co., New York (1915).

Crump, Mrs. Josephine B., *Echoes from the Ozarks*, Muskogee, Okla. (1913).

Francis, David R., Collected papers. In Missouri Historical Society, St. Louis.

Hubbard, Freeman H., *Railroad Avenue*, McGraw-Hill Book Co., New York (1945). Revised and republished by Golden West Books, San Marino, Calif. (1965).

Interstate Commerce Commission, Accident *Bulletin* No. 53, 28-30 (1914).

McKnight, E. T., *Zinc and Lead Deposits of Northern Arkansas*, U. S. Geological Survey *Bulletin* 853, Washington, Government Printing Office (1935).

Missouri & North Arkansas Railroad, *Oak Leaves* magazine, issues for 1910-1915 period.

Missouri Public Service Commission, Case No. 462, *Tipton Ford Collision*, August 1914.

Railway Age Gazette 57, No. 20, 904 (1914), *Report on Tipton Ford Collision.*

Ruhl, Otto, *Past and Present of Zinc Mining in Arkansas*, Min. & Eng. *World* 35, 373 (1911).

St. Louis Republic, *The Book of St. Louisans*, 2nd Edition (1912).

Sanford, George A., *Helena, Arkansas — The Natural Gateway to the South and Southwest*, Illinois Central Magazine, 17-23 (January 1918)

Shaw, R. B., *Down Brakes*, P. R. Macmillan, New York (1961).

Shiras, Tom, *Early Days in the North Arkansas Zinc District*, Eng. Min. Journal *110*, 165 (1920).

CHAPTER 5

Bradley, W. F., *An Industrial War*, Bradley and Russell, Harrison, Arkansas (1923).

Farris, J. K., *The Harrison Riot: The Reign of the Mob on the Missouri & North Arkansas Railroad*, Wynne, Arkansas (1924).

Gooden, Orville T., *The Missouri & North Arkansas Railroad Strike*, Columbia University Press, New York (1926).

Interstate Commerce Commission, *In the Matter of Divisions of Joint Rates, Fares, and Charges on Traffic Interchanged Between the Missouri & North Arkansas Railroad Company and its Connections,"* ICC Reports *68*, 47-70 (1922).

Interstate Commerce Commission, *In the Matter of the Applications of* . . . *the Organizers of the Missouri & North Arkansas Railway Company for a Loan from the United States under Section 210 of the Transportation Act, 1920, as Amended,* ICC Reports 71, 395-405 (1922).

Koach, K. H., *Missouri & North Arkansas Railroad Resumes Operation,* Railway Age 72, 1341-1343 (June 10, 1922).

Railroad Telegrapher 38, 929-931 (August 1921), *Missouri & North Arkansas 'Junked.'*

Ripley, W. Z., *Consolidation of Railroads,* ICC Reports 63, 465-660 (1921).

Railway Age 71, 196 (July 30, 1921), *Missouri & North Arkansas Discontinues Operation.*

CHAPTER 6

Missouri & North Arkansas Railway Company, annual reports to stockholders, 1926-1932 incl.

Saxon, Lyle, *Father Mississippi,* The Century Company, New York (1927).

Simpich, F., *The Great Mississippi Flood of 1927,* National Geographic Magazine 52, No. 3, 243-289 (September 1927).

CHAPTER 7

American Locomotive Co., *Motive Power Study for Missouri & Arkansas Railway,* Schenectady, N. Y.    (January 1945).

Coverdale and Colpitts (Consulting Engineers), *Report on Missouri & Arkansas Railway,* New York, (May 10, 1947). By M. C. Kennedy.

Interstate Commerce Commission, *Missouri & Arkansas Railway Company Acquisition and Stock,* ICC Reports 207, 641-644 (1935).

Missouri & Arkansas Railway Company, minute book, 1935-1946.

Office of Defense Transportation, *Report on Missouri & Arkansas Railway,* Washington (May 21, 1944). By Sam Fordyce III.

Railroad Stories 20, No. 2, 88-89 (July 1936), *Locomotives of the Missouri & Arkansas Railway.*

Railway Age 104, No. 24, 970-971 (1938), *Missouri & Arkansas Rail Cars.*

Railway Age 105, No. 24, 846-847 (1938), *Rail Motor Cars Solve Problems.*

Reconstruction Finance Corporation (Railroad Division), *Report on Missouri & Arkansas Railway Company,* Washington (June 1, 1939). By W. W. Sullivan and T. A. Hamilton.

Watkins, L. A., *How One Railway Created New Freight Business,* Railroad Magazine 29, No. 2, 65-69 (January 1941).

CHAPTER 8

Arkansas & Ozarks Railway Corp., *Application for Abandonment and Return to Questionnaire,* June 28, 1960.

Deane, Ernie, *The A & O.: Historic Railroad has its Troubles,* Arkansas *Gazette,* April 24, 1960.

Foresman, Bob, *Railroad Revives under a New Name,* Tulsa *Tribune,* Feb. 9, 1950.

Helena & Northwestern Railway, *Application for Financial Aid to I.C.C. and R.F.C.,* Helena, Arkansas (Nov. 15, 1950).

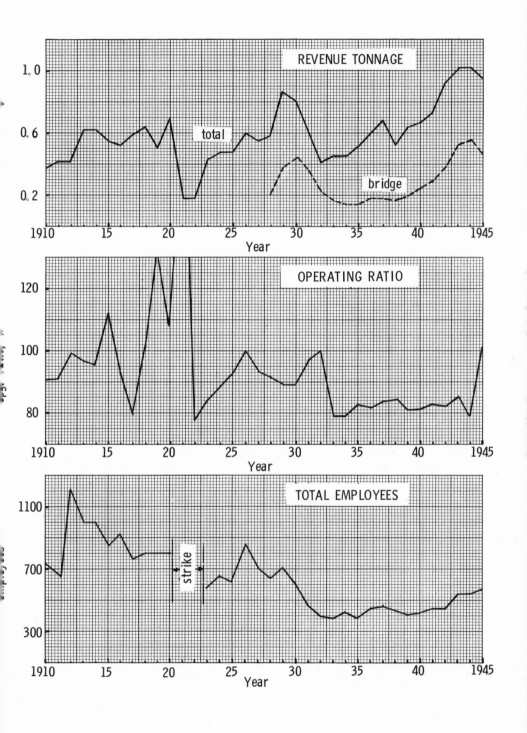

Caboose 305 arrived in September 1907, outfitted as a private car for vice-president George Sands. It was later converted to regular caboose service. Furniture car 3967 was one of fifty received in June 1912; it sported insignia used during E. M. Wise's general managership. After 1915 very few new freight cars were placed in revenue service. Exceptions were M. & N. A. 2648, bottom, and the car pictured above opposite. No. 2648 was one of 50 new boxcars leased in 1933 from the Mather Humane Stock Transport Co. N.W.X. 519 was leased from the North Western Refrigerator Line Co. by the Missouri & Arkansas and was used for strawberry shipments.

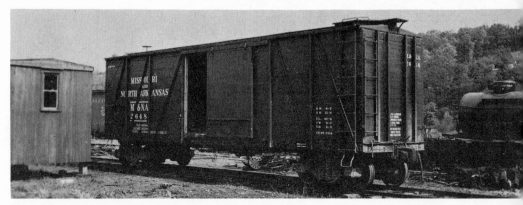

Combination car 60, in the middle picture, was purchased secondhand in 1911 as a wooden coach and numbered 16. In 1926 it was converted to a combination car, seating 12, and given steel sheathing; at that time it was renumbered. Coach 5, in the bottom picture, was purchased new in 1907 and was sheathed in 1926-1927. Both cars were around in 1946, but the combine had been placed on the inactive list.

*(Four pictures: E. G. Baker)*

## LOCOMOTIVE ROSTER – MISSOURI & NORTH ARKANSAS RAILWAY

| Fin. No. | Orig. No. | Builder & Type | Bldr. No. | Date Built | Date Acquired | Date Retired | Cylinder dim., in. | Driver o.d., in. | Boiler Pressure psig | Wt. on Drivers lbs. | Wt. of Engine lbs. | Tractive Effort lbs. |
|---|---|---|---|---|---|---|---|---|---|---|---|---|
| 1-1 | | 2-8-0 Pittsburgh | 631 | 1882 | 1882 | 1900 | 18x24 | 44 | | | | |
| 1-2 | | 4-4-0 Dickson | 457 | 1884 | 1907 | 1920 | 19x24 | 68 | 160 | 68,000 | 92,000 | 17,500 |
| 1-3 | | 4-4-0 Baldwin | 38054 | 1912 | 1912 | 1912 | 18x24 | 68 | | | | |
| 1-4 | | 2-8-0 Baldwin | 29561 | 1906 | 1927 | 1933 | 20x24 | 50 | 180 | 122,000 | 139,000 | 30,000 |
| 2-1 | | 4-4-0 Rogers | 450 | 1883 | 1883 | 1915 | 17x24 | 66 | 140 | 42,000 | 64,000 | 12,500 |
| 2-2 | | 4-4-0 Rogers | | | 1916 | 1916 | | | | | | |
| 2-3 | | 2-8-0 Baldwin | 31095 | 1907 | 1927 | 1933 | 20x24 | 50 | 180 | 122,000 | 139,000 | 30,000 |
| 3 | | 4-6-0 Dickson | 1145 | 1900 | 1900 | 1929 | 18x24 | 56 | 180 | 92,000 | 116,000 | 20,900 |
| 4 | | 4-6-0 Cooke | 2674 | 1901 | 1901 | 1929 | 19x26 | 56 | 180 | 107,000 | 130,000 | 25,600 |
| 5 | | 4-6-0 Cooke | 2675 | 1901 | 1901 | 1929 | 19x26 | 56 | 180 | 107,000 | 130,000 | 25,600 |
| 6 | | 2-6-0 Baldwin | 21456 | 1903 | 1903 | 1929 | 19x26 | 56 | 180 | 115,000 | 135,000 | 25,600 |
| 7 | | 2-6-0 Baldwin | 21462 | 1903 | 1903 | 1929 | 19x26 | 56 | 180 | 115,000 | 135,000 | 25,600 |
| 8 | | 2-6-0 Baldwin | 8938 | 1887 | 1903 | 1925 | 19x24 | 56 | 145 | 83,000 | 99,000 | 19,100 |
| 9 | | 2-6-0 Baldwin | 23354 | 1903 | 1907 | 1929 | 18x24 | 56 | 180 | 102,000 | 120,000 | 20,900 |
| 10 | | 2-8-0 Baldwin | 31314 | 1907 | 1907 | 1933 | 22x28 | 56 | 180 | 168,000 | 182,000 | 37,000 |
| 11 | | 2-8-0 Baldwin | 31335 | 1907 | 1907 | 1933 | 22x28 | 56 | 180 | 168,000 | 182,000 | 37,000 |
| 12 | | 2-8-0 Baldwin | 31336 | 1907 | 1907 | 1933 | 22x28 | 56 | 180 | 168,000 | 182,000 | 37,000 |
| 13 | | 2-8-0 Baldwin | 31337 | 1907 | 1907 | 1933 | 22x28 | 56 | 180 | 168,000 | 182,000 | 37,000 |
| 14-1 | | 2-8-0 Baldwin | 31338 | 1907 | 1907 | 1933 | 22x28 | 56 | 180 | 168,000 | 182,000 | 37,000 |
| 14-2 | | 2-6-0 Baldwin | 55519 | 1922 | 1943 | 1949 | 18x26 | 50 | 180 | 108,000 | 123,000 | 25,600 |
| 15-1 | | 4-4-0 Baldwin | 32666 | 1908 | 1908 | 1933 | 18x24 | 63 | 180 | 73,000 | 115,000 | 18,900 |
| 15-2 | | 2-6-0 Baldwin | 55520 | 1922 | 1943 | 1949 | 18x26 | 50 | 180 | 108,000 | 123,000 | 25,600 |
| 16 | | 4-4-0 Baldwin | 32856 | 1908 | 1908 | 1935 | 18x24 | 63 | 180 | 73,000 | 115,000 | 18,900 |

## LOCOMOTIVE ROSTER – MISSOURI & NORTH ARKANSAS RAILWAY (Continued)

| Fin. No. | Orig. No. | Builder & Type | Bldr. No. | Date Built | Date Acquired | Date Retired | Cylinder dim., in. | Driver o.d., in. | Boiler Pressure psig | Wt. on Drivers lbs. | Wt. of Engine lbs. | Tractive Effort lbs. |
|---|---|---|---|---|---|---|---|---|---|---|---|---|
| 17-2 |  | 4-4-0 Baldwin | 37069 | 1911 | 1911 | 1938 | 18x24 | 63 | 180 | 76,000 | 113,000 | 19,200 |
| 18-1 |  | 4-6-0 Baldwin | 34188 | 1910 | 1910 | 1933 | 18x26 | 62 | 200 | 116,000 | 150,000 | 26,600 |
| 18-2 |  | 4-6-0 Alco | 38827 | 1905 | 1936 | 1949 | 19x24 | 63 | 180 | 115,000 | 150,000 | 21,000 |
| 19-2 | 17-1 | 4-6-0 Baldwin | 34187 | 1910 | 1910 | 1936 | 18x26 | 62 | 200 | 116,000 | 150,000 | 26,600 |
| 20-2 |  | 4-6-0 Baldwin | 41297 | 1914 | 1914 | 1949 | 20x26 | 62 | 180 | 124,000 | 168,000 | 25,700 |
| 21-2 |  | 4-6-0 Baldwin | 40671 | 1913 | 1927 | 1949 | 21x26 | 65 | 200 | 125,000 | 159,000 | 29,500 |
| 30 | 19-1 | 2-8-2 Baldwin | 34201 | 1910 | 1910 | 1933 | 22x26 | 56 | 180 | 159,000 | 194,000 | 37,000 |
| 31 | 20-1 | 2-8-2 Baldwin | 34202 | 1910 | 1910 | 1933 | 22x26 | 56 | 180 | 159,000 | 194,000 | 37,000 |
| 32 | 21-1 | 2-8-2 Baldwin | 38827 | 1912 | 1912 | 1949 | 23x28 | 56 | 180 | 163,000 | 198,000 | 40,500 |
| 33 | 22 | 2-8-2 Baldwin | 38828 | 1912 | 1912 | 1949 | 23x28 | 56 | 180 | 163,000 | 198,000 | 40,500 |
| 34 |  | 2-8-2 Baldwin | 41315 | 1914 | 1914 | 1949 | 23x28 | 56 | 180 | 162,000 | 194,000 | 40,500 |
| 35 |  | 2-8-2 Baldwin | 41316 | 1914 | 1914 | 1949 | 23x28 | 56 | 180 | 162,000 | 194,000 | 40,500 |
| 36 |  | 2-8-2 Baldwin | 41317 | 1914 | 1914 | 1949 | 23x28 | 56 | 180 | 162,000 | 194,000 | 40,500 |
| 37 |  | 2-8-0 Alco | 27758 | 1903 | 1929 | 1936 | 21x28 | 57 | 200 | 164,000 | 184,000 | 36,800 |
| 40 |  | 2-8-0 Alco | 49343 | 1911 | 1928 | 1949 | 23x32 | 63 | 200 | 214,000 | 240,000 | 45,700 |
| 41 |  | 2-8-0 Alco | 40078 | 1907 | 1928 | 1949 | 23x32 | 63 | 200 | 208,000 | 229,000 | 45,700 |
| 42 |  | 2-8-0 Alco | 44105 | 1907 | 1928 | 1939 | 23x32 | 63 | 200 | 208,000 | 229,000 | 45,700 |
| 43 |  | 2-8-0 Alco | 49345 | 1911 | 1928 | 1949 | 23x32 | 63 | 200 | 214,000 | 240,000 | 45,700 |
| 44 |  | 2-8-0 Alco | 49371 | 1911 | 1928 | 1938 | 23x32 | 63 | 200 | 214,000 | 240,000 | 45,700 |
| 45 |  | 2-8-0 Alco | 49347 | 1911 | 1929 | 1933 | 23x32 | 63 | 200 | 214,000 | 240,000 | 45,700 |
| 46 |  | 2-8-0 Alco | 49359 | 1911 | 1929 | 1935 | 23x32 | 63 | 200 | 214,000 | 240,000 | 45,700 |
| 47 |  | 2-8-0 Alco | 49361 | 1911 | 1929 | 1935 | 23x32 | 63 | 200 | 214,000 | 240,000 | 45,700 |
| 48 |  | 2-8-0 Alco | 49365 | 1911 | 1929 | 1935 | 23x32 | 63 | 200 | 214,000 | 240,000 | 45,700 |

## LOCOMOTIVE ROSTER – MISSOURI & NORTH ARKANSAS RAILWAY (Continued)

| Fin. No. | Orig. No. | Builder & Type | Bldr. No. | Date Built | Date Acquired | Date Retired | Cylinder dim., in. | Driver o.d., in. | Boiler Pressure psig | Wt. on Drivers lbs. | Wt. of Engine lbs. | Tractive Effort lbs. |
|---|---|---|---|---|---|---|---|---|---|---|---|---|
| 49 | | 2-8-0 Alco | 49366 | 1911 | 1929 | 1949 | 23x32 | 63 | 200 | 214,000 | 240,000 | 45,700 |
| 50 | | 2-8-2 Baldwin | 40306 | 1913 | 1939 | 1949 | 24x30 | 56 | 180 | 187,000 | 249,000 | 47,700 |
| 51 | | 2-8-2 Baldwin | 38933 | 1912 | 1939 | 1949 | 24x30 | 56 | 180 | 187,000 | 249,000 | 47,700 |
| 52 | | 2-8-2 Baldwin | 38934 | 1912 | 1939 | 1949 | 24x30 | 56 | 180 | 187,000 | 249,000 | 47,700 |
| 53 | | 2-8-2 Baldwin | 40302 | 1913 | 1939 | 1949 | 24x30 | 56 | 180 | 187,000 | 249,000 | 47,700 |
| 54 | | 2-8-2 Baldwin | 38935 | 1912 | 1939 | 1949 | 24x30 | 56 | 180 | 187,000 | 249,000 | 47,700 |
| 55 | | 2-8-2 Baldwin | 40303 | 1913 | 1939 | 1949 | 24x30 | 56 | 180 | 187,000 | 249,000 | 47,700 |
| 60 | | 2-8-0 Rogers | 6128 | 1904 | 1944 | 1949 | 22x32 | 62 | 200 | 187,700 | 212,000 | 42,500 |
| 61 | | 2-8-0 Alco | 29117 | 1903 | 1944 | 1949 | 24x32 | 61 | 180 | 182,900 | 206,000 | 45,100 |
| 62 | | 2-8-0 Alco | 29135 | 1904 | 1944 | 1949 | 22x32 | 63 | 200 | 182,900 | 206,000 | 42,100 |
| 1915 | | 2-8-0 Alco | 42459 | 1907 | 1944 | 1949 | 24x30 | 63 | 185 | 187,000 | 210,500 | 43,100 |
| 1972 | | 2-8-0 Alco | 46817 | 1909 | 1944 | 1949 | 23½x30 | 63 | 195 | 195,000 | 219,000 | 43,600 |

## MOTOR CARS

| No. | Type | Builder | Date Built | Date Acquired | Date Retired | Length ft. | Seating Capacity | Weight lbs. | Horsepower |
|---|---|---|---|---|---|---|---|---|---|
| 102 | Gasoline-Electric | G.E. | 1912 | 1912 | 1927 | 70.5 | 62 | 94,000 | 200 |
| 103-1 | Gasoline-Electric | G.E. | 1912 | 1912 | 1914 | 70.5 | 62 | 94,000 | 200 |
| 103-2 | Gasoline-Electric | G.E. | 1914 | 1914 | 1927 | 70.5 | 62 | 94,000 | 200 |
| 605 | Gasoline | Brill | 1937 | 1937 | 1949 | 43.0 | 28 | 32,600 | 92 |
| 705 | Gasoline | A.C.F. | 1938 | 1938 | 1946 | 75.5 | 33 | 66,000 | 200 |
| 726 | Gasoline | A.C.F. | 1938 | 1938 | 1949 | 75.5 | 33 | 66,000 | 200 |

# LOCOMOTIVE NOTES

1-1  Purchased new for Eureka Springs Railway. Boiler later used for stationary steam generation at Eureka Springs shops.

1-2  Purchased 6/8/07 from DL&W. Ex-DL&W 186; to 933 in 1889; to 488 in 1904.

1-3  Ordered as 3rd No. 1, but diverted directly to Tremont & Gulf No. 50.

1-4  Purchased 12/27 from Midland Valley Rwy. (along with 2-3 and 21-2). Ex-MV 16.

2-1  Purchased new for Eureka Springs Railway as ES 2.

2-2  Purchased used from Fitzhugh-Luther Co., 3/16. Not on roster at end of 1916. Disposition unknown.

2-3  Purchased 12/27 from Midland Valley Rwy. (along with 1-4 and 21-2). Ex-MV 17.

3  Purchased new. Retired officially in 1929 but not scrapped until 1934.

4  Purchased new. Retired officially in 1929 but not scrapped until 1935.

5  Purchased new. Sold to Doniphan, Kensett and Searcy in 1929; DK&S 7.

6 & 7  Purchased new. Retired officially in 1929 but not scrapped until 1934-35.

8  Purchased from CNO&TP. Ex-CNO&TP 25; to 525; to 614. May have had a replacement boiler. Sold in 1925; disposition unknown.

9  Purchased 1/07 from Illinois Terminal RR. Ex-IT 8. Retired officially in 1929 but not scrapped until 1934.

10 through 14-1  Purchased new. Retired as a group in 1933, and scrapped in 1934.

14-2 through 15-2  Leased from Wichita Falls & Southern in 1943. Ex-WF&S 14 and 15. Were converted from oil- to coal-burners. Purchased in 1945. Scrapped at Harrison in 1949.

15-1 and 16  Purchased new. No. 15-1 scrapped in 1935. Boiler from 16 sold to Silica Sand Co., Everton, Ark., in 1936.

17-2  Purchased new; order diverted from Midland Pennsylvania No. 1. Delivered as M&NA 23. Renumbered 1914. There has been some speculation that this locomotive was formerly NOGN 105 (Baldwin 28339, 1906) but this appears to be in error. Scrapped at Harrison in 1939.

18-1 and 19-2  Purchased new. No. 19-2 delivered as 17-1 and renumbered in 1911 or 1912. No. 18-1 retired in 1933 and scrapped in 1934. No. 19-2 retired in 1936 and scrapped in 1939.

18-2  Purchased used from Akron, Canton & Youngstown, 9/36. Was originally NYC&StL 40-2; to 300 in 1910; to AC&Y 300 in 1920. Driver o.d. was 62″.

20-2  Purchased new. After 1949 abandonment was used in track salvaging. Was transferred to A&O books and used in rehabilitation work. Scrapped 1949.

21-2     Purchased 12/27 from Midland Valley Rwy. (along with 1-4 and 2-3). Was initially Kansas City and Memphis 7; later MV 7. Scrapped at Harrison in 1949.

30 and 31     Purchased new and delivered as 19-1 and 20-1. Both renumbered in 1914. Retired in 1933 and scrapped in 1934-5.

32 and 33     Purchased new and delivered as 21-1 and 22. Both renumbered in 1914. At Heber Springs during 1946-9 inactivity and scrapped there in 1949.

34 through 36     Purchased new. Nos. 34 and 36 at Kensett during 1946-9 inactivity and scrapped there in 1949. No. 35 scrapped at Harrison in 1949. Driver o.d. changed to 55″, increasing TE rating to 41,200 lbs.

37     Purchased used from Southern Iron & Equipment Co. Formerly Buffalo, Rochester & Pittsburgh No. 310, and was sold to SI&E in 1923. Little used on M&NA. Retired in 1933 and scrapped in 1936.

40 through 49     Purchased used from New York Central (Big Four) through Hyman-Michaels Co. The M&NA Mechanical Department rated these locomotives at 48,365 lbs. tractive effort, possibly due to an increase in steam pressure. Former numbers were:

|     |        |      | Scrapped |
| --- | ------ | ---- | -------- |
| 40  | CCC&StL | 6812 | 1949 |
| 41  |        | 6728 | 1949 |
| 42  |        | 6755 | 1939 |
| 43  |        | 6814 | 1949 |
| 44  |        | 6840 | 1939 |
| 45  |        | 6816 | 1934 |
| 46  |        | 6828 | 1936 |
| 47  |        | 6830 | 1936 |
| 48  |        | 6834 | 1936 |
| 49  |        | 6835 | 1949 |

50 through 55     Purchased used from Atlanta, Birmingham & Coast through Southern Iron and Equipment Co. All were scrapped at Harrison in 1949. Former numbers were:

| 50 | AB&A | 101 | AB&C | 210 |
| -- | ---- | --- | ---- | --- |
| 51 |      | 92  |      | 201 |
| 52 |      | 93  |      | 202 |
| 53 |      | 97  |      | 206 |
| 54 |      | 94  |      | 203 |
| 55 |      | 98  |      | 207 |

60 through 62     Purchased used from St. Louis Southwestern. All originated on the Erie and in 1942 were sold to the StLSW. All were scrapped at Harrison in 1949. Former numbers were:

| 60 | Erie | 1624       | StLSW | 530 |
| -- | ---- | ---------- | ----- | --- |
| 61 |      | 1579       |       | 533 |
| 62 |      | 1597; 2101 |       | 532 |

1915 and 1972     Leased and then purchased from the Rock Island. Formerly CRI&P 1915 and 1972. Scrapped at Harrison in 1949.

# References

Arkansas *Gazette*, Centennial Edition: 1819-1919, November 20, 1919.

Arkansas *Gazette*, State Centennial Edition: 1836-1936, June 15, 1936.

Arkansas Railroad Commission, Annual Reports, 1899-1905.

Brown, Lynn, *The Missouri & North Arkansas Railroad*, unpublished manuscript, Harrison, Arkansas, April 27, 1964. In Regional Library, Harrison.

Campbell, Donald K., *A Study of Some Factors Contributing to the Petition for Abandonment by the Missouri & Arkansas Railroad in September, 1946*, Arkansas Historical Quart. 8, 267-326 (1949).

Clark, Ira G., *Then Came the Railroads*, University of Oklahoma Press, Norman (1958).

Eureka Springs *Daily Times-Echo*, "Special Edition Commemorating the 25th Anniversary of the Incorporation of Eureka Springs, Arkansas," April 24, 1905.

Eureka Springs *Daily Times-Echo*, "The Arkansaw Traveler's Illustrated Souvenir Edition," April 6-8, 1907.

Fletcher, John G., *Arkansas*, University of North Carolina Press, Chapel Hill (1947).

Harrison *Daily Times*, Arkansas Centennial Edition, July 1936.

Herndon, Dallas T., *Centennial History of Arkansas*, S. J. Clarke Publishing Co., Chicago/Little Rock (1922).

Hull, Clifton E., *The Eureka Springs Railway*, unpublished manuscript, North Little Rock, Arkansas, ca 1964. In Little Rock Public Library.

Interstate Commerce Commission, *Engineering Report Upon Missouri & North Arkansas Railroad Company*, Howard M. Jones, Supervising Engineer, February 14, 1922.

Interstate Commerce Commission, *Statistics of the Railways in the United States*, Annual Reports for the years 1883-1960, Washington, Government Printing Office.

Interstate Commerce Commission, *Valuation Docket No. 511,* — *Missouri & North Arkansas Railroad Company,* decided June 20, 1927. ICC Reports, *125,* 639-673 (1927).

Makris, George A., *A Survey of Transportation in the State of Arkansas,* M. A. Thesis, University of Arkansas (1937).

Missouri Public Service Commission, Annual Reports by Missouri & Arkansas Railway and Predecessors, 1909-1949. (Earlier known as Railroad and Warehouse Department of State of Missouri.)

Moody's *Transportation Manual,* 1925-1949.

Poor's *Manual of Railroads,* 1877-1924.

Russell, Jesse L., *Behind These Ozark Hills,* Hobson Book Press, New York (1947).

Schick, Robert, *The Turbulent North Arkansas,* Railroad Magazine, *46,* No. 1, 10-25 (June 1948).

Thomas, D. Y. *Arkansas and Its People,* American Historical Society, New York (1930).

Wood, Stephen E., *The Development of Arkansas Railroads,* Arkansas Historical Quart. 7, 103-140, 155-193 (1948).

Writers' Program, *Arkansas — A Guide to the State,* American Guide Series, Hastings House, New York (1941).

Files of newspapers and magazines:
Arkansas *Gazette,* Little Rock, Arkansas
*Commercial and Financial Chronicle*
Harrison *Times,* Harrison, Arkansas
Helena *World,* Helena, Arkansas
Marshall *Mountain Wave,* Marshall, Arkansas
Neosho *Daily Democrat,* Neosho, Missouri
*Railway Age*
St. Louis *Globe-Democrat*
St. Louis *Post-Dispatch*
St. Louis *Republic*

# Index

# SECOND DISTRICT

| | SOUTHWARD | | | | | | | | | | | NORTHWARD | |
|---|---|---|---|---|---|---|---|---|---|---|---|---|---|
| THIRD CLASS | SECOND CLASS | FIRST CLASS | Siding Capacity | | Distance from Joplin | Maximum Grade | TIME TABLE No. 7 | Maximum Grade | Station Numbers | Telegraph Call | FIRST CLASS | SECOND CLASS | THIRD CLASS |
| **325** Local Freight | **11** Manifest Freight | **1** Passenger | Pass. | Other | | | Effective 12.01 A. M. SUNDAY February 25, 1945 | | | | **2** Passenger | **12** Freight | **326** Local Freight |
| Mon. Wed. Fri. | Daily | Daily | | | | | STATIONS | | | | Daily | Daily | Tues. Thurs. Sat. |
| Lv 6.00AM | Lv 7.00PM | Lv 11.59AM | Yd. | | 126.33 | 1.75 | DN......HARRISON......CTWX | | 126 | DS | Ar 1.41PM | Ar 5.00AM | Ar 2.05PM |
| | | | | | | | 4.69 | | | | | | |
| 6.20 | 7.20 | f 12.11PM | 27B | | 131.02 | 1.75 | BELLEFONTE......* | 1.75 | 131 | | f 1.30 | 4.35 | 1.50 |
| | | | | | | | 5.59 | | | | | | |
| 6.30 | 7.44 | f 12.24 | 28B | | 136.61 | 1.75 | OLVEY......* | 1.75 | 137 | | f 1.17 | 4.13 | 1.31 |
| | | | | | | | 4.75 | | | | | | |
| 6.45 | 8.05 | s 12.36 | 32B | 18 | 141.36 | 1.60 | D......EVERTON......W | 1.75 | 141 | RN | s 1.06 | 3.50 | 1.15 |
| | | | | | | | 6.92 | | | | | | |
| 7.10 | 8.30 | s **12.51** M2 M326 | 36B | | 148.28 | 1.75 | PINDALL | 0.64 | 148 | | s **12.51** M1-P326 | 3.20 | **12.51** M1 2-P |
| | | | | | | | 7.06 | | | | | | |
| 7.40 | 9.00 | s 1.03 | 39B | | 155.34 | 1.60 | ST. JOE | 1.75 | 155 | | s 12.34 | 2.45 | 12.16PM |
| | | | | | | | 6.38 | | | | | | |
| 8.10 | 9.30 | s 1.23 | 25B | | 161.72 | 1.30 | GILBERT......W | 1.67 | 162 | | s 12.19 | 2.15 | 11.55AM |
| | | | | | | | 5.49 | | | | | | |
| 8.35 | 9.55 | f 1.40 | 13B | | 167.21 | 1.30 | ZACK......* | 1.37 | 167 | | f 12.02PM | 1.45 | 11.30 |
| | | | | | | | 3.67 | | | | | | |
| 8.55 | 10.15 | 1.49 | 41B | | 170.88 | 1.75 | JAMESON | 0.00 | 171 | | 11.53AM | 1.32 | 11.17 |
| | | | | | | | 1.89 | | | | | | |
| 9.02 | 10.22 | s 1.53 | 16B | 4 | 172.77 | 1.75 | D......MARSHALL | 0.75 | 173 | MR | s 11.49 | 1.25 | 11.10 |
| | | | | | | | 2.12 | | | | | | |
| 9.10 | 10.30 | f 1.59 | 9B | | 174.80 | 0.44 | BAKER......* | 1.28 | 175 | | s 11.43 | 1.10 | 10.55 |
| | | | | | | | 6.86 | | | | | | |
| 10.08 | 11.15 | 2.14 / 2.34 | 44B | 53 | 181.75 | 0.30 | DN......LESLIE......WY | | 182 | K | 11.28 / 11.08 | 12.45AM | 10.30 |
| | | | | | | | 4.79 | | | | | | |
| 10.23 | | f 2.46 | 7N | | 186.54 | 0.00 | RUMLEY......* | 0.60 | 187 | | f 10.56 | | 9.42 |
| | | | | | | | 5.27 | | | | | | |
| 10.43 M2 | 11.50PM M12 | 2.59 | 21B | | 191.81 | 0.00 | ELBA | 0.60 | 192 | | s 10.43 M325 | 11.50PM M11 | 9.22 |
| | | | | | | | 9.19 | | | | | | |
| 11.17 | 12.25AM | 3.19 | 38B | | 201.00 | 0.50 | ARLBERG......W | 0.60 | 201 | | s 10.23 | 11.17 | 8.48 |
| | | | | | | | 4.90 | | | | | | |
| 11.32 | | f 3.30 | 7N | | 205.90 | | LYDALISK | | 205 | | f 10.12 | | 8.33 |
| | | | | | | | 4.38 | | | | | | |
| 11.52AM | 1.00 | f 3.39 | 34B | | 210.28 | 0.15 | OAKVALE | 0.50 | 210 | | f 10.03 | 10.43 | 8.13 |
| | | | | | | | 4.75 | | | | | | |
| 12.22PM | 1.30 | s 3.50 | 34B | 79 | 215.03 | 0.00 | D......SHIRLEY......W | 0.45 | 215 | SN | s 9.53 | 10.25 | 7.43 |
| | | | | | | | 9.26 | | | | | | |
| 12.52 | 2.00 | f 4.12 | 20B | | 223.29 | 0.50 | PARTAIN | 0.60 | 223 | | f 9.31 | 9.45 | 7.13 |
| | | | | | | | 4.10 | | | | | | |
| 1.07 | 2.15 | s 4.21 | | 25S | 227.39 | 0.30 | EDGEMONT | 0.50 | 227 | | s 9.22 | 9.29 | 6.58 |
| | | | | | | | 2.23 | | | | | | |
| 1.15 | 2.23 | s 4.27 | 28B | 22 | 229.62 | 0.50 | HIGDEN | 0.60 | 230 | | s 9.16 | 9.20 | 6.50 |
| | | | | | | | 7.23 | | | | | | |
| 1.42 | 2.50 | s 4.42 | 33B | | 236.85 | 0.60 | MILLER......* | 0.50 | 237 | | s 9.01 | 8.55 | 6.23 |
| | | | | | | | 6.47 | | | | | | |
| Ar 2.05PM | Ar 3.15AM | Ar 4.57PM | Yd. | | 243.32 | 0.45 | DN......HEBER SPRINGS......CWY | 0.60 | 243 | HB | Lv 8.46AM | Lv 8.30PM | Lv 6.00AM |
| Mon. Mon. Fri. | Daily | Daily | End Connected B—Both N—North S—South | | | | 116.99 | | | | Daily | Daily | Tues. Thur. Sat. |
| **325** | **11** | **1** | | | | | | | | | **2** | **12** | **326** |

# Northward trains are superior to trains of the same class in the opposite direction.

All trains must get proper clearance card at Harrison and Heber Springs.

### SIDINGS AND SPURS BETWEEN STATIONS

See Page 8

### ADDITIONAL FLAG STOPS FOR PASSENGER TRAINS

Shain,   Mile 189.03 no track

Barnett,   Mile 196.52 no track

Sendeff,   Mile 222.09 no track

Karber,   Mile 225.76 car capacity 6, connected north end.

See Page 4 for "special instructions" second district.

See Page 4 for speed restrictions.

See Page 4 for overhead structures that will not clear man on top or side of car.